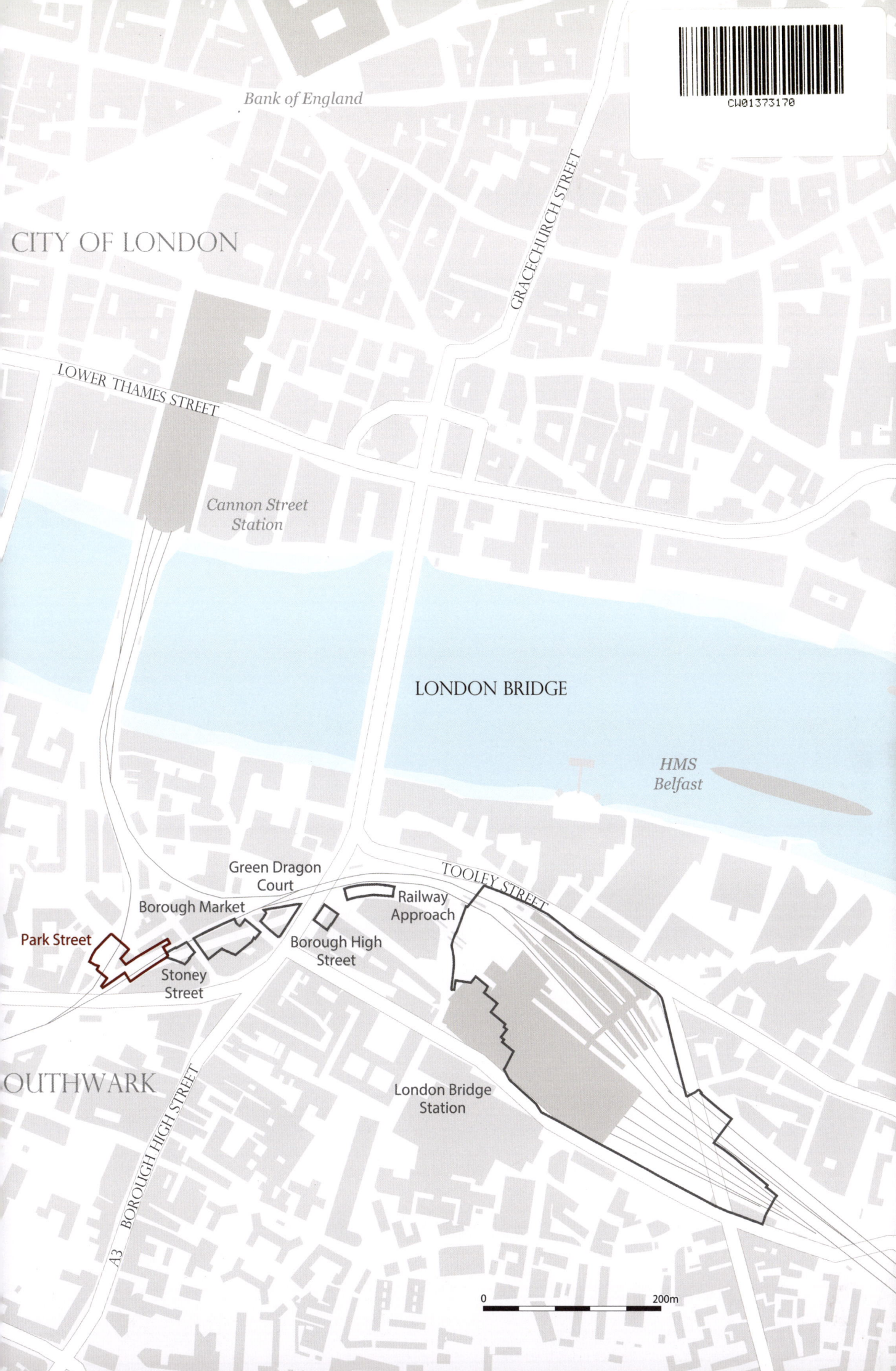

Living and Dying in Southwark 1587–1831

Excavations at Cure's College Burial Ground, Park Street

by Louise Loe, Kate Brady, Lisa Brown,
Mark Gibson and Kirsty Smith

with contributions from
Brian Dean, Rowena Henderson, Peter Moore, Julian Munby, Daniel Poore,
Ian Scott, Steven Teague and Helen Webb

Illustrations by
Victoria Hosegood, Gary Jones, Sophie Lamb, Steven Teague
and Magdalena Wachnik

Thameslink Monograph Series No. 3

The publication of this volume has been generously funded by Network Rail

Published by OAPCA as part of the Thameslink Monograph series

Designed by Oxford Archaeology Graphics Office

Edited by Lisa Brown

© 2017 OAPCA

Front cover: View of Cure's College Almshouses (1808) by George Smith (© London Metropolitan Archives)

Back cover: Excavation of burials (© Museum of London Archaeology)

Map underlay © MOTCO

ISBN 978-0-9956636-1-9

This book is part of a series of four monographs about the Thameslink project, which can be bought from all good bookshops and internet bookshops.
For more information visit www.oxfordarchaeology.com and www.pre-construct.com

Typeset by Production Line, Oxford

Printed in Great Britain by Latimer Trend & Company Ltd., Plymouth, UK

Contents

List of Figures vii
List of Tables ix
Summary xi
Foreword xiii
Acknowledgements xv

Chapter 1: Introduction *by Lisa Brown and Louise Loe* 1
    Project background 1
    Geology and topography 1
    Park Street, St Saviour's parish, Southwark 2
    Methodology 2
    Textual and graphical conventions 3
    Monograph structure 5
    The archive 5
    The reburial of the human remains 6

**Chapter 2: Documentary evidence for burials at Park Streeet and other post-medieval
cemeteries in Southwark** *by Kirsty Smith and Louise Loe* 7
    Introduction 7
    Historical background of Southwark 7
    St Margaret's new churchyard 8
    Cure's College burial ground 10
    Other contemporary burial grounds in St Saviour's parish 18
    Burial fees for St Saviour 1613–1838 19
    Burial registers and fees books for St Saviour's parish 20
    Summary and conclusion 23

Chapter 3: Archaeological results *by Kate Brady and Lisa Brown* 25
    Introduction 25
    Recording methodology 27
    Chronological sequence 28
        Phase 1 28
        Phase 2 28
        Phase 3 30
    Multiple burials 31
        Grave [969] Pile Cap D 32

Grave [971] Pile Cap D 32
Grave [3078] Pile Cap C1–G1 33
Multiple burials in Pile Cap E–H 33
Structures bounding the burial ground 37
Discussion 38
        Orientation 38
        Burial density and depth 38
        Burial status 38
        Family plots 38

Chapter 4: The people: scientific analyses of the human skeletons
    by Louise Loe with Brian Dean, Mark Gibson, Rowena Henderson and Helen Webb 41
Osteological analysis 41
Terminology 43
Methods 43
Results 43
    Condition and completeness 43
    Ancestry 44
        Demography 44
    Physical attributes 47
        Stature 47
        Child growth 48
        Indices 48
        Enthesial changes 49
    Non-metrical analysis 50
        Cranial non-metric traits 50
        Post-cranial non-metric traits 50
        Spatial analysis for shared traits 50
    Dental status 53
        Adult dentitions 53
        Juvenile dentitions 57
    Skeletal pathology 57
        Infection 57
        Metabolic disorders 64
        Joint disease 66
        Trauma 72
        Circulatory disorders 76
        Neoplastic disease 77
        Congenital and developmental conditions 78
        Miscellaneous pathological conditions 79
Isotope analysis *by Rowena Henderson* 80
    Background 80
    Isotope analysis research questions 80
    Sample selection and method 81
    Results 81
    Conclusions 82

Scientific analyses of the human skeletal remains: summary and conclusions *by Louise Loe* 82
    Mortality patterns 83
    Behavioural changes 85
    Childhood health 86
    Cultural and fashionable practices 88
    Overall health and well-being: Park Street in context 90
    Conclusions 91

Chapter 5: Coffins and coffin furnishings *by Mark Gibson* 93
  Background to post-medieval coffins 93
  Methodology 93
  Results 93
  Discussion 99

Chapter 6: Discussion: social history, funerary practice and skeletal studies
    by Louise Loe and Kirsty Smith 103
  Summary of the main findings 103
  Archaeological context 103
    Appearance, organisation and management 104
  Funerary practice at Cure's College 108
    Funerals 108
    Coffins and coffin furniture 110
  Who was buried at Cure's College burial ground? 112
  Health status and cause of death 114
    Living conditions and disease 114
    Mass fatality 116
  Comparison of mortality and morbidity at Cure's College with Cross Bones and St Saviour's
    burial grounds 118
  Conclusions: Living and dying in Southwark, the perspective from Cure's College 120

Bibliography 123

Index 137

List of Figures

1.1	The Thameslink route in Central London	Endpapers
1.2	Location of the Park Street site	4
1.3	Key to drawing conventions	4
1.4	Reburial of unknown Londoner (© Network Rail)	5
1.5	Memorial for the Park Street individuals at Kemnal Park, Chislehurst (© Network Rail)	6
2.1	Possible location of St Margaret's New Churchyard 1536–c 1587 (later the location of Cure's College)	9
2.2	Possible location of the new churchyard, later Cure's College, on Londinvm Feracissimi Angliæ map c 1572 (© Southwark Council)	9
2.3	(a) Thomas Cure's plaque, Southwark Cathedral (obscured by a later monument); (b) stone tablet dedicated to Thomas Cure at 9 Park Street	11
2.4	Newcourt's map of 1658 showing Cure's College burial ground (labelled I) (© Southwark Archives)	12
2.5	Morgan's map of 1676–1682 showing College Church Yard (© Southwark Archives)	13
2.6	Rocque's map of 1746 showing College Yard and College Almshouses (© MOTCO)	14
2.7	Horwood's map of 1792–1799 showing Almshouses (© MOTCO)	15
2.8	Gwilt's 1814 survey of Cure's College (after an original held by London Metropolitan Archives)	15
2.9	Gwilt's 1821 survey of Cure's College (© London Metropolitan Archives)	16
2.10	Jn. Howe's 1844 plan of Cure's College, showing the rebuild of 1831 (© London Metropolitan Archives)	17
2.11	12th century–19th century burial grounds of St Saviour's parish	19
2.12	Cost of six burial locations in St Saviour's parish in 1613, 1709, 1792 and 1838	20
3.1	Location of the Park Street burials	25
3.2	Phase 2 burials	26–7
3.3	The cemetery and associated structures	29
3.4	Wall [4065] (Structure PM5) and excavation of adjacent burials (top of photograph)	34
3.5	Plan of excavated burials overlying Howe's 1844 plan of Cure's College	35
3.6	Plan showing locations of preserved coffin remains and fittings	36–7
4.1	Completeness of skeletons	44
4.2	Condition of skeletons	44
4.3	Fragmentation of skeletons	44
4.4	Age distribution of the total assemblage (n=331)	45
4.5	Age/sex distribution of the total assemblage (n=331)	45
4.6	Mass grave and non-mass grave mortality profiles compared A: as a percentage of each sample; B: as a percentage of the total assemblage	45
4.7	Prevalence of ATML and caries	53
4.8	SK [911] Prime adult male. Large internally (right) and externally (left) draining cavity associated with the right maxillary first molar	55

4.9	SK [841] prime adult male with extreme dental attrition and grooves on the occlusal surfaces of maxillary teeth (arrowed)	56
4.10	Dental overcrowding, SK [2352]	56
4.11	Inflammation, left parietal bone (copper staining on left), SK [4038]	58
4.12	Prevalence of periostitis by element	59
4.13	Inflammation, right maxilla and mandible of SK [962]. Likely related to the maxillary periapical cavity (arrowed)	59
4.14	SK [833] Older child. Anteriorly bowed right and left tibiae with thickening and periostitis	60
4.15	Bony changes on the tibia, femur and manubrium of SK [4009], indicative of syphilis	62
4.16	Evidence of possible ulceration as a complication of systemic infection. Left tibia, SK [2317]	63
4.17	Fracture of the left femoral neck and secondary arthritis of the hip joint, SK [789]	65
4.18	Unsexed adult, SK [4040]. Concave fracture involving the thoracic spine ('cod fish vertebrae')	65
4.19	Prevalence of extra-spinal OA by element	67
4.20	Osteoarthritis, left knee joint of SK [627]	67
4.21	Prevalence of spinal joint disease	69
4.22	SK [2160] Adult female with lytic lesions around the acetabulum of the right hip ('Egger's cysts')	70
4.23	SK [631] Unsexed adult. Osteoarthritis and erosive changes involving the first metatarso-phalangeal joint (post-mortem damage is also present on the head of the first metatarsal)	71
4.24	Bamboo type ankylosis, second to fifth cervical vertebrae, SK [956]	71
4.25	SK [2217] Male adult. Healed fractures involving the left radius (radiograph only), left tibia and left fibula. There is marked overlap of the fracture margins and shortening of the bones	73
4.26	Prevalence of fractures by element (lefts and rights combined)	74
4.27	Dislocation involving the left gleno-humeral joint, SK [880]	75
4.28	Dislocation involving the left talo-calcaneal joint, secondary to fracture of the talus, SK [2222]	76
4.29	Bilateral osteochondritis dissecans involving the knee joint, SK [2314]	77
4.30	An illustration of segments of the tooth taken and the age brackets assigned to them. Adapted from Henderson *et al.* (2014)	81
4.31	Box and whisker plots of the first and third molars showing the $\delta^{15}N$ and $\delta^{13}C$ results from each age bracket. Taken from Henderson *et al.* (2014)	82
5.1	Coffin fixing nails from coffin [2202]	94
5.2	Grip from coffin [710] (top) and PQC 7152 (middle and bottom) for comparison	95
5.3	Grips from coffin [2128]	95
5.4	Breastplate type CCS6 with fragments recovered from coffins [890] (blue) and [915] (red)	96
5.5	Breastplate from coffin [4030]	97
5.6	Breastplate from coffin [604]. Dashed lines are extrapolated edges	97
5.7	Studs embedded in mineralised coffin wood, coffin [915]	98
5.8	Grips from pit fill [2072] (of type PQC7152, shown in Fig. 5.2)	98
6.1	Cure's College Almshouses and burial ground facing north-west, 1851 (© British Museum)	105
6.2	Cure's College Almshouses and burial ground facing north, 1851 (© British Museum)	106
6.3	Cure's College Almshouses and burial ground facing south-east towards the chapel, 1852 (© British Museum)	107
6.4	Cure's College Almshouses showing the chapel on the left, prior to the rebuild of 1831 (© London Metropolitan Archives)	110
6.5	Interior view of the chapel of Cure's College Almshouses showing benches, the pulpit and a painting hanging on the wall, 1825 (© London Metropolitan Archives)	111
6.6	(a) The Ship Inn, Borough High Street (1827) by John Chessel Buckler (© London Metropolitan Archives); (b) view of Pepper Alley, Southwark (1827) by John Chessel Buckler (© London Metropolitan Archives)	116

List of Tables

1.1	Summary of the Thameslink archaeological investigations in Central London	2-3
1.2	Pile cap impact levels	3
2.1	Comparison between the burial fees of burial grounds in St Saviour	18
2.2	Comparison of burial fees at each of the main parochial burial grounds of St Saviour (in pence)	20
2.3	Methodology of sampling the St Saviour's parish fees books	21
2.4	Cure's College burial ground, 1782–91. Entries which record cause of death from fees book P92/SAV/3093	21
2.5	Cure's College burial ground, 1782–97. Mentions of occupations in burial registers P92/SAV/3093 and P92/SAV/3094	22
3.1	Phasing	28
3.2	Multiple burials (omitting mass burial [969])	31–2
3.3	Skeletons in mass burial [969]	33
4.1	Definition of osteological and medical terms used in the text	41
4.2	Comparative assemblages referred to in the present report	42
4.3	Completeness of skeletons	43
4.4	Condition of skeletons	43
4.5	Fragmentation of skeletons	43
4.6	Numbers of skeletons in each age category	45
4.7	Park Street mortality patterns compared with other post-medieval assemblages (adapted from Bekvalac and Kausmally 2008, 43)	46
4.8	Park Street male and female mortality patterns compared with other post-medieval assemblages	46–7
4.9	Age and sex distribution: Pile Cap D mass grave	47
4.10	Comparison between Park Street non-mass grave and mass grave demographic trends with other assemblages associated with plague/epidemic	47
4.11	Comparison of statures	48
4.12	Juvenile femur age (Scheuer and Black 2000) compared with dental age (Moorees et al. 1963, a and b)	49
4.13	Femoral shaft index	49
4.14	Tibial shaft index	49
4.15	Age and sex distribution of skeletons with pronounced muscle/ligament/tendon sites	50
4.16	Prevalence of pronounced sites by sex and skeletal region	50
4.17	Prevalence of cranial non-metric traits	51
4.18	Prevalence of post-cranial non-metric traits	52
4.19	Comparison of adult dental status	54–5
4.20	Inter-site comparison of crude prevalence rates for periostitis/surface inflammation	58
4.21	Adult and juvenile TPR for periostitis/surface inflammation	59
4.22	Distribution of elements with periostitis/surface inflammation (skeletons with multiple element involvement only)	60–1
4.23	Skeletons with probable/possible rickets	64

4.24	Cribra orbitalia, true prevalence	66
4.25	Inter-site comparison of crude prevalence rates for cribra orbitalia	66
4.26	Age and sex distribution of skeletons with OA	67
4.27	Frequency of joints affected with OA	67
4.28	Skeletons with generalised OA	68
4.29	Inter-site comparison of extra-spinal OA	68
4.30	Inter-site comparison of spinal OA	69
4.31	Crude prevalence of adults with Schmorl's nodes	69
4.32	True prevalence of Schmorl's nodes, spondylosis deformans and vertebral body marginal osteophytosis	69
4.33	Crude prevalence of adults with spondylosis deformans	69
4.34	Inter-site comparison of fracture crude prevalence rates	72
4.35	Fracture true prevalence rates by element	74
4.36	Skeletons with multiple fractures	75
4.37	Skeletons with osteochondritis dissecans	77
4.38	Inter-site comparison of CPR for osteochondritis dissecans	77
4.39	Details of skeletons with congenital and developmental conditions	78–9
4.40	Non-breastfed individuals	88
4.41	Breastfed individuals	89
5.1	Coffin grips	94
6.1	Summary of sizeable, key historic burial grounds excavated from the Borough of Southwark	104–5
6.2	Summary comparison of pathology, Park Street and Cross Bones	119

Summary

This volume presents the results of archaeological investigations of 16th- to early 19th-century burials at Park Street, Southwark, believed to be from Cure's College Almshouse burial ground, established in the parish of St Saviour in 1587. The burials were excavated as part of the Thameslink Project, an infrastructure upgrade which involved substantial construction works at Blackfriars Station and London Bridge Station, and along the New Borough Viaduct.

Fieldwork undertaken by Museum of London Archaeology (MOLA) involved the excavation of nine pile caps, and monitoring during the installation of drains. This covered approximately 34% of the burial ground and revealed some 250 earth-cut graves which contained a total of 331 individuals. The graves were characterised by heavy intercutting. They were generally east-west aligned and contained single and multiple stacked inhumation burials numbering up to nine individuals. One mass grave, apparently less well organised than the others, contained 36 men, women and children, possibly victims of an epidemic and/or famine, some contained within coffins and others not. Overall, these patterns are consistent with existing historical and archaeological evidence which reflects a London suburban parish struggling to provide burial space and cover the cost of burial at a time of high mortality rates.

A small number of artefacts found with the individuals and in the disturbed cemetery soils include (primarily) coffin remains, but also occasional dress items such as pins and buttons. None of the individuals could be identified, except for a William Pope who died in 1816, whose remains were found in direct association with a coffin nameplate. Less direct information about the individuals was obtained from burial records, in particular fees books. Cure's College was founded for the sick and poor, but the records point to a group that did not just represent inmates from the almshouse, but also individuals from the wider parish and other London parishes. They included locals and immigrants from the Home Counties, continental Europe, Ireland and Scotland. Further, they were not among the poorest members of society. Although some had their burials paid for by the parish most, especially from the 18th century, were earning a living as, amongst other trades, labourers, skilled craftsmen, and trades people, and they paid their own fees, which were not the cheapest in the parish.

All 331 skeletons underwent full osteological analysis. They comprised 245 adults (104 males, 73 females, 68 unsexed individuals), and 86 juveniles (individuals less than 18 years of age). A high number of individuals were aged between 18 and 35 years, an unusual figure compared with other assemblages from London. One explanation is that it reflects high numbers of working age immigrants in Southwark, who were more susceptible to earlier deaths than the local population because of exposure to new diseases, possibly epidemics, against which they lacked immunity. If correct, this finding is consistent with historic sources which document a high intake of immigrants and migrants into London between the 17th and 19th centuries.

A range of diseases was observed on the skeletons, most notably scurvy, rickets, and syphilis. This is in keeping with local historical sources which depict an inadequately nourished population experiencing living conditions which were detrimental to health, in particular, overcrowding, poor sanitation, and atmospheric pollution. Compared with other assemblages from the rest of London and the country, these and other health indicators (for example, cribra orbitalia, enamel hypoplasia, and non-specific infection) were not very prevalent, possibly because the Park Street individuals had weaker constitutions and had succumbed to disease faster, before conditions affected the skeleton. This was supported by estimated adult statures which were found to be lower than most other populations, and considered to relate to physiological health stress in childhood, inadequate nutrition, and poor maternal/carer health in particular. There was also little evidence for trauma, but the high number of incomplete skeletons in the assemblage was probably a key factor in this.

Further insight into childhood nutrition was provided by incremental isotope analysis, a relatively new method which provides the opportunity to explore childhood dietary patterns over relatively small timeframes (for example, years and months) using adult teeth. This showed that diets were varied, including some individuals who had been breastfed as babies and others not. During their first eight years of life, boys and girls had consumed different diets, and this may reflect either physiological differences between the sexes or cultural practice.

Other observations were that patterns in the Park Street osteology, in particular the mortality profile and disease among juveniles, are different to lower status and higher status burial grounds elsewhere in the parish, namely, Cross Bones and St Saviour's. The osteology, therefore, seems to be consistent with the sector of society that Cure's College burial ground served, that is working class individuals who were not the poorest members of society, but were also not particularly wealthy.

Cure's was one of nine burial grounds in the parish of St Saviour's and is the sixth sizeable burial ground assemblage from Southwark to be archaeologically excavated and analysed. It is also the first sizeable post-medieval almshouse burial ground assemblage to be archaeologically examined from the country and, as such, contributes valuable new information on burial practice, population trends and patterns of disease in London during the 16th–19th centuries.

Foreword

The Thameslink Programme will transform north-south travel through London and has included, amongst other works, the rebuilding of London Bridge and Blackfriars stations and the construction of a new viaduct through Borough Market in Southwark. This massive undertaking required the bringing together of teams of highly skilled individuals over many years to ensure that the work was designed, planned and constructed to the highest standards and with the minimum impact on the environment, people using the existing railway and those who lived or worked nearby.

From the earliest planning stages, Network Rail recognised that some of the key areas of construction were located in the very heart of historic London and that it was highly likely that important archaeological remains would be discovered during building work. From the outset provision was made to integrate archaeological specialists within the Thameslink teams to ensure that any archaeological work was planned and undertaken to the highest standards.

Now that we have finished our archaeological work it is clear that the discoveries have lived up to expectations and Network Rail is pleased to make them known to the public in the four Thameslink archaeological monographs. These volumes represent the culmination of a massive programme of archaeological site work that started in a small carpark off Redcross Way, Southwark, and then spread through Borough Market and across Borough High Street, crossed the Thames to Blackfriars Station, and finally ended in the arches beneath London Bridge Station. That this work kept ahead of and did not delay construction is a testament to the skill, dedication, professionalism and sheer hard work of the archaeologists at Oxford Archaeology, Pre-Construct Archaeology and the Museum of London Archaeological Service, as well as the unwavering support of Thameslink's construction teams at Skanska, Costain and Balfour Beatty.

Our finds have been many and varied, but perhaps the most exciting was the discovery of an unknown Roman bathhouse beneath Borough High Street, which is discussed in Monograph 1. The importance of this find was recognised immediately and steps were taken to modify our works to ensure that it could be preserved beneath a new building planned for the site. The remains have since been deemed to be of national importance by Historic England and now have legal protection as a Scheduled Monument. Today, the building is occupied by a well-known restaurant chain and office workers and tourists eat their sandwiches and sip coffee just a few centimetres above the remains of a building that once provided a refuge to the tired and dust-covered inhabitants of Roman London.

As part of our project planning, we anticipated that we would uncover the remains of Londoners buried in the old Park Street burial ground. We weren't sure how many to expect, but not many were anticipated as the graveyard should already have been cleared in the 1860s when the first Borough Viaduct was built. We were surprised, then, to have to exhume over 300 individuals and many cubic metres of charnel that the Victorian engineers had left behind them. The work has provided a fascinating insight into the lives and deaths of the urban poor in 18th and 19th century London and we report on these finds in Monograph 3. The remains have all now been re-buried in a new burial ground belonging to the Diocese of Southwark, preceded by a ceremony at Southwark Cathedral in which the remains of a single, unknown parishioner were carried to and from the cathedral on a horse drawn bier.

Should anyone require greater detail on our discoveries, the archive of the project is housed with the London Archaeological Archive and Research Centre at the Museum of London.

Simon Blanchflower
Major Programme Director – Thameslink

Acknowledgements

Oxford Archaeology and Pre-Construct Archaeology (OAPCA) wish to thank Network Rail for funding the Thameslink archaeological works and for commissioning this book. Network Rail's Project Director was Graham Campbell, Brian Richards was the Construction Manager, Tony Carter the Senior Project Manager and Ankur Amin and Sarah Williams were Project Managers for the scheme. Network Rail's Environmental Co-ordinator was Elizabeth Wood-Griffiths. Their contributions are all gratefully acknowledged.

OAPCA are also grateful to Chris Place, who acted on behalf of Network Rail as Project Archaeologist, for his assistance, constructive advice, and guidance throughout the course of the fieldwork and post-excavation stages of the project. We would also like to thank Bridgit Choo-Bennett, the Consents Manager at Network Rail, for her involvement and support.

OAPCA are grateful to the numerous other organisations and individuals involved in the fieldwork stage of the Park Street works. Skanska was the Principal Contractor for Network Rail. Susan Fitzpatrick was Skanska's Bid Director, and Nadeem Rajwani, Alex Hoyos, Adam Clarkson, and Kierin Giblin were Section Engineers on the project. OAPCA would especially like to thank Tim Ovington and James Ruck for their co-operation on this site.

OAPCA wish to acknowledge the kind support shown throughout the course of the project by the Very Reverend Colin Slee (deceased), former Dean of Southwark Cathedral, who officiated at the funeral service of the 'unknown parishioner', and by the Very Reverend Andrew Dunn, current Dean of Southwark Cathedral. Barry Albin-Dyer (deceased) and Simon Dyer of F A Albin and Sons, Funeral Directors, generously donated the handmade coffin and hand-engraved coffin plate for the burial. John Hughes, Development Manager for Network Rail, liaised closely with Southwark Cathedral, and oversaw the burial.

The Museum of London Archaeology (MOLA) undertook the first major phase of the cemetery excavation, with the second smaller phase carried out by OAPCA. OAPCA gratefully acknowledge the contributions and co-operation of MOLA, especially Project Managers Derek Seeley and Lesley Dunwoody. We also wish to extend thanks to their site staff for their contribution to the excavation, especially Project Supervisor Joanna Taylor, and fieldwork supervisors Iain Bright, Alex McAuley, and Ashley Pooley.

Dr Chris Constable, the Senior Archaeology Officer for the London Borough of Southwark, monitored and advised on the archaeological fieldwork investigations, and we would like to thank him for his support throughout.

Dan Poore and Peter Moore managed the project for OAPCA throughout all stages of the project, supported by Nick Sheperd, Frank Meddens and Alistair Douglas. The Post-Excavation and Publication Managers were Jon Butler, Lisa Brown, Victoria Ridgeway and Leo Webley, and their considerable efforts in bringing such an enormous archaeological archive first to assessment then publication is appreciated. Kirsty Smith undertook the documentary background research with the assistance of Julian Munby, and obtained high resolution versions and copyrights for the historic maps and images. Ian Scott prepared the small finds catalogue (excluding coffin furniture) for the archive.

OAPCA are grateful to several specialists who contributed to the scientific analyses presented in Chapter 4. Stable isotope analysis was supervised by Professor Julia Lee-Thorpe. Peter Ditchfield and Rick Schulting are also thanked for their assistance. The radiography was carried out by Mark Viner, Kim Viner, Mark Farmer and Wayne Hoban of Reveal Imaging, who are acknowledged for their unwavering commitment and patience in producing some excellent images. We are indebted to Iain Watt, who generously gave his time to read the radiographs and discuss differential diagnoses with us. Our report would be lacking without his input.

The tireless work of Finds Administrators Märit Gaimster and Leigh Allen, with the assistance of Geraldine Crann, facilitated the processing, exchange, and tracking of finds between the two offices. Nicola Scott and Tiziana Vitali arranged for the security copying of the archives and of their preparation for deposition.

The publication illustrations were produced by graphics staff Sophie Lamb, with the assistance of Gary Jones and Steven Teague, who produced the GIS-generated site drawings. Victoria Hosegood drew the coffin fittings, and Magdalena Wachnik oversaw the graphics work.

Finally, the authors are gratefully indebted to John Schofield, who reviewed an earlier draft of the entire report, and to Margaret Cox, who read and commented on Chapters 4 and 6. The monograph has benefited greatly from their input, and any shortcomings are our own.

Chapter 1

Introduction

by Lisa Brown and Louise Loe

This volume describes the 16th- to early 19th-century burial assemblage excavated between 2009 and 2011 at Park Street, St Saviour's parish, Southwark. The assemblage comprises 331 skeletons, most likely from Cure's College burial ground, and is an important contribution to current knowledge of the life – and death – of London's working classes between the 16th and 19th centuries.

Project background

The principal objective of the Thameslink Programme was to reduce crowding on London's commuter services. The infrastructure upgrade necessitated substantial construction works at Blackfriars Station and London Bridge Station and along the course of the New Borough Viaduct, a raised twin-track railway extending from Metropolitan Junction (Park Street) to London Bridge Station (Fig. 1.1 – endpapers). The numerous archaeological investigations undertaken along the 2.4km route to discharge planning conditions attached to the consents infrastructure programme are presented in Table 1.1. The archaeological work was undertaken from Park Street to London Bridge Station and its eastern approaches, and on both the north and south sides of the Thames in the vicinity of Blackfriars Station.

The Thameslink excavations produced abundant evidence for land use from the prehistoric periods through to the modern era, and the findings have transformed our understanding of these areas of London across this time span. The archaeological work was conducted between 2009 and 2010 by Museum of London Archaeology (MOLA), and between 2010 and 2013 by Oxford Archaeology and Pre-Construct Archaeology (OAPCA), and funded by Network Rail.

The results of the Thameslink archaeological investigations are published as four monographs, of which this report forms *Monograph 3* (Table 1.1). *Monograph 1* presents the evidence for prehistoric and Roman activity discovered at the sites along the course of the New Borough Viaduct and at London Bridge Station. *Monograph 2* explores the story of these sites during the period following the abandonment of the Roman settlement, through the Saxon and medieval periods, and up to the introduction of the railway. *Monograph 4* presents the results of geotechnical and archaeological work on both banks of the River Thames at Blackfriars.

Geology and topography

London is located within the Thames Basin, a broad syncline of chalk filled by Tertiary sands and clays, which is overlain by the Pleistocene gravel terraces of the River Thames. In the City the Tertiary bed-rock consists predominantly of the London Clay Formation, laid down in a marine environment 56–59 million years ago. The sequences of Pleistocene river terraces in the London area generally date from the period following the Anglian glaciation (*c* 450,000 years ago) when the Thames was diverted from an earlier course through the Vale of St Albans to broadly its current position.

On the north bank of the river, in the vicinity of Blackfriars, lie the Taplow and Hackney terraces, which rise steeply away from the river up towards Ludgate Hill (BGS sheet 256). On the south bank of the Thames the topography is more low-lying. The younger Shepperton terrace gravel, deposited towards the end of the last glacial period (the Devensian), lies buried beneath more recent alluvium and river silts. However, the original post-glacial topography consisted of a series of gravel islands or eyots, separated from each other and the southern bank of the river by channels, which would have been wet or marshy depending on the river level during various periods.

The Borough Viaduct sites lie within the boundaries of the northern eyot, which is known as the 'Bridgehead Island' (MoLAS 2003) or 'Northern Island'. The island extends between Joiner Street to the east and Southwark Bridge Road to the west, Union

Table 1.1: Summary of Thameslink archaeological investigations in Central London

Site code	Site name	Archaeological contractor	Supervisor	Date of excavation
THB09	Blackfriars Station, New Bridge St, Queen Victoria St and Blackfriars North	MOLA	Isca Howell, Louise Fowler, and Ruth Taylor	Nov 2009-Oct 2010
BVQ09	Pile Caps A-H rear of Southwark St and Park St; Test Pits 14 and 17 Redcross Way and Test Pits 10–12, 15–16 Park St	MOLA	Portia Askew, Isca Howell, and David Saxby	Sept 2009–March 2010
BVB10	Arches 12–16 Park St	OAPCA	Joanna Taylor	July–Sept 2010; June 2011
BVT09	Rear of 6-7 Stoney St and Test Pits 1–2, 8–9, 13, Stoney St and The Wheatsheaf	MOLA	David Saxby	Nov 2009–Feb 2010
BVE11	The Wheatsheaf	OAPCA	Ashley Pooley	Feb 2011; May–Sept 2011
BVF10	Borough Market	OAPCA	James Langthorne	Nov 2010; Aug–Sept 2011
BVU10	Pile Locations K1, K2, L1, L2, M1 and M2 Borough Market	MOLA	Portia Askew and Ken Pitt	Jan-March 2010
BVG10	2–4 Bedale St	OAPCA	James Langthorne	July-Nov 2010; Aug–Nov 2011
BVJ10	Pile Cap P, Green Dragon Court	OAPCA	Ashley Pooley	Sept–Oct 2010
BVX09	Pile Cap P and Pile Locations 1–6, 16–26 Borough High St and 1–7 Green Dragon Court	MOLA	Tony Mackinder, Ken Pitt, and David Saxby	May–Sept 2010
BVW10	Pile Locations N1 and N2	MOLA	Tony Mackinder, Ken Pitt, and David Saxby	June 2010
BVK11	11-15 Borough High St	OAPCA	Amelia Fairman and Jacek Gruszczynski	Jan–Nov 2010
BVL10	Vaults 2, 5 and 9, Railway Approach	OAPCA	Audrey Charvet and Amelia Fairman	June–Nov 2010; Feb 2011
BVC12	Western Approach Viaduct (formerly Station Approach Viaduct)	OAPCA	Amelia Fairman, James Langthorne, and Joanna Taylor	Feb–June 2010
BVM12	London Bridge Station Improvement Works	OA-PCA	Amelia Fairman, Carl Champness, James Langthorne, Mark Beasley, and Paw Jorgensen	July 2012–March 2013

Street and Southwark Street to the south, and the River Thames to the north. The sites are generally located within areas of high ground, with the natural sands and gravels occurring between 1.00–1.20m OD and the land set back from the tidal channels at a remove from the surrounding foreshores. When untruncated natural deposits occur below these heights, it is generally an indication that the land surface is 'dropping' towards a channel edge, and it can be assumed that the land would have been susceptible to flooding, especially during high tides.

Park Street, St Saviour's parish, Southwark

The Park Street investigations (BVQ09 and BVB10) extended between NGR TQ 32484 80159 (west) and TQ 32562 80204 (east). The site boundary incorporated part of two extant Victorian viaducts, constructed to carry the railway between London Bridge and Charing Cross Stations and to Cannon Street Station. The Park Street and Hop Exchange section of Borough Viaduct was built on nine pile caps founded on clusters of 550mm or 750mm diameter piles located either side of the existing 19th-century viaduct, connected by ground beams passing beneath the viaduct arches (Fig. 1.2). The site is bounded by properties fronting on Park Street to the north-west, the rear of 7a Stoney Street to the north-east, the rear of the Hop Exchange to the south-east, a short section of Southwark Street to the south, and the rear of properties fronting Redcross Way to the west.

Natural sands and gravels deposits were not exposed to the rear of the Hop Exchange and Park Street, where they lay below the depth to which it was practicable to excavate. However, undisturbed levels were found in the deeper excavations in Pile Caps A, B and D within the western part of the site. Here the natural sand and gravel appeared to slope slightly away from west to east. They were at their highest level of 1.18m OD within Pile Cap A, 1.28m OD within Pile Cap B, and 1.21m OD within Pile Cap D. The nearest water source is the River Thames, which lies approximately 250m to the north of the Park Street excavations.

Methodology

To allow construction it was necessary to remove the rear extensions of 1-13 Park Street. The brick viaduct arches were not founded directly on Terrace Gravel, but rather were underlain by a cemented granular fill.

National grid ref (centroid)	Assessment area	Assessment reference	Monograph volume	Monograph area
TQ 3172 8087 (north); TQ 3170 8055 (south)	TAA8	Teague, S. 2013	4	Blackfriars Station
TQ 3253 8017	TAA7	Teague, S, Loe, L, and Taylor, J 2013	1, 2, and 3	Park St
TQ 3255 8019	TAA7	Teague, S, Loe, and Taylor, J 2013	1, 2, and 3	Park St
TQ 3256 8019	TAA6	Taylor, J 2013	1 and 2	Stoney St
TQ 3257 8018	TAA6	Taylor, J 2013	1 and 2	Stoney St
TQ 3262 8020	TAA5	Teague, S, and Taylor, J 2013	1 and 2	Borough Market
TQ 3265 8020	TAA5	Teague, S, and Taylor, J 2013	1 and 2	Borough Market
TQ 3265 8021	TAA4	Langthorne, J, and Taylor, J 2013	1 and 2	Borough Market
TQ 3267 8022	TAA3	Brady, K, and Taylor, J 2013	1 and 2	Green Dragon Court
TQ 3267 8022	TAA3	Brady, K, and Taylor, J 2013	1 and 2	Green Dragon Court
TQ 3269 8023	TAA3	Brady, K and Taylor, J 2013	1 and 2	Green Dragon Court
TQ 3273 8023	TAA2	Fairman, A and Taylor, J 2013	1 and 2	Borough High St
TQ 3277 8025	TAA1	Hughs, V and Taylor, J 2013	1 and 2	Railway Approach
TQ 3291 8023	TAA9	Taylor, J, and Champness, C 2013	1 and 2	London Bridge Station
TQ 3293 8022	TAA10	Fairman, A, Champness, C, and Taylor, J 2014	1 and 2	London Bridge Station

Therefore, excavation was locally restricted to pile cap formation level (between 2.3m and 2.9m OD) in order to avoid any risk to the integrity of these structures and adjacent buildings. Excavation through the full archaeological sequence was completed in those areas sufficiently distant from susceptible foundations. The impact level, including piles, varied across the site, but in all pile cap areas it penetrated the complete archaeological sequence (Table 1.2).

Archaeological recording was undertaken using the single context recording system specified in the Museum of London Site Manual (MoL 1994) and Pre-Construct Archaeology's Operation Manual I (Taylor and Brown 2009). Recording was undertaken with reference to a 5m square grid imposed over the excavation area. The excavation of human remains was carried out in accordance with the written instructions of the Ministry of Justice, and relevant guidance set out by the BABAO (2010a; 2010b), the IFA (1993), and English Heritage (2005).

Modern overburden was reduced by mechanical means under archaeological guidance to the top of the burial horizon or significant archaeological deposit. Human remains which lay within the development area were hand excavated, recorded and recovered in a controlled and systematic manner. All spoil was checked for charnel and, when present, it was removed and stored for reburial, but not analysed in detail because it generally holds limited scientific value (EH 2004).

Skeleton recording sheets captured information on orientation, the attitude and preservation status of the bones, and location with reference to OD heights. Coffin records captured information on coffin shape, dimensions and distinguishing characteristics. The presence of associated coffin furniture (eg breastplates, grips, grip plates, fixing nails) was noted and this material was retained for analysis where preservation was deemed to be sufficient.

In addition to the viaduct construction works, new drainage associated with the refurbishment of the Park Street properties was monitored as an archaeological watching brief.

Table 1.2: Pile cap impact levels

Area	Impact level (mOD)
Pile Cap C	2.2
Pile Cap C1–G1	2.3
Pile Cap D	0.6
Pile Cap E–H	2.3

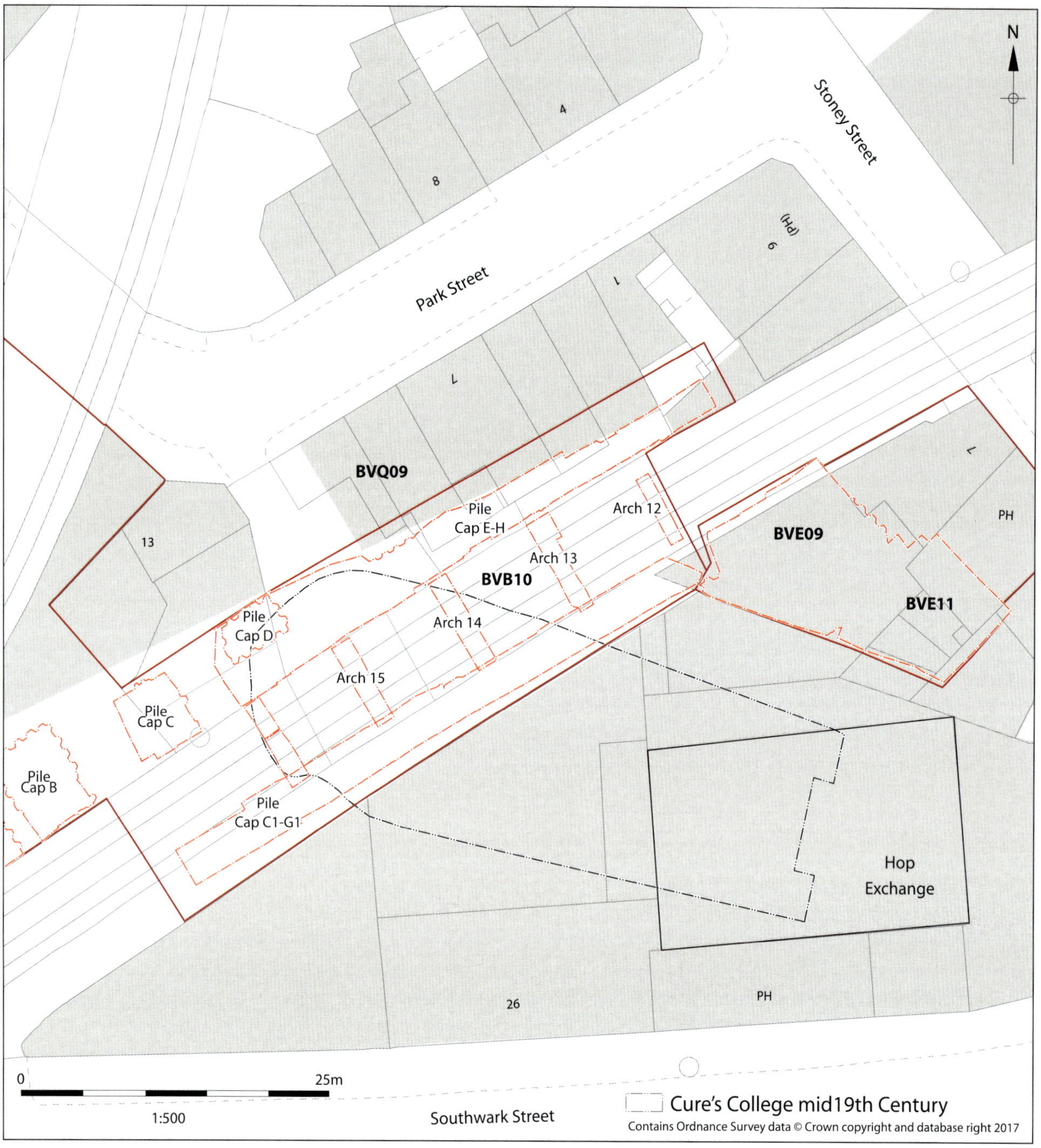

Fig. 1.2 Location of the Park Street site

Textual and graphical conventions

The basic unit of cross-reference throughout the archive for the Thameslink project is the site code and context number. This is a unique number given to each archaeological 'event' within a particular site (eg layer, wall, grave cut, pit cut or fill, road surface, etc), only cited in the publication text where a specific reference is required, eg 'BVB10 [3023]'. Small finds are individually identified by site code and a unique small find number, eg 'BVB10 SF6', whilst environmental samples are identified by site code and a

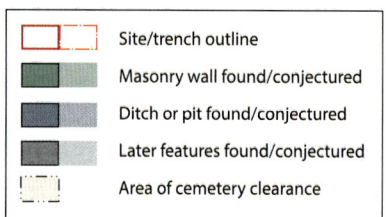

Fig. 1.3 Key to drawing conventions

unique environmental sample number, eg 'BVB10 {9}'. Dating evidence is presented selectively by land use, referenced to key contexts, fabrics present (in the case of pottery and ceramic building materials), and the date for the assemblage assigned by specialists. The period plan illustrations are largely interpretative and show significant features as well as found and conjectured structural evidence. A key to the drawing conventions used in the plans in this publication is provided in Figure 1.3. Levels on plans are expressed in metres above Ordnance Datum and scales of reproduction are given in the figure captions.

The archaeological data presented in the chronological narratives is organised by dated periods. These are unique to the Thameslink site sequence and generally based on a combination of stratigraphic interpretation and dating evidence. Divisions within periods are defined by major topographic changes, such as the effects of a widespread fire or the construction of new buildings, and for each period are numbered in chronological order. The Thameslink periods are:

- Period 1 – natural
- Period 2 – prehistoric
- Period 3 – Roman
- Period 4 – Saxon
- Period 5 – medieval
- Period 6 – post-medieval

The archaeology of the Cure's College burial ground falls entirely within post-medieval Period 6. Pre-Period 6 levels impacted in some pile caps are dealt with in Monographs 1 and 2.

Monograph structure

The integration of stratigraphic, documentary, osteological and finds data underlies the structure of this report, which is divided into the following chapters:

Chapter 1 – Introduction

Chapter 2 – Documentary evidence for burials at Park Street and other post-medieval cemeteries in Southwark

Chapter 3 – Archaeological results

Chapter 4 – The people: scientific analyses of the human skeletons

Chapter 5 – Coffins and coffin furnishings

Chapter 6 – Discussion: social history, funerary practice and skeletal studies

Fig. 1.4 Reburial of unknown Londoner (© Network Rail)

The archive

The fieldwork and research archives for the Park Street site (site codes BVQ09 and BVB10) and other sites along the Thameslink route have been deposited with the Museum of London. The archive may be consulted by prior arrangement with the archive manager at the London Archaeological Archive (LAA), Mortimer Wheeler House, 46 Eagle Wharf Road, London N1 7ED.

The reburial of the human remains

Exhumation was undertaken in accordance with a licence from the Coroner's Unit at the then Department of Constitutional Affairs. The skeletons and associated funerary remains were reburied at Kemnal Park, Chislehurst. The reburial process was marked by the formal funeral of a single individual, selected to represent all the parishioners buried at the Park Street cemetery. The 'unknown parishioner' was buried in a handmade ceremonial coffin, designed and made by Albin's undertakers, a family firm based in Bermondsey, which also donated and engraved an original 19th-century coffin plate from its archives (Fig. 1.4). The funeral service was held at Southwark Cathedral on 18 June 2012 and was followed by burial with the other individuals found in the excavation (Figs 1.4–1.5).

Fig. 1.5 Memorial for the Park Street individuals at Kemnal Park, Chislehurst (© Network Rail)

Chapter 2

Documentary evidence for burials at Park Street and other post-medieval cemeteries in Southwark

by Kirsty Smith and Louise Loe

Introduction

A wealth of documentary source material exists for post-medieval cemeteries and their populations, and those that are most relevant to Park Street are considered here. They include cartography dating from the 16th century which charts the physical origins and development of the burial ground. Contemporary or near-contemporary accounts and surveys provide information on London burial grounds (eg Holmes 1896; Walker 1839), Southwark society (Rendle 1878), St Saviour's parish (eg Taylor 1833) and the county (eg Malden 1912). Further, Boulton's (2005) studies on Southwark's population, economy and society during the 17th century employs extensive research of primary sources (eg taxation assessments, parish registers, vestry minutes) to explore the lives of the inhabitants with reference to demography, wealth and other such factors.

The parish records are a key source of information and document deaths and burials in the parish of St Saviour. Those primarily consulted for this research include fees books and burial registers (see below), which provide information on numbers of deaths, ages at death, causes of death, occupations, location of burial and fees paid for burial. However, as with all forms of evidence they have their limitations. Most notable is that many entries are incomplete or missing. In addition, the relevance and reliability of entries are questionable. For example, recorded ages at death may differ from real ages at death; some people were not aware of their real ages (Roberts and Cox 2003, 290). Molleson and Cox (1993) observed that, at Christchurch Spitalfields, some males were reported to be older than they were because of fashionable practices at the time. Similarly, recorded causes of death are often not accurate, their being reflective of contemporary understanding of disease and whatever physical manifestations were present at the time of death (Roberts and Cox 2003, 290).

This chapter presents an appraisal of the documentary evidence relating to the burial ground and its occupants. First, it considers the wider context with a brief review of the historical background to Southwark. Next, the chapter explores the origins of the Park Street burials. The burials were located in an area of Southwark where a number of contemporary burial grounds existed, the boundaries of which expanded and/or retracted with time. St Margaret's New Churchyard is most relevant in this respect, and therefore in order to properly appreciate the origin of the Park Street burials it is necessary to begin here. This is followed by a review of the sources on the establishment and development of Cure's College Almshouse and burial ground. Other contemporary burial grounds within the parish are then considered. The following section focuses on Cure's College burial ground fees in relation to the other burial grounds in the parish, as they provide an informative perspective on the relative wealth and status of the population that used the burial ground, and document how this changed over time. The final section of this chapter considers burial registers and fees books, to develop a broader understanding of the Park Street burial population. Attention has been given to information which is most substantive and which can best be employed to interpret the archaeological and osteological record, described in Chapters 3 to 5. It includes information on occupation, ages at death, causes of death and funeral costs.

Historical background of Southwark

The ancient borough of Southwark initially comprised the medieval Surrey parishes of St George the Martyr,

St Olave, St Margaret and St Mary Magdalene. In 1540, the parish of Southwark St Saviour was formed by amalgamating St Mary Magdalene and St Margaret. Further reorganisation resulted in the creation of Southwark St Thomas in 1555 and Southwark St John Horsleydown in 1733 by splitting them from St Olave. It is these parishes which are most relevant here because they date to the period during which it is most likely that the present Park Street burials were made.

During the medieval period Southwark was dominated by a number of high-status manors and sub-manors of religious orders and wealthy individuals. The Bishop of Winchester owned a large area to the west of Borough High Street from the 12th century, and this area became the manor of the Clink. The manor of the Paris Garden, located to the west of the Clink during the medieval period, was owned by the Knights Templar religious order.

All of Southwark became the 26th ward of the city in 1550, called Bridge Ward Without. Even so, the borough was independent of the city's jurisdiction and this continued until 1889 when it became part of the county of London. This status meant that the Paris Garden and Clink manors had considerable influence over the borough's society and economy. It also meant that the borough, which was not subject to the London Councillors' disapproval of plays, became a focus for theatre and leisure, with the Rose Theatre built in 1592 and the Globe in 1599.

Bankside, within the Paris Garden and the Clink, became associated with prostitution, possibly as early as the 13th century. During the 14th century this area became known as the Stews where a large number of brothels operated (Carlin 1996, 40; 49). These became known as leisure ground areas with bear, dog and bull baiting by the late 15th to 16th centuries. However, during the 17th century, such activities did not conform to the interests of increasing urban expansion, and landlords attempted to annul them. In 1655, for example, Thomas Walker, who owned the Clink, ordered soldiers to shoot seven of the bears to death and pulled down a playhouse to build tenements.

Located on the south bank of the Thames, Southwark was very well connected for trade and commerce, being accessible to Surrey and Kent, the Upper Thames and the Lower Thames estuary, as well as coastal and international destinations. In addition, Southwark's economic development greatly benefited from London Bridge, which until 1750 was the only bridge over the Thames in London, and afforded direct access to important markets lying north of the river. It was the accessibility of the borough, coupled with its status outside London's jurisdiction, that encouraged considerable, rapid growth of commerce and industry. For example, the Borough Market became an important centre of commerce, and Southwark was populated by taverns, inn-keeping and associated trades. Leather-works, breweries, vinegar and glassworks, and tanning were all established and by the 19th century Southwark, along with South London, had become the capital's industrial quarter.

Many of Southwark's inhabitants were poor and, like elsewhere in London, the borough's rapid expansion was characterised by poor public health amenities and a high prevalence of infectious diseases. Very high rates of mortality and morbidity were experienced among the working classes as a result of poor air quality, overcrowding, malnutrition, and poor working conditions. Contributing to this were several outbreaks of plague, in 1577–78, 1603, 1625, 1635–36, 1637 and 1641. There was also a devastating fire on 26 May 1676, which resulted in a number of fatalities, believed to have been higher than the number resulting from the Great Fire of London 10 years previously.

St Margaret's New Churchyard

The church of St Margaret's was located on the west side of Borough High Street at the junction with Stoney Street, and was in existence by the early 12th century (Fig. 2.1). The medieval burial ground for this church was originally located in a triangular plot of land between Borough High Street and a street called Counter Lane on Rocque's map of 1746.

On 20 August 1536 the size of the churchyard was allowed to be increased by an Act of Parliament. The churchwardens must have anticipated the need for a new churchyard as they purchased an acre of ground from Thomas Ouley esq. in 1533. A memorandum of 1534 gives details of the reason for the new churchyard in the parish of St Margaret:

> Let it be known by the ? ? year of our Lord 1534. This be consent of the inhabitants of the parish of Saint Margaret in Southwark ? by their good ? brought and purchased from Thomas Ouley esquire and his wife a certain old place in the ground belonging to the same sometimes called the Lord Ferres Place set and being within the said parish. The buyers there of Thomas Bully, John Smith William Cutter, John Ritten, Wraffe Copwood, John Garner, John Crosse, Robert Petty, William Jefferson, William Chandler. Nicolas ? Bridge, John Sparrow with the aid of all the whole body of the parish for the sum of one hundred and ten pounds sterling which was gathered among the for said buyers and the inhabitors of this same parish withy ten pounds that the prior of Saint Mary Overies gave to the same purchases and all they willing to make a churchyard they having so

Documentary evidence

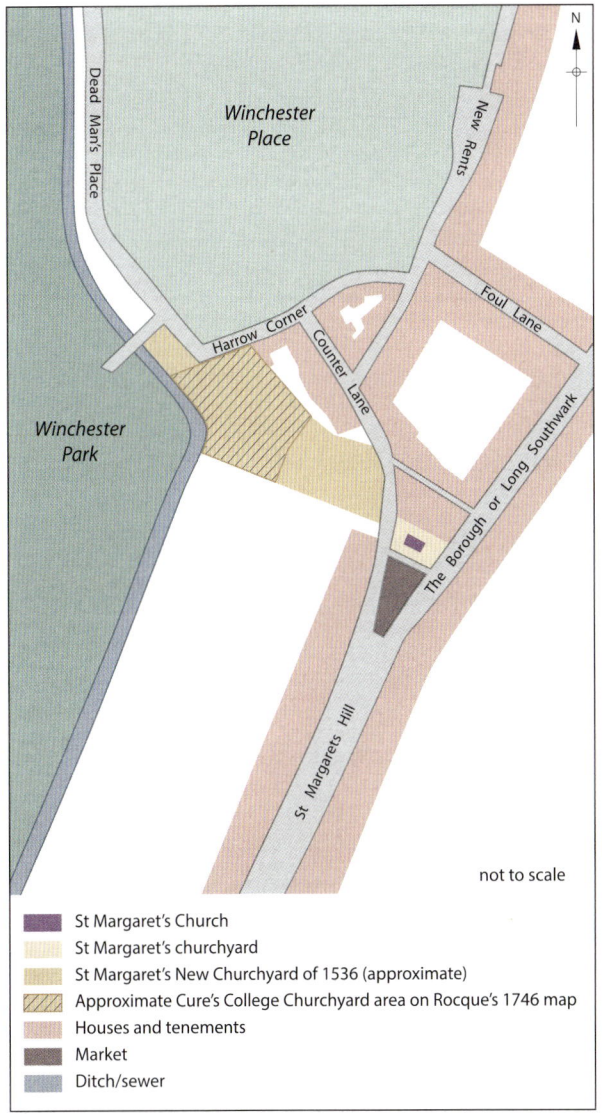

small and scant room in the time of necessity that they were faine to bury three or four dead bodies within one sepulchre one upon another. The which churchyard was ? and hallowed the ? day of September base in the year of our Lord one thousand five hundred and thirty six it is to be known by this record that out sovereign Lord King Henry the eight supreme head in the earth ? god of the church of England and the 27th year of his most noble reign (LMA P92/SAV/0025).

Carlin (1983, 162) describes the location of this churchyard as lying west of the corner of Counter Lane and south of Harrow Corner (later the site of Cure's College; see Fig. 2.1 for conjectured location). The acre of ground that was brought in 1533 contained eight dilapidated houses and five gardens that were later turned into the new burial ground (Carlin 1983, 163).

The new churchyard is not depicted on a schematic plan of Southwark dated to 1550 (Carlin 1983). It may possibly be shown on Braun and Hogenberg's *Londinvm Feracissimi Angliae* map of c 1572 (Fig. 2.2), where a rectangular plot of land is shown located on the corner of Dead Man's Place and Counter Lane (named on Morgan's map of 1682; see below). The map also shows houses to the west of Counter Lane and fronting the road that became known as Dead Man's Place. On the western and southern side of the rectangular space appear to be trees or shrubs indicating there may not have been houses on these two sides. Several dashes are indicated

Fig. 2.1 Possible location of St Margaret's New Churchyard 1536 –c 1587 (later the location of Cure's College)

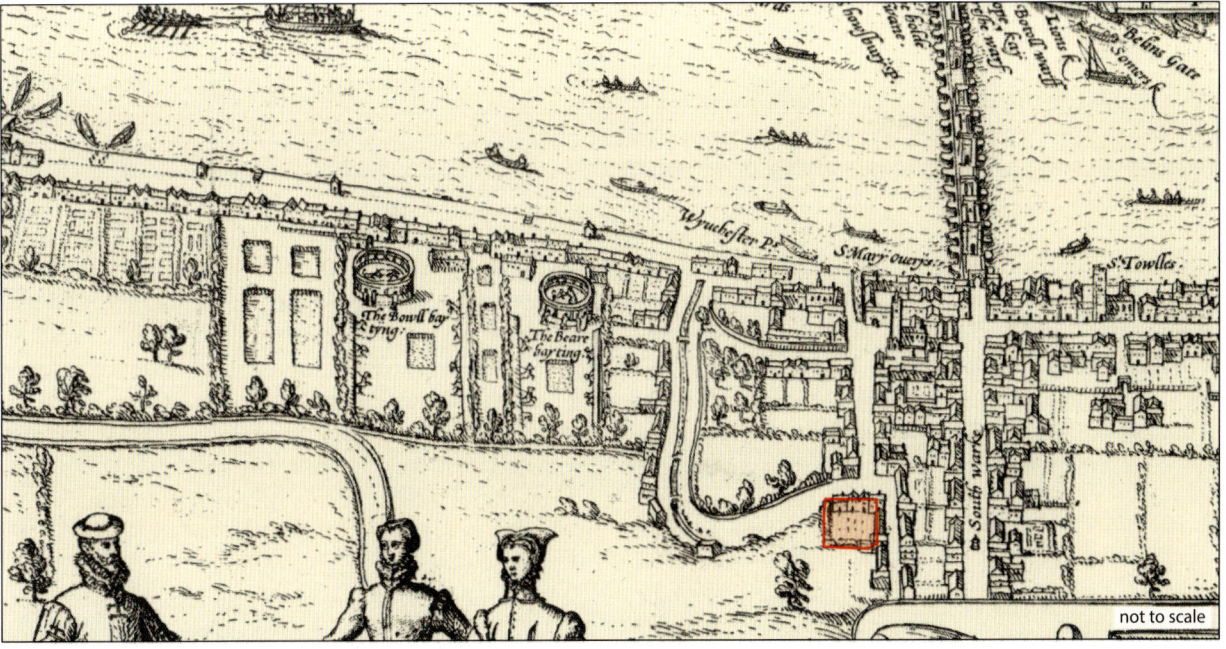

Fig. 2.2 Possible location of the new churchyard, later Cure's College, on Londinvm Feracissimi Angliæ map c 1572 (© Southwark Council)

within the open space which may indicate grave markers but this is speculative.

Any burials within this acre between 1536 and 1540 are likely to have been general parishioners from the parish of St Margaret. Between 1540 and the later 16th century St Saviour's became the parish church, and the primary choice of burial location may have become one of the burial grounds around St Saviour's Church. It is possible, however, that burials may have continued in the new churchyard as an interim arrangement. Alternatively, it may have been used as a lower status burial ground as the burial fees show that interment around the parish church appeared to be the most expensive option between 1613 and 1838 (Table 2.2).

St Margaret's Church declined in use after the formation of St Saviour's parish in 1540. Soon after this the church was converted into a courthouse and may have survived until the fire of Southwark in 1676 (Carlin 1983, 155–6). The burial ground associated with St Margaret's Church became the responsibility of the churchwardens of St Saviour's after 1540. Part or all of this burial ground may have spread across Counter Lane as in 1573–4 the church was ordered to not supply room for burials as the churchyard was located in the middle of the highway (Malden 1912, 151–61). This could indicate that this acre burial ground had begun to decline in use by the later 16th century. By the time of Rocque's map of 1746 the area west of Counter Lane appears to have been built on.

Cure's College burial ground

The burial ground is variously referred to as Cure's College, St Saviour's Almshouse, or College Yard burial ground (Londonburials.co.uk). It was a fee-paying burial ground, used by the poorer members of the parish who were either sponsored or who could not afford a burial at the more expensive parish church of St Saviour.

Foundation of the College
In 1579 Thomas Cure (Fig. 2.3) bought Waverley House and lands adjoining from Lord Montague. Waverley House, located north-west of St Margaret's New Churchyard, had previously belonged to the Abbot of Waverley before the dissolution. The church-wardens ceased renting it out in 1587:

> ...it is agreed at this Vestry that Waverley Howse shall not be let by lease to any man.
>
> Item it is also agreed at this Vestry that the church-wardens and vestrymen shall enter into Waverley Howse at Michaelmas next, and then see how every house is rented and so dispose the same according to their discretions (P92/SAV/450, Vestry Minutes 1582-1628, 225, Tuesday 20 June 1587).

This corresponds with a period of change for St Margaret's New Churchyard, as parts of it appear to have been divided up as parcels of land and sold on during the late 16th century. By 1580 the wardens of the parish of St Saviour had already built six almshouses on part of the new churchyard (Roberts and Godfrey 1950, 82–3). The names of the first inhabitants of the almshouses are recorded in the vestry minutes:

> At which Vestry these poor people hereunder named were placed in the new churchyard, in the new almshouses there, *viz*
>
> Father Wriggs
>
> Father Wrighte, Father Rodes, Mother Noble, Mother Mase, Mother Buglesse
>
> Also it was further agreed at the said Vestry that every one of the above named poor people should have weekly towards their relief 20d apiece (P92/SAV/449, Vestry Minutes 1557-81, 162, Saturday 8 October 1580).

In 1584 Thomas Cure commissioned the building of a hospital or college for poor and sick people on his land (Roberts and Godfrey 1950, 82–3). He organised the building of another ten almshouses that were added to the six existing ones. The sixteen almshouses became known as Cure's College (Malden 1912, 161–2).

> Lastly it is agreed at this Vestry that the chimneys of the three old houses in the churchyard shall be removed reared and builded up according as the former almshouses be within the houses, and also fenced up with brick above the doors, towards the which Mr. Cure hath promised to give 40s, who shall be a surveyor of the same. And also give his opinion therein (P92/SAV/450, Vestry Minutes 1582–1628, 225, Tuesday 20 June 1587).

Cure's College could be thought of as an early workhouse, perhaps with more favourable conditions, that is, an income. The College admitted certain people and gave them a pension of 20d a week. In order to be accepted the inmates had to be elected by a sponsor, and members of the parish vestry voted on who to admit. Those admitted were tested on knowledge of the Christian faith and had to agree to strict house rules, which included no drinking or swearing. They were allowed to be accompanied by their husband or wife and children, to share a single pension, and any able-bodied had to work. They had to wear a badge outside of the College, and were locked in at night. Residents included people who had worked as labourers and lived in the parish for several years;

Documentary evidence

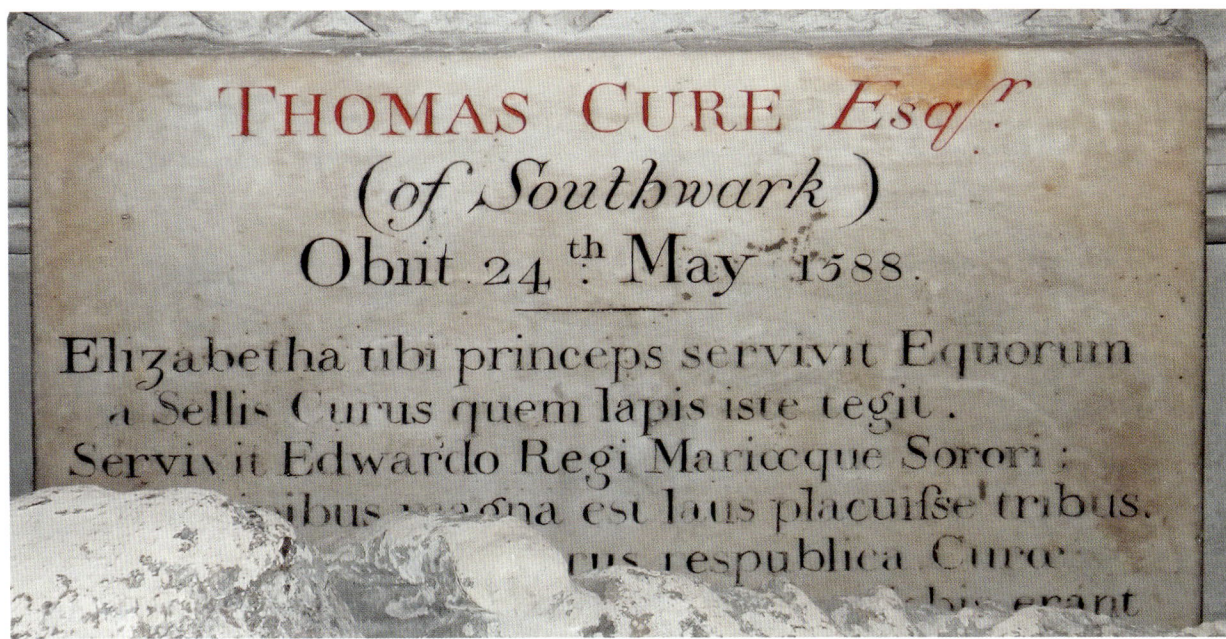

Fig. 2.3 (a) Thomas Cure's plaque, Southwark Cathedral (obscured by a later monument)

Fig. 2.3 (b) stone tablet dedicated to Thomas Cure at 9 Park Street

the blind; the long term ill but not contagious; people impoverished through no fault of their own (eg fire or shipwreck); and those overburdened by children.

The physical setting of Cure's College is considered in Roberts and Godfrey (1950). The almshouses were set back from Park Street, but were surrounded by other abodes and businesses, including the nearby Borough Market. Soap Yard, where soap was manufactured during the 16th and 17th centuries, occupied part of the property between Park Street and the almshouses, and a brewhouse encroached on the property in the early 18th century. In addition, some properties were endowed to Cure's, including no. 7 (The Wheatsheaf), nos 8 and 9 (The Harrow) and nos 1–13 (Harrow Corner).

In 1587, the vestry had decided to partition part of the new churchyard off and make the College and its burial ground a separate entity. The Vestry minutes for St Saviour record details of this change of boundary on 30 July 1587:

> …it is agreed at this Vestry that the pale in the new churchyard at the charges of the parish shall be removed and set elsewhere at the discretion of the churchwardens, and surveyors (viz) Mr Cure, Mr. Hedd, Mr. Pynder, and Mr. Dodsonne. Item it is also agreed at this Vestry that the common privy within the new churchyard aforesaid shall likewise at the charges of the parish be taken down and set elsewhere according to the discretion of the churchwardens and surveyors first above named, whereby the College and churchyard may be severed and kept by itself (P92/SAV/450, Vestry Minutes 1582–1628).

This change may have been because St Margaret's New Churchyard had already gone out of use by this point. The minutes above suggest that the new churchyard was being used partly as a common privy, and therefore not respected as a burial place at this time. Vestry minutes from 1603 suggest that the only decent place for burial was around St Saviour's Church by this date:

> Also it was agreed that concerning the place of burial betwixt chain and chain in the uttermost

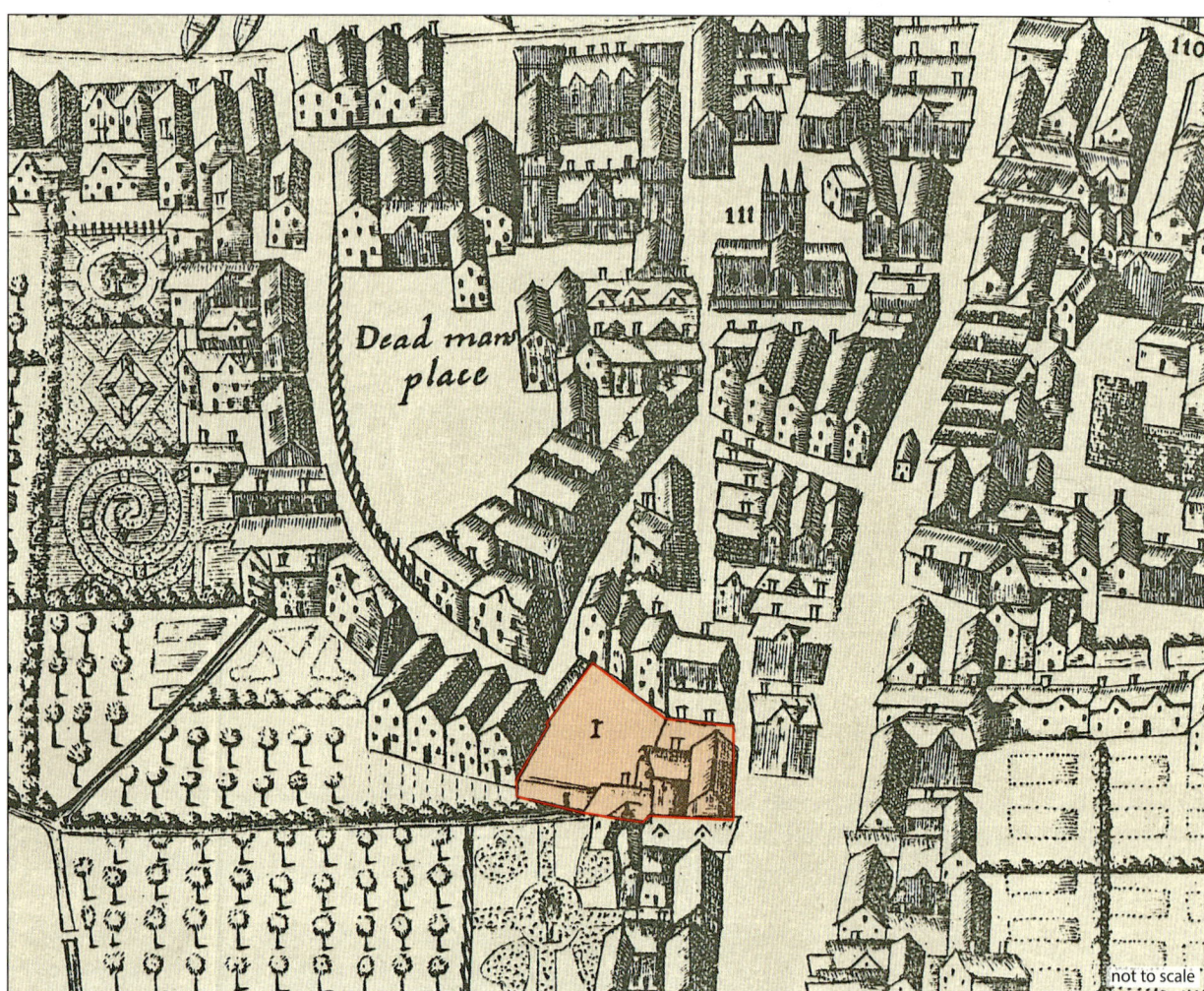

Fig. 2.4 Newcourt's map of 1658 showing Cure's College burial ground (labelled I) (© Southwark Archives)

Churchyard sometimes St. Mary Magdalene's, and the making up of the Church walls and all other things thereunto belonging, shall be referred to the churchwardens' discretions, as also the paving and graveling of the said Churchyard for keeping of it decent for burial, seeing now there is no other meet place for burial (P92/SAV/450, Vestry Minutes 1582–1628, 372, Thursday 24 November 1603).

Thus, the area formally set out in 1587 as Cure's College burial ground possibly encompassed land containing parish burials dating from 1536, but the archaeological investigations did not produce any evidence to support this either way (see Chapter 3). There is no record of any distinct area being used for burials for the short period between the foundation of the almshouses in 1580 and 1584 and the establishment of Cure's College burial ground in 1587.

17th and 18th centuries
Newcourt's map of 1658 (Fig. 2.4) shows what may be Cure's College burial ground (labelled I), with tenements both to the north and east of it. To the south of Cure's College there appears to be a boundary wall with a doorway within it, and a boundary wall to the north-west of the College grounds, which separated the burial ground from Park Street.

Morgan's Map of 1676–82 (Fig. 2.5) shows that the original almshouses of the late 16th century may have been located on the south-west side of the College, and possibly on the north-east side by this date. The College burial ground appears to lead straight onto Park Lane to the north (called Dead Man's Place at the time). A wall runs along the south-western side of the College, separating it from an area of open ground. It is possible that the wall followed a boundary line of medieval origin, namely the ditch separating Winchester Place from Winchester Park (see Thameslink Monograph 2).

Rocque's map of 1746 (Fig. 2.6) indicates that by this time more buildings had been constructed to the north of the College, and the entrance onto Harrow Corner had become narrower. Rocque also labelled a block of buildings on the north-east side of the College as 'Coll. Al. H'. By this date the open space to the south-

Fig. 2.5 Morgan's map of 1676–1682 showing College Church Yard (© Southwark Archives)

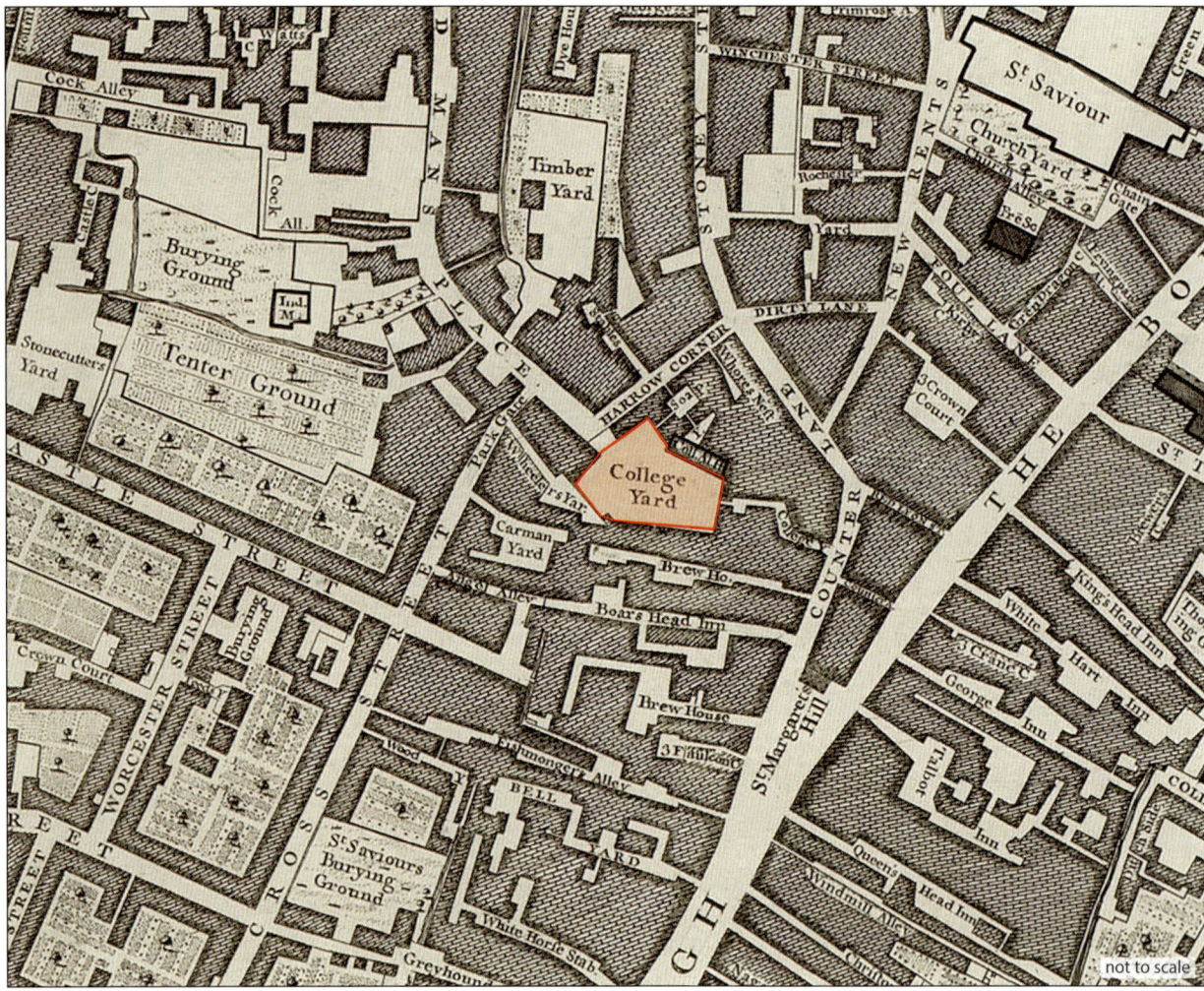

Fig. 2.6 Rocque's map of 1746 showing College Yard and College Almshouses (© MOTCO)

west of the College Yard appears to have been built on.

Horwood's map of 1792–9 (Fig. 2.7) shows the College buildings in greater detail. Six almshouses are visible on the north-east side, seven beside the passageway to the east, two buildings on the east side of the yard, seven buildings to the south, and two buildings on the west side of the quadrangle. The buildings on the west side do not appear on Rocque's map, where the boundary wall to the west abuts Wheelers Yard.

Gwilt's surveys of 1814 and 1821
George Gwilt surveyed many buildings in the St Saviour's area during the early 19th century. His detailed survey of the College almshouses in 1814 (Fig. 2.8) shows how they were arranged around the burial ground in the centre. By this date the area of the College burial ground is known to have reduced in size. Prior to this it is possible that the burial ground may have extended up to the almshouses on all sides.

On Gwilt's survey, a pathway appears to frame the outside of the burial ground. The burial ground itself appears to have been formalised into an uneven rectangular shape, with most of it on an east-south-east and west-north-west alignment, and the western side facing north-west. This uneven alignment may have been the result of using the plot of St Margaret's New Churchyard which ran from the corner of Counter Street westwards. A gate or boundary appears to be blocking off the entrance to the burial ground from Park Street, suggesting that the College and burial ground had become a private and restricted space by this date.

Gwilt also surveyed the College burial ground in 1821 (Fig. 2.9) and included the date at which some of the buildings were constructed. The erection date of the buildings to the north of the quadrangle is 1820, and these no doubt replaced earlier almshouses shown on the same plot. The buildings to the south and east are not labelled. Three almshouses in the centre of the southern elevation are labelled with a construction date of 1820, and as 'raised six feet higher than the old tenements'. The building to the west of these is labelled as 1695, the building in the north-west corner as 1694, and the building next to it is labelled 'Chapel'. The

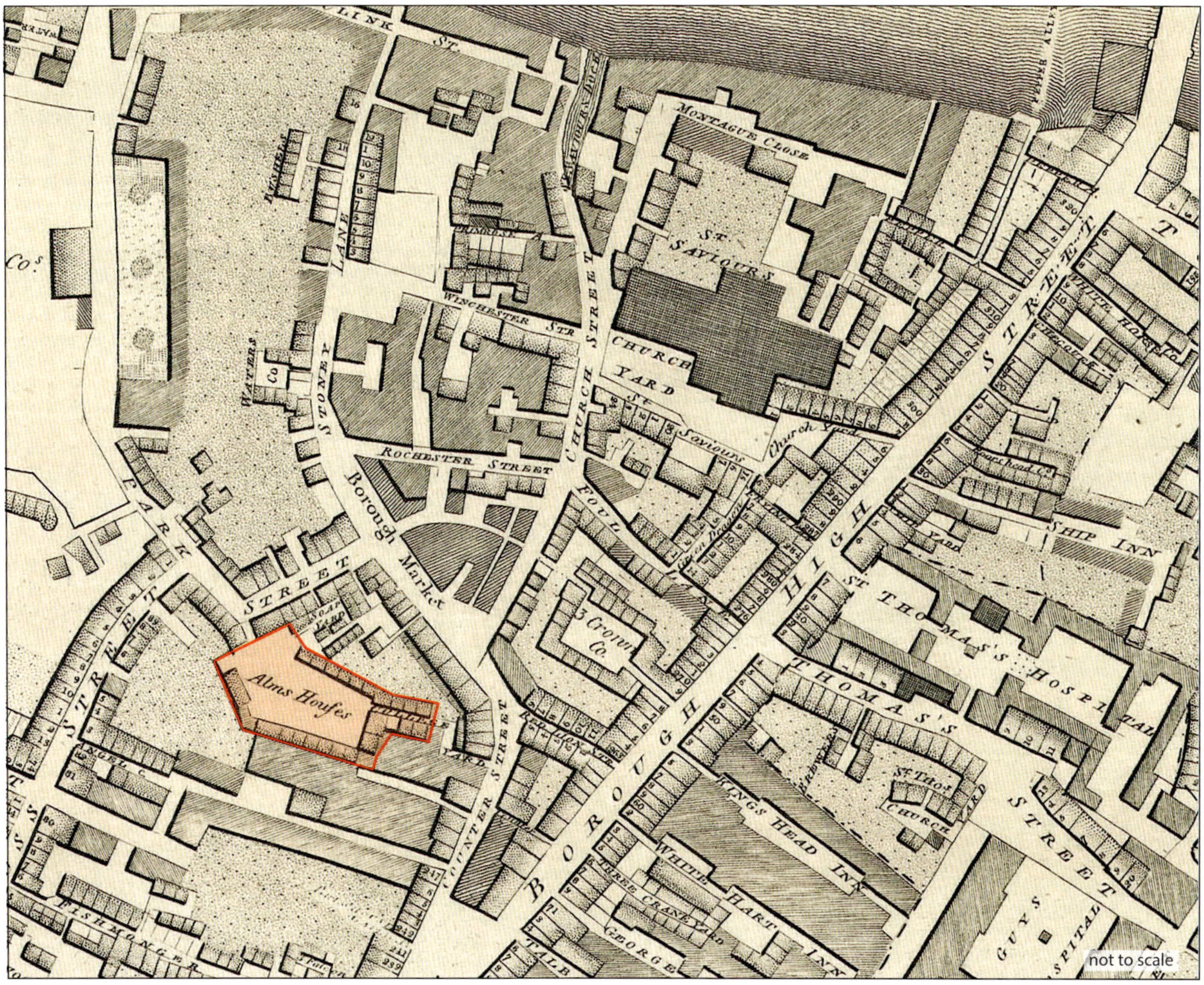

Documentary evidence 15

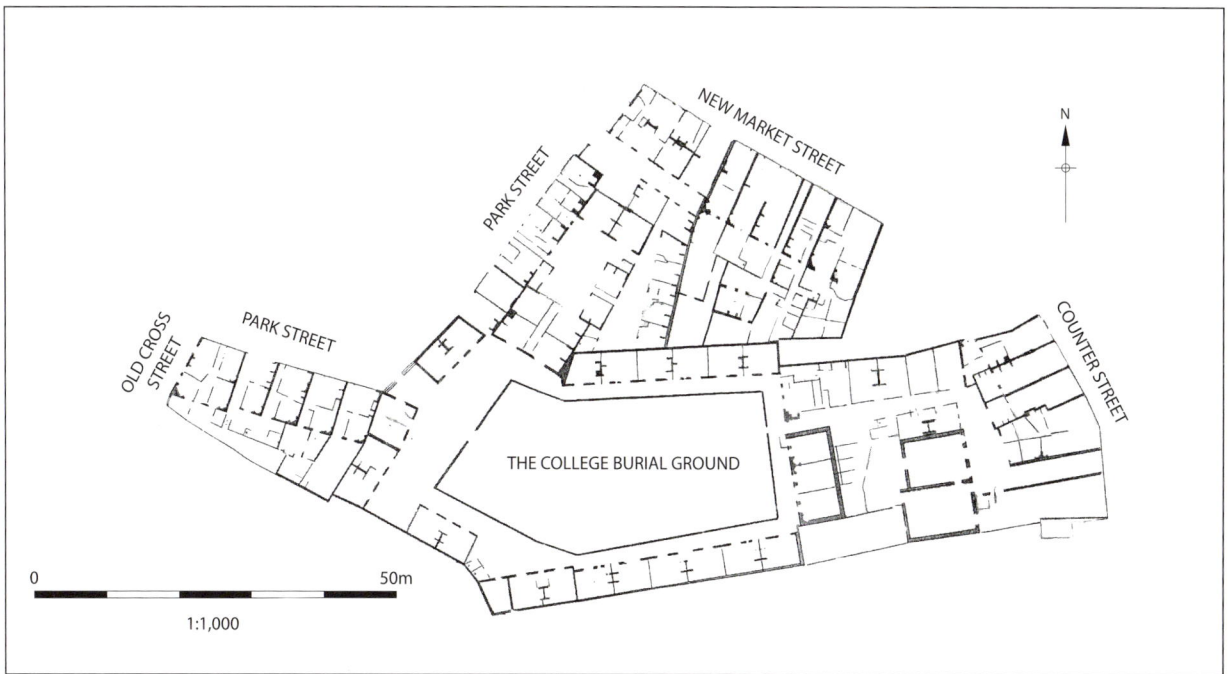

Fig. 2.7 Horwood's map of 1792–1799 showing Almshouses (© MOTCO)

Fig. 2.8 Gwilt's 1814 survey of Cure's College (after an original held by London Metropolitan Archives)

building in the north corner, adjoining Park Street, is labelled 1709.

By 1821 the western end of the formalised burial ground had been modified to a more rounded shape than the rectangle shown on Gwilt's earlier survey of 1814. The rounded end of the burial ground appears to be off-centre.

1831–1862

In 1831 the College almshouses were rebuilt and the western end of the burial ground reorganised (Roberts and Godfrey 1950, 82–3). This can be seen on Howe's plan of the College dated 1844 (see Fig. 2.10). The plan shows that the College burial ground had been reshaped into a more symmetrical design in 1831. The amount of open yard space was reduced at the north-western end of the site and replaced with three adjacent buildings.

Howe's plan also shows that ten inmates of the College were from the Borough, six from the Clink liberty, three were sponsored by named individuals (Jackson, Young and Spratt), and three by unnamed individuals, making a total of 22 inmates. The five inmates of Soap Yard are also listed. Soap Yard appears to have been associated with the College as the entrance yard to it is shown leading eastwards from the College yard.

Burials may have continued in the College burial ground until the 1853 burial ground closure Act of Parliament which banned the burying of the dead within urban areas, or possibly as late as 1863 when the almshouse was closed and the land sold to Charing Cross Railway Company. The vestry minutes of 1849 show that the College Yard was still in use until at least during the late 1840s:

> That in Cure's College which entirely surrounds the college grave yard there have been 27 deaths during the last 12 years and that of these 11 persons lived to upwards of 80 years of age, 8 upwards of 75, 4 upwards of 67, 1 upwards of 62 showing that interring the dead in this ground was not to prejudicial to the health of those persons.
>
> That only one case of cholera has occurred in the college during the present awful visitation and that case was not fatal (Extract from the report of the wardens as to burials, 11 September 1849).

On 24 September 1853 the burial board of St Saviour's met to receive tenders for the conveyance of the dead of

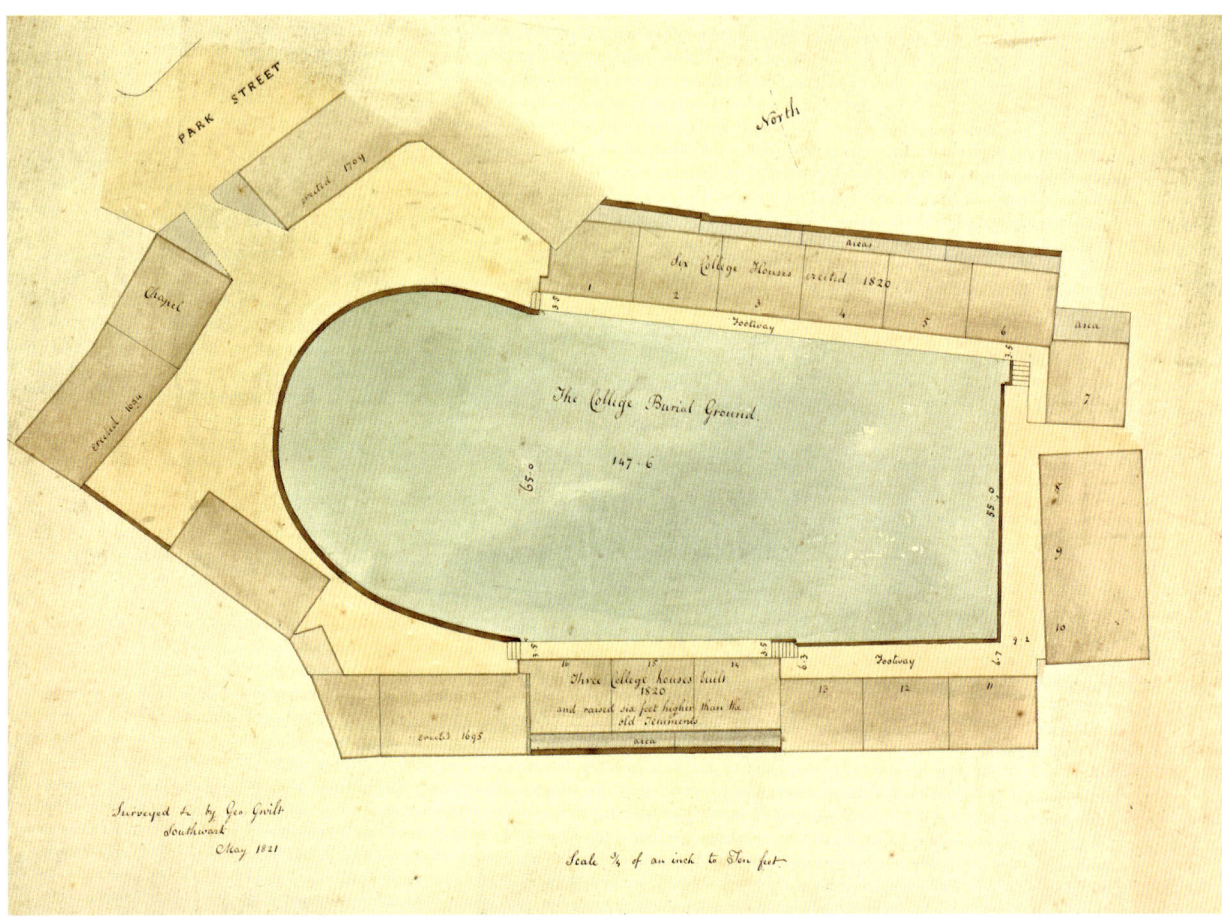

Fig. 2.9 Gwilt's 1821 survey of Cure's College (© London Metropolitan Archives)

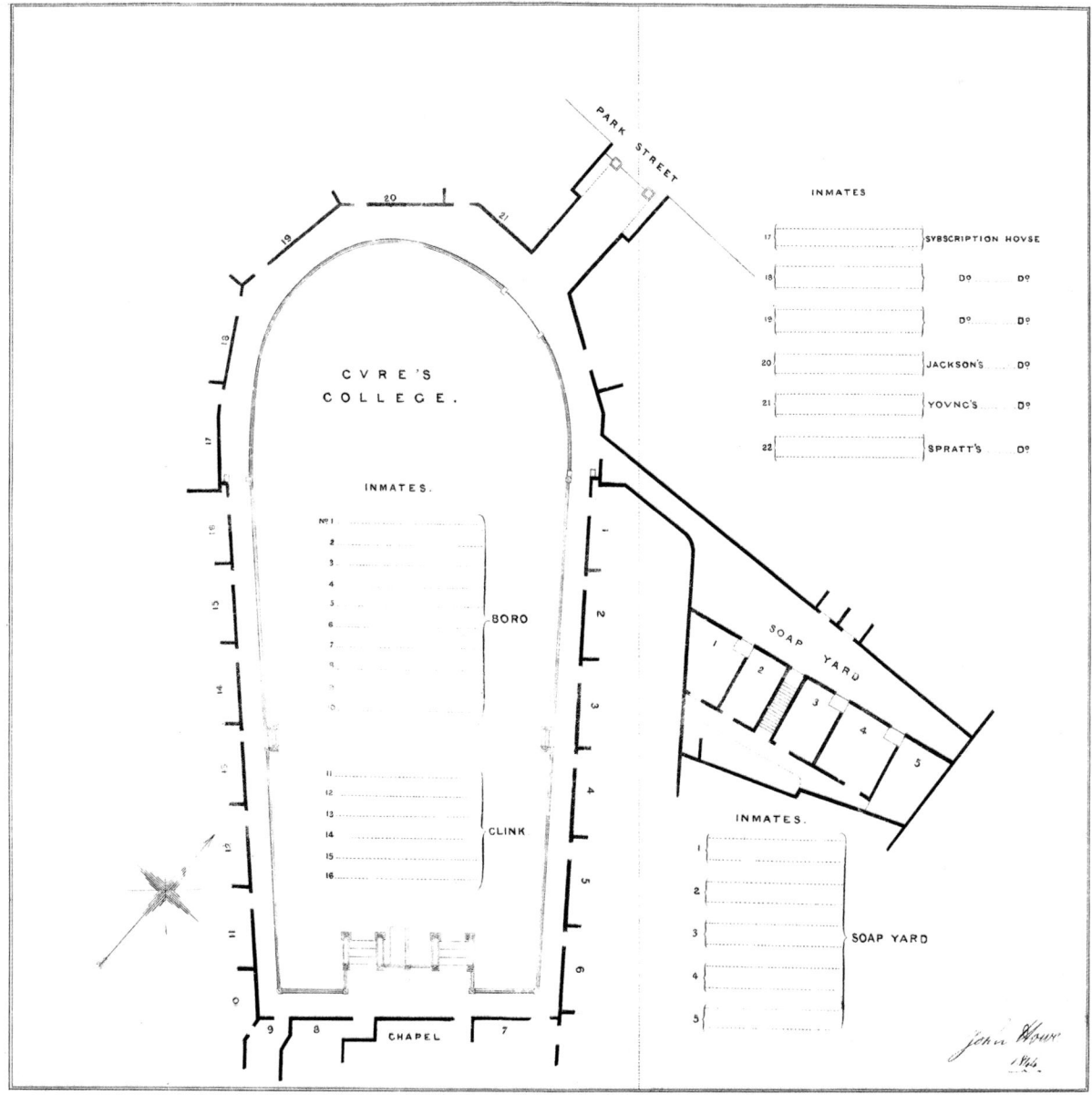

Fig. 2.10 Jn. Howe's 1844 plan of Cure's College, showing the rebuild of 1831 (© London Metropolitan Archives)

St Saviour's to the burial yard of Victoria Park cemetery, Mile End Road. This was primarily a meeting to discuss the conveyance of poor inhabitants of the parish from the Union in Marlborough Street. They also wanted tenders for 'other classes of inhabitants' to be taken from their dwellings with mourners (Daily News, Issue 2293, Monday, 26 September 1853).

In 1862 the Charing Cross Railway Company bought Cure's College. At least 7950 burials were cleared and taken for reburial at Brookwood Cemetery, Woking and Nunhead Cemetery, South London (National Archives, RAIL 107/3). The land was subsequently developed as a viaduct for the London Bridge to Charing Cross railway and a builder's yard, the latter now part of Borough Market. The almsmen and women were moved to newly-built almshouses in Lower Norwood.

The Park Street excavation demonstrated that the clearance was far from complete, with 331 articulated burials and much disarticulated bone recovered. Clearance appears to have taken place only within the post-1831 extent of the burial ground. Burials sealed beneath buildings and paths built in 1831 were left in place (see Chapter 3).

Today, Cure's Almshouse survives as St Saviour's Court, Purley, which is in the care of the Corporation of Wardens of the Parish of St Saviour's (or United St Saviour's Charity), founded during the reign of Henry VI as the Guild of the Fraternity of the Blessed Virgin Mary. The guild was later incorporated under Henry

> **Thomas Cure (d. 1588)**
>
> Thomas Cure was a wealthy individual who earned a living as master of the saddle horses to Edward VI, Queen Mary, and Queen Elizabeth I. According to the wardrobe accounts he earned over £500 in 1583 and over £1500 in 1584 (Hasler 1981). Such was his wealth that, in addition to founding Cure's Almshouse, he owned a ship and its cargo in 1573, acquired a manor of Widefleete in Southwark in 1580, and paid for the engraving of a new silver seal for East Grinstead's coat of arms in 1572. A warden at St Saviour's, Southwark by 1559, he served as an MP for the borough of Southwark in 1563, 1571, and 1586. He served on committees concerned with foreign tradesmen, work for the poor, inn holders and tipplers, tanned leather and the preservation of woods (Hasler 1981).
>
> Cure died on 24 May 1588 and in his will he passed the responsibility of making annual payments to the poor living in his almshouse to his son, George. Cure is buried in Southwark Cathedral (see Fig. 2.3).

VIII to manage parish affairs and local charities for the people of north Southwark.

Other contemporary burial grounds in St Saviour's parish

Burial grounds in use in the parish around the time of Cure's College included St Saviour's Church and churchyard (Fig. 2.11; and see Table 2.2 below), now Southwark Cathedral, the most popular place of burial (in particular, the southern churchyard), used between 1540 and 1853 by non-parishioners as well as parishioners. St Mary Magdalene Chapel churchyard, dating from the 13th century and associated with St Mary's Priory, was amalgamated into St Saviour's south churchyard in c 1540. St Margaret's New Churchyard, described above, was an extension of the 12th century churchyard and may or may not have been in use at the time of Cure's burial ground. Cross Bones burial ground (c 1594–1853) was for the poorest members of the parish, as well as St Saviour's Union burial ground, of a slightly later date (1780–1853), established for inmates of the workhouse. St Saviour's, Cure's, and Cross Bones were the three burial grounds used by the parish authorities. Other burial grounds within the parish included Dead Man's Place, possibly dating from the 1660s until at least 1843. It was originally

Table 2.1: Comparison between the burial fees of burial grounds in St Saviour (Churchwardens of St Saviour broadsheet 1613; Concanen and Morgan 1795, 161–6; Turner 1838).

	1613	1709	1792	1838
St Saviour's Church (interior)	20 shillings (not including extras), grave maker 16d	Varies depending on location. Between £3–£10 and £1–£2 in the vaults. Under 7 years cheaper	Same as 1709, no change in fees for church and vault burials	Unknown
St Saviour's, vaults under church	NA	Adults £1, 10 shillings. 7–14 years 15 shillings. Under 7 years 15 shillings	Adults £1, 10 shillings. 7–14 years 15 shillings. Under 7 years 15 shillings	Must be in lead. Adult £3 13s 8d. Under 10 years £2 12s
St Saviour's churchyards (in 1709 probably Bull or Green Church-Yard)	2 shillings with a coffin, 16d without	Adults 5 shillings. 7–14s 2 shillings 6d, under 7 years 1 shilling 8d	Adults and over 7s 10 shillings, under 7 years 5 shillings	Adults £1, 5s, 10d. Under 10 years 16s 2d
Cure's College burial ground	Adults 12d with coffin/ 8d without. Childe 4d with coffin, 2d without	Adults 2 shillings 8d, 7–14 years 1 shilling 4d, under 7 years 8d	Adults and 7–14s 7 shillings and 6d, under 7 years 3 shillings 6d	Adults £2 10d, Under 10 years £1, 3s
Old Burying Ground (in 1709) Probably Cross Bones	Unknown	Adults 1 shilling, 4d, 7–14 years 8d, under 7 years 4d	Adults and 7–14 years 2 shillings, 6d. Under 7 years 1 shilling 6d	Cross Bones: 4 feet grave Adult 12s 20d, Child 8s 2d
St Saviour's New Burying Ground from c 1792? This could be the Union Workhouse burial ground from 1780 onwards	NA	NA	Adults and 7–14 years 1 shilling, Under 7 years 3d	Unknown

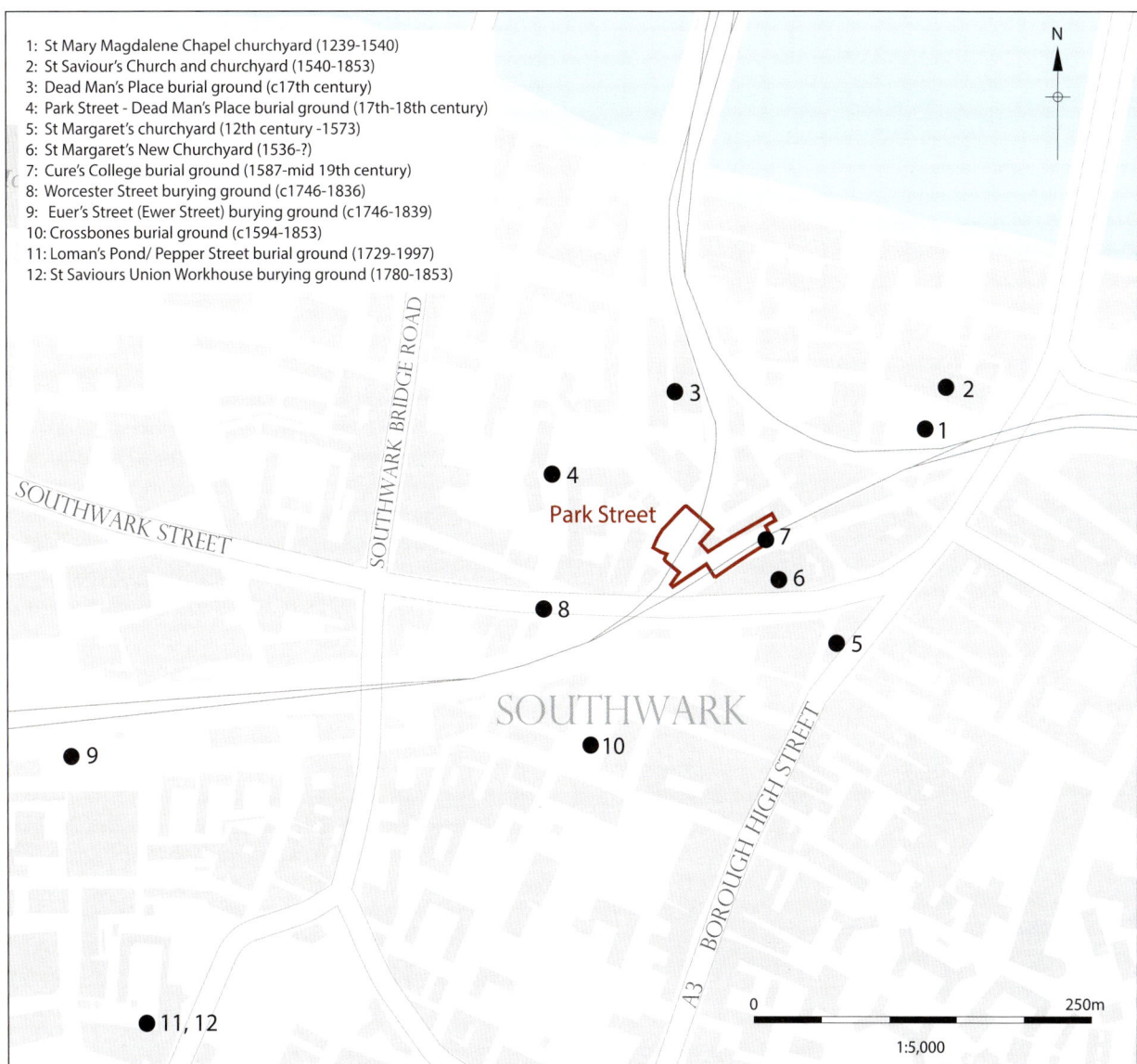

Fig. 2.11 12th century–19th century burial grounds of St Saviour parish

established for victims who died of plague in 1665, but the west side was later used as an independent minister's burial ground. The burial grounds at Worcester Street, Euer's Street (Ewer Street) and Pepper Street (Loman's Pond) date to between the 18th and early 19th centuries and were used by non-conformists, Quakers and Baptists, respectively.

Burial fees for St Saviour 1613–1838

The churchyard to the south of St Saviour became the premier burial location for the people of St Saviour's parish, and between 1613 until 1795 the cost of burial is known to have increased steadily (Table 2.1). The increasing costs of burial over time in St Saviour's Church itself and the vaults show that pressures of burial space increased with the population of St Saviour.

If the burial fees per burial ground in St Saviour's are converted from pounds and shillings into pence, a comparison of the costs can be made over time. Table 2.2 shows the increasing costs of burial in pence for an average adult burial at each of the burial grounds. For burial inside St Saviour's Church £3 has been used as an average amount of fees.

Figure 2.12 shows that in 1613 the most expensive burial location in St Saviour's was burial inside St Saviour's Church. This trend continued in the 18th century, when it was still by far the most expensive place to be buried. The costs of burial inside St Saviour's are not known for the 19th century, but it is likely they would have been substantially higher than for the 18th century. The price of burial within the vaults of St Saviour's Church are the same for both 1709 and 1792, whereas the cost of burial in the vaults in 1838 had more than doubled. The costs of burial

Table 2.2: Comparison of burial fees at each of the main parochial burial grounds of St Saviour (in pence)

	1613	1709	1792	1838
St Saviour's Church (interior)	256	720	720	
St Saviour's Church vaults		360	360	884
St Saviour's churchyards	24	60	120	310
Cure's College burial ground	12	32	90	490
Old Burying Ground (Cross Bones)		16	30	164
St Saviour's New Burying Ground (Union Workhouse)			12	

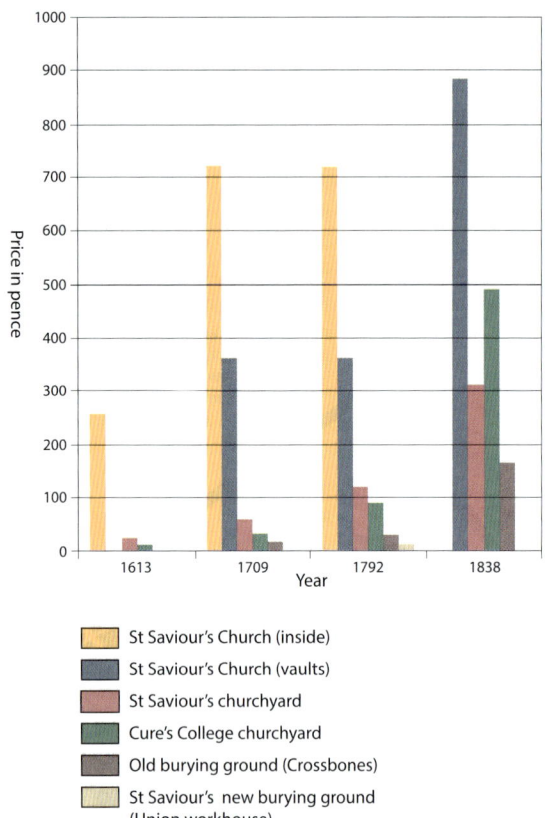

Fig. 2.12 Cost of six burial locations in St Saviour's parish in 1613, 1709, 1792 and 1838

within St Saviour's churchyards increased greatly over time. The cost of burial in the Old Burying Ground (probably Cross Bones) also increased over time, particularly in 1838. The cheapest place to be buried in 1792 was the St Saviour's New Burying Ground, which was most likely to have been the Union Workhouse burial ground, which opened around 1780.

Between 1613 and 1792 the Cure's College burial ground was one the cheapest places to be buried within St Saviour. During the 17th century the College burial ground was the cheapest location for burial, in 1702 it was the second cheapest, and in 1792 the third cheapest burial location. However, during the 19th century the cost of burial in the College burial ground appears to have increased to a higher rate than the churchyards around St Saviour's Church. In the 19th century Cure's College burial ground became the second most expensive place to be buried after the St Saviour's Church vaults.

If the average burial fees are also used as an indicator of social status it would suggest that burial within St Saviour's Church was reserved for the wealthiest residents during the 17th and 18th centuries. The vaults may have later become the next most favourable place for the wealthy to be buried. The status of the people buried within the College burial ground may have changed over time, it possibly being a burial ground for the poor during the 17th century. This is supported by research from Boulton (2005), who found that during the 17th century parishioners in St Saviour's on an adequate income could afford to pay at least 1 shilling for a burial. Therefore, it is likely that in the 17th century people buried at the College burial ground would have been amongst the 26% of the population Boulton classed as poor. This group of people would have needed their burial fees to be paid for by the parish, and are likely to have been unemployed, sick or aged.

During the 18th century the College burial ground was not the only location for burial of the poorer population. In 1792 the Old Burying Ground and the workhouse may have been allocated for the poorest residents of St Saviour's, and so the demographic of the people buried in the College burial ground may have changed in the 18th century.

In the 19th century Cure's College burial ground may have become more exclusive as the cost of burial increased to nearly 500d (£2, 10d). Perhaps by 1838 the College burial ground had become so full that very few people were buried there, and so the burial cost had risen steeply. This may be explained by a decrease in the amount of space in the burial ground after the 1831 rebuilding works at the College, which reduced the size of the burial ground by approximately one-fifth.

Burial registers and fees books for St Saviour's parish

Burial registers
The St Saviour parish records are held at the London Metropolitan Archives under reference code P92/SAV. These records have been gathered from several different

sources, including separate sets of administrative papers relating to the wardens of St Saviour, and the vestry records. Seven burial registers are catalogued for the period 1722–1848, but these cover only periods of a few years each, interspersed with large gaps. The original registers were not available for access at the time of research, but they have been digitised and made available online (www.ancestry.co.uk; www.findmypast.co.uk). A search of these resources produced only limited results for 'Cure + College', 'College' and other variants.

Additionally, more basic summary burial registers for St Saviour's parish dating to the early 19th century are held on microfilm in the Southwark Archives. These list the first name and surname of the deceased, their abode, burial date, and the name of the person who officiated at the ceremony, but not the burial location. The parish burial registers, therefore, provide limited information on the population interred at Cure's College.

Fees books
The parish records in the London Metropolitan Archives also include four fees books dating to between 1766 and 1802. These provide the names, age of death, and crucially the location of burial, with Cure's College burial ground indicated by the word 'college'. They state the cost of the burial, in some cases giving a breakdown of the various fees. The occupation and cause of death of the deceased are also sometimes listed. Although not burial registers as such, these give a much more detailed account of burials within the parish for the periods of time they cover.

The four fee books examined include two which were classed as at risk, and so the pages could not be counted quickly. Page numbers were estimated by the stacks of pages within bindings which fell at regular intervals of about 15 pages. Table 2.3 shows that during the period 1766–1802 the use of the College burial ground may have changed, with a peak of use between 1782–1791.

The first book (1766–1774 P92/SAV/3091) did not always include the age of death for Cure's College burial ground individuals. Therefore, it was decided to sample the books with the highest occurrences of College burial ground entries (P92/SAV/3093 and P92/SAV/3094), covering 1782–97, and these were transcribed. Details of the burials listed in these books are available in the archive.

Of the 399 burials recorded, 186 of the burial entries concern male individuals and 211 concern females. Two entries refer to individuals of unknown sex due to illegible handwriting. Over 80 of the burials appear to be infants under one year old. Most ages are represented within the fee books, but people over 45 appear to be the most numerous, with 147 out of 399 of the individuals aged between 45 and 105 years. The oldest individual was Mary Piliatt, who was a pensioner in the College and who died aged 105 years. Inmates of the college accounted for 43 of the 399 burials.

Fees book P92/SAV/3093 also records cause of death for the first few pages and, therefore, the first few entries of the College burials. Only six entries record cause of death, with four of the six being infants one year or under (Table 2.4). In the case of the infants the cause of death appears to have been convulsions, measles, teeth and smallpox. Although the diagnosis of the 18th-century recorder may not have been accurate it does demonstrate that the 80 or so infants under one

Table 2.3: Methodology of sampling the St Saviour parish fees books

Burial register	Years	No. of years	Number of pages (approx)	Entries per page	Total burials (approx)	College burials	College burial percentage
P92/SAV/3091	1766–1774	8	150	11	1650	1/33	3.0
P92/SAV/3093	1782–1791	9	300	4	1200	262	21.8
P92/SAV/3094	1791–1797	6	360	4	1440	136	9.4
P92/SAV/3095	1797–1802	5	550	4	2200	1/40	2.5

Table 2.4: Cure's College burial ground, 1782–91. Entries which record cause of death from fees book P92/SAV/3093

First name	Surname	College inmate	Other information	Age	Address	Occupation	Cause of death
Amon	Cotton	No	S. of R. Cotton	8m	Foul Lane		Convulsions
John	Dewe	No		76	Maid Lane	Clock Maker	Asthma
Sarah	Cowiden	No	D. of Taylor	9m	Pye Garden	F – Colourman	Measells (sic)
Mary Ann	Broom	No	D. of Charles Broom	10m		F – A barber	Teeth
Sarah	Arnold	No		16	Castle Court		Mortification
Rich	Bell	No	S. of Ric Bell	1	Castle Street	F – Glass Grinder	Small pox

Table 2.5: Cure's College burial ground, 1782–97. Mentions of occupations in burial registers P92/SAV/3093 and P92/SAV/3094

Occupation	No.	Occupation	No.
Apothecary	1	Fireman	1
Baker	2	Fishmonger	2
Barber	3	Fruiterer	1
Basket maker	3	Gentleman	8
Beam maker	1	Glass grinder	2
Bearer in the Marshleigh	1	Glazier	1
Bellman	1	Green grocer	1
Boat builder	1	Horse-seller	1
Book keeper	4	Joiner in the College	1
Box maker	1	Labourer	25
Brazier	1	Lighterman	10
Brewer	1	Mans servant	1
Brewers servant	3	Mason	1
Bricklayer	4	Milk man	1
Brush maker	3	Mustard maker	1
Butcher	15	Painter	2
Cabinet maker	2	Pawn broker	3
Carman	5	Porter	9
Carpenter	6	Print cutter	1
Cheesemonger	1	Sawyer	3
Clark/Clerk	6	Scale maker	1
Clock maker	2	Servant	1
Coach hangers maker?	1	Setter in the yard	1
Coachman	1	Smith	5
Coloursman	5	Soap maker	1
Collector of the Kings Tax	1	Stone mason	1
Cooper	6	Taylor	3
Cordwainer	4	Tobacconist	1
Currier	2	Victualler	18
Customs House Office	1	Vintner	2
Distiller	1	Waterman	7
Draper	1	Weaver	3
Drawer	1	Wheelwright	3
Dyer	7	Wooling draper	1
Excise man	2	Worsted maker	1
Farrier	1		
Felt maker	1	TOTAL	226

year may have died from a range of causes. The 16 year old Sarah Arnold appears to have died from mortification, a term referring to infected tissue. John Dewe appears to have died from asthma at 76 years old.

Of the 226 individuals whose occupations were listed, most seem to have been in manual trades. Many of the occupations noted are of fathers whose children died, so some may have been listed several times. Table 2.5 shows the number of times each occupation is mentioned in the burial registers.

Of the total of 226, only eight are listed as gentleman of independent means. The occupations that stand out as most numerous are 25 labourers, 18 victuallers, 15 butchers and 10 lightermen (barge/river men). Many of the other occupations appear to be either a skilled craft, or providers of a service or selling role, especially related to food and drink.

Thirty-nine of the 399 list their address as outside the parish. These were mostly south London parishes, but there were also a few from north London parishes.

Funeral costs
The St Saviour parish fees books for 1782–1791 (P92-SAV-3093) provide the most detailed information on funeral costs. They indicate that the only people in the parish who did not pay for their burial were paupers buried in the workhouse burial ground (WH in the burial registers). In these entries it appears that some people may have been buried together in the same grave as they are listed together. Amongst the entries are references to 'Old Ground', which may have been the Cross Bones burial ground. The fees books indicate that the 'Old Ground' was a cheap place to be buried, and it seems that most of those buried there were older adults.

There appear to have been a variety of types of funerals and fees paid at Cure's College burial ground. The most basic funerals seem to relate to some pensioners who actually lived in the College, which perhaps paid part of their fees. Most of the entries for the College burial ground include additional funeral costs, such as minister, register, clerk, sexton, grave making, bearers and, in some cases, bell ringing. The contrast between a basic burial and one with a number of extras added is noteworthy. For example, three types of bell were available at Cure's College burial ground: the small bell, the lady bell, and the great bell. The great bell cost 6s 19d, the lady bell cost 4s 4d and the small bell cost 1s 8d. The most expensive funerals at over £1 at the College burial ground also had a desk service. These more expensive funerals tended to be of older adults who were not resident pensioners at the College, but general parishioners who either had a trade or were pensioners with enough capital for a funeral. The cheapest funerals at the College burial ground from the period 1782–91 appear to have been a number of infants under one year, with a funeral cost of around 6 shillings.

The St Saviour's records for 1782–1791 shows that the types of people buried within the College burial ground in the late 18th century were not the wealthiest in the parish, but also not the poorest. They appear to have been split between those on an adequate income (perhaps even some on surplus income) and those who were poor but had sufficient savings (or family and friends) to pay for a funeral. The College pensioners may have been poor, but the College or parish may have paid some of their funeral costs, or they would have saved for funeral costs with their allocated income (Boulton 2005, 163).

Summary and conclusion

Although earlier burial activity is known at the site, map regression suggests that the Park Street assemblage relates to the burial ground of Cure's College, established in 1587, within the parish of St Saviour. The burial ground was in use until the 1850s, possibly as late as 1862, but the present assemblage probably dates to a period up to 1831, before the burial ground was re-ordered and reduced in size. The burial ground was initially used by some of the poorest members of the parish, but an increase in fees over time suggests that it subsequently became more exclusive and was then used primarily by working class individuals with some financial means. Additional details of funeral costs suggest that various types of funeral took place at Cure's College burial ground with a range of options that could be included for a fee.

The parish registers were found to be very limited in their scope, perhaps a surprising finding considering the wealth of information that has been obtained from this source for other, similar, studies. Far more informative were the fees books, which have helped to characterise the population most likely to have been excavated at Park Street. These are extensive in terms of the number of years they cover, and it was therefore necessary to limit the present research to a sample. This sample suggests that most individuals were engaged in manual work relating to service industry occupations, and some were from outside the parish. There were more females than males, a large number of infants, and a good number of individuals over the age of 45 years. While this information is limited by the sampling strategy employed, it nevertheless provides a useful context with which to explore the archaeological and osteological evidence from Park Street.

Chapter 3

Archaeological results

by Kate Brady and Lisa Brown

Introduction

The 2010–11 excavation of the Park Street and Hop Exchange section of Borough Viaduct was confined to the footprint of nine pile caps located on either side of an existing Victorian viaduct (Fig. 3.1). All of the pile caps were excavated at least in part to impact level, which varied across the site from Roman (Period 3), medieval (Period 5) and post-medieval (Period 6) horizons (see Chapter 1, Table 1.2). The construction design required that the underside of the pile caps be between 2.3m and 2.9m below the upper archaeological horizon previously recorded for this part of Southwark (NWR 2009a).

The excavation of the burial ground exposed 331 discrete skeletons interred in earth-cut single and multiple graves. The evidence suggests that all of the burials were supine and extended. Highly decayed

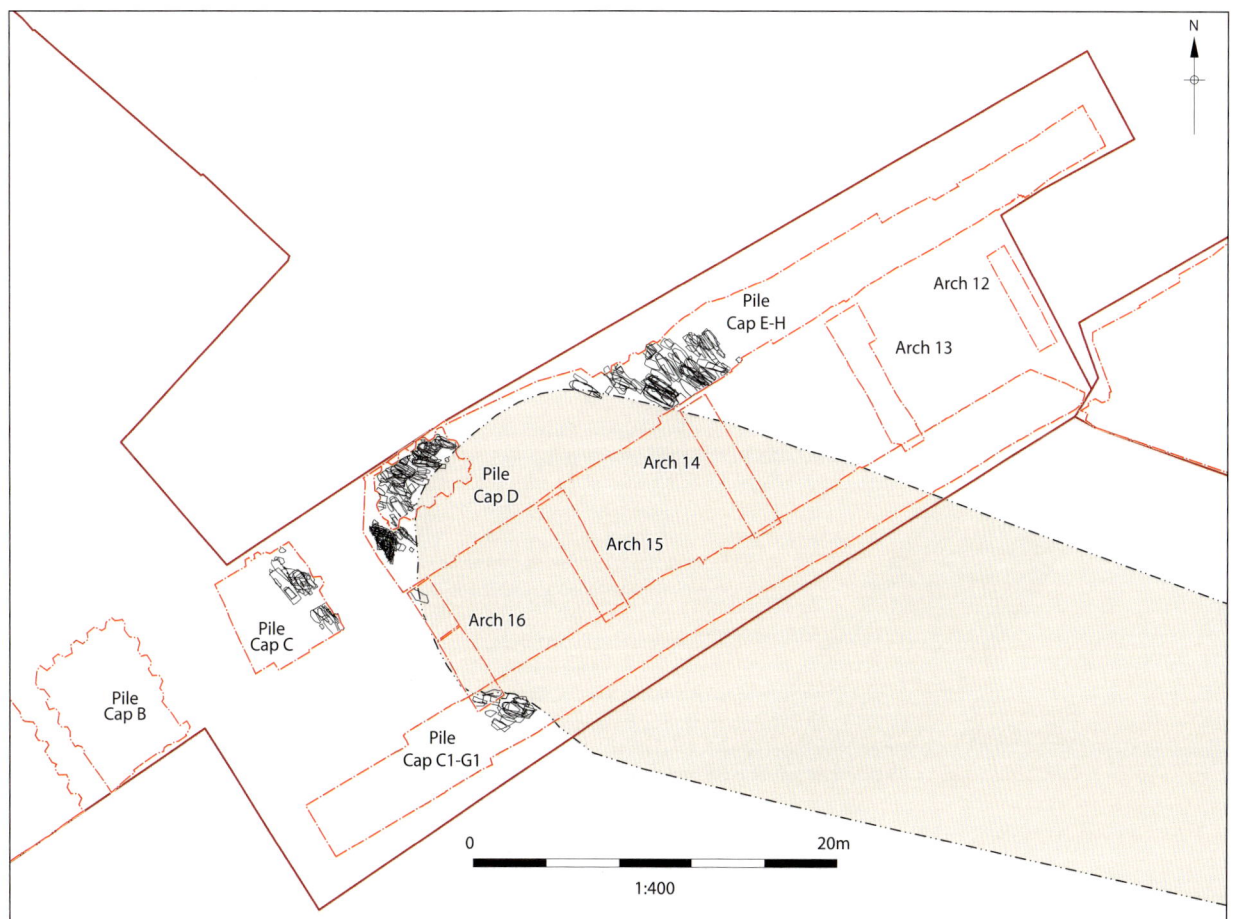

Fig. 3.1 Location of the Park Street burials

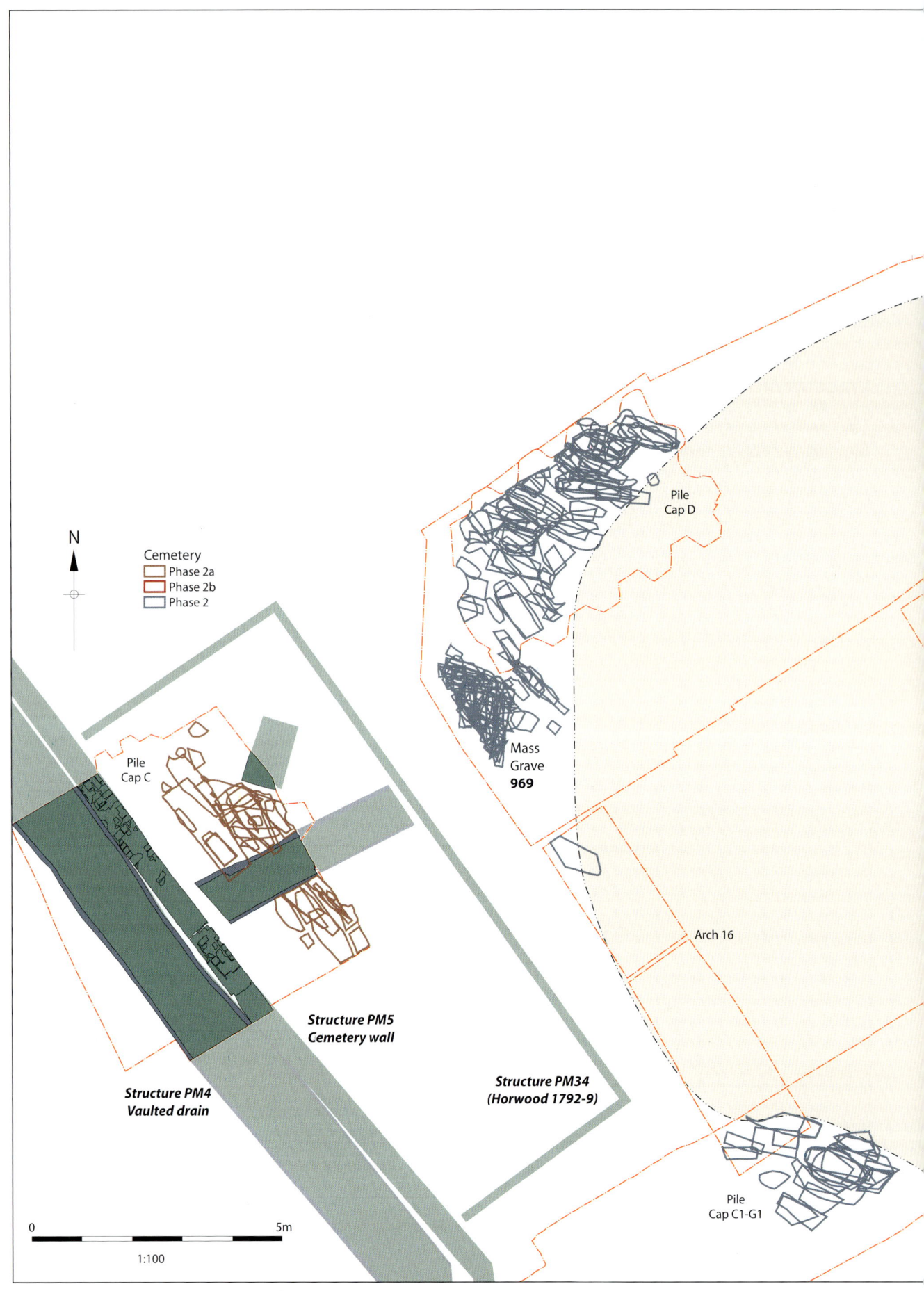

Archaeological results

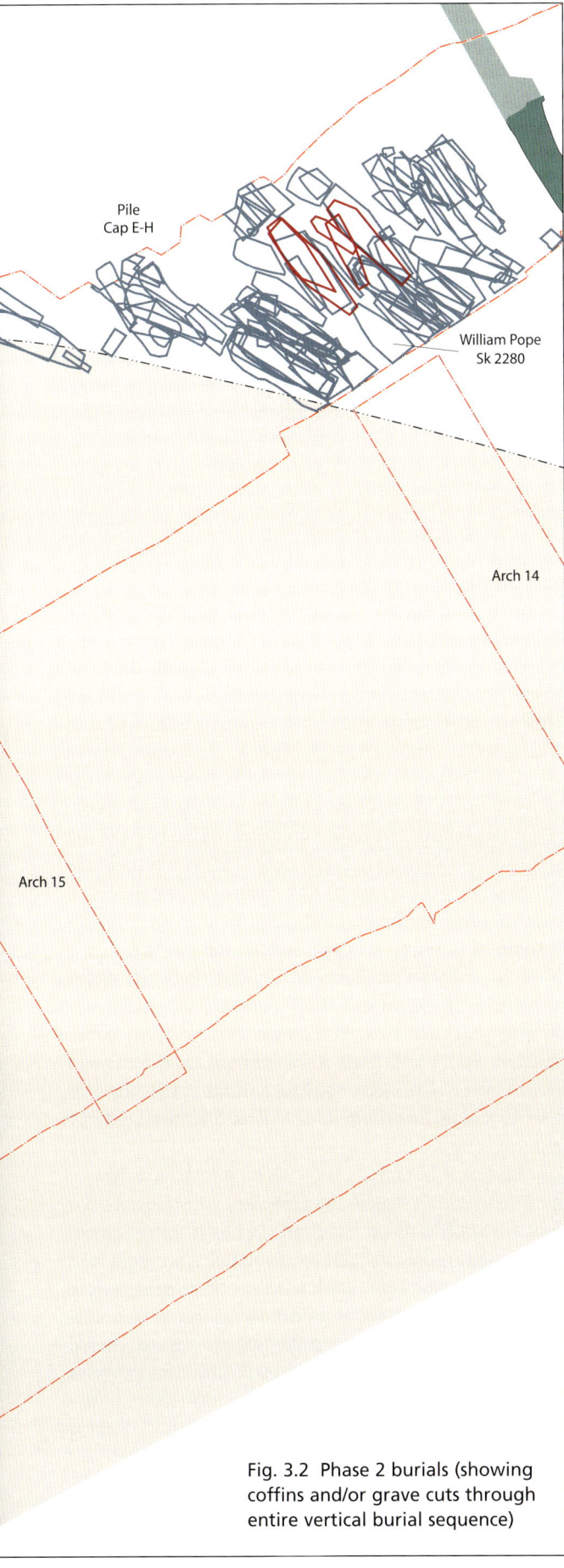

Fig. 3.2 Phase 2 burials (showing coffins and/or grave cuts through entire vertical burial sequence)

remains of wood, iron and copper alloy coffin fittings provided evidence that at least some of the burials were coffined, whereas others were clearly not. Burials were essentially restricted to four areas: Pile Caps C, D and E–H, and the south-western part of Pile Cap C1–G1. These burials can be dated to 1587–1831. Historic map evidence suggests that they lay beneath buildings and paths constructed in 1831 (Chapter 2), and hence survived the cemetery clearance of the 1860s. They covered an area of 448m², an estimated 34% of the total area of the pre-1831 burial ground, and extended across an area of the site measuring 28m NE-SW by 16m NW-SE (Fig. 3.1). The only burial datable to a single year was an individual accompanied by a breastplate which bore the name William Pope, who was shown in the parish burial records to have died in April 1816 (see below and Chapters 2 and 5). The remainder of the site was largely devoid of burials as a result of the cemetery clearance, though one partial burial and a charnel pit found in Arch 16 appear to have escaped the clearance. A second charnel pit was found in Arch 13, beneath the remains of an almshouse building known to have existed by 1814 (Fig. 3.3). The charnel pits have been excluded from the analysis.

Recording methodology

The methodology for fieldwork has been set out in Chapter 1. In summary, all of the burials were removed down to pre-cemetery levels within all of the pile caps, and a number were excavated through the underlying medieval (Period 5), Roman (Period 3) and natural (Period 1) deposits in Pile Cap D. A comprehensive list of the skeleton, grave cut and coffin numbers, orientation, associated coffin remains and coffin furniture is available in the archive. Dimensions of the grave cuts were recorded where possible (details available in the archive), but some burials were not completely exposed within the limits of excavation. In these cases the grave dimensions were uncertain so the records represent the best indication of the grave size, or measurable portion, but not always the precise size of the cut.

The key cemetery structures (walls, drains, buildings) and features (eg charnel pit) are numbered on the figures using the structure numbers assigned for post-medieval period structures (PM) in Monograph 2, in which the results for the entire Park Street excavation are described. For example, western cemetery boundary walls [3023] and [4065] are shown on the figures as Structure PM5, an eastern boundary wall [2033] as Structure PM6, and culvert/drain [4014] as Structure PM4.

Table 3.1: Phasing

Phase	Description	Date range
Phase 1	Natural features and pre-burial ground activity	Before 1587
Phase 2	Burial ground activity	1587–1831
Phase 2a	Early phase of burial ground activity in Pile Cap C	1587–1799
Phase 2b	Later phase of burial ground activity in Pile Cap E–H	1816–1831
Phase 3	Post-burial ground activity	1831 onwards

Chronological sequence

The archaeological remains are divided into three phases (Table 3.1) within the Thameslink scheme Periods 1–6 (see Chapter 1). The cemetery activity dates entirely to the post-medieval period (Period 6), but the earliest burials were cut through pre-cemetery natural gravels (Period 1), which was overlain by Roman to early post-medieval deposits (Periods 3–5).

The pre-cemetery activity (Phase 1) across the site is summarised below and described more fully in Thameslink Monographs 1 and 2, while the cemetery sequence of Phase 2 and the post-burial ground activity of Phase 3 are presented here.

Phase 1

Natural gravels were encountered in Pile Cap D at 1.21m OD. Above this and in Pile Caps E–H a sequence of Roman floors, make-up layers, beam slots and walls were exposed, remains of buildings of the early to late Roman Period 3. Traces of an early Roman episode of fire destruction possibly date to the time of the Boudican revolt (see Thameslink Monograph 1).

In the eastern part of Pile Caps E–H Roman activity was succeeded by the accumulation of soils that appear to have been reworked during early medieval Period 5. A few pits of this date also attest to early medieval occupation in the vicinity.

Activity of 15th- to 16th-century date recorded in the Pile Caps E–H areas was represented by a pit that contained a large quantity of pottery dated to 1500–1550. A soil layer in Pile Cap C produced pottery dated to 1480–1600, suggesting late medieval to early post-medieval occupation nearby (see Thameslink Monograph 2).

Phase 2

The Phase 2 burials were exposed in an area covering 28m NE-SW and 16m NW-SE within Pile Caps C, D, C1–G1 and E–H (Fig. 3.2). All of the burials lay within an area defined by wall Structure PM5 to the west and Structures PM8 and PM35 to the east (Fig. 3.3). No grave markers or marker settings were found. A notable absence of burials was identified in the south-eastern part of Pile Cap D and in a small area in the north-western part of Pile Cap E–H.

The Phase 2 burials were cut into cemetery soils 0.62–1.1m thick, observed in all of the excavated areas. These soils consisted of tenacious clayey silts incorporating mortar, chalk, charcoal, ceramic building material (CBM) fragments, stone fragments and oyster shell. The burials were heavily intercutting in all areas of the site, and in many cases only partial remains survived. Many extended beyond the limits of excavation. However, the earliest burials were well spaced, perhaps laid out in rows.

The alignment of the graves was generally NW-SE, but some deviations were noted. However, the earliest burials in Pile Cap D, which directly cut the pre-cemetery soil and cut no other graves, can be separated into two distinct groups. In the south-western part of Pile Cap D one group of nine burials was aligned precisely NW-SE, and another group of five in the north-eastern part of this pile cap was aligned WNW-ESE. Occasionally, some significant deviations from the NW-SE alignment were noted. Most obvious was the case of mass grave [969], where a wide range of orientations was recorded (Fig. 3.2). Three other burials in proximity to grave [969] deviated from the NW-SE orientation. Burial [673], which cut the upper fill of the pit, was aligned E-W, and burial [659], later in the sequence, was orientated NE-SW. No other features of these burials were unusual, and both had clearly been coffined. Coffined burial [835] in Pile Cap D was also oriented E-W, but also featured the common traits.

Across Pile Caps D, C1–G1 and E–H, areas of coffined burials were interspersed with burials for which no coffin traces survived. Two concentrations of burials that mostly lacked coffin remains were located within mass grave pit [969], where coffin remains were associated with only four of the 36 burials, and in Pile Cap C1–G1, where none of the burials was associated with coffin remains. In contrast, all burials in a sequence of three consecutive burial stacks in the western part of Pile Cap E–H (graves [2424], [2414] and [2384]) were coffined.

Most of the burials can only be broadly assigned to Phase 2. However, some burials can be dated to before 1799 (Phase 2a) or to after 1816 (Phase 2b).

Archaeological results

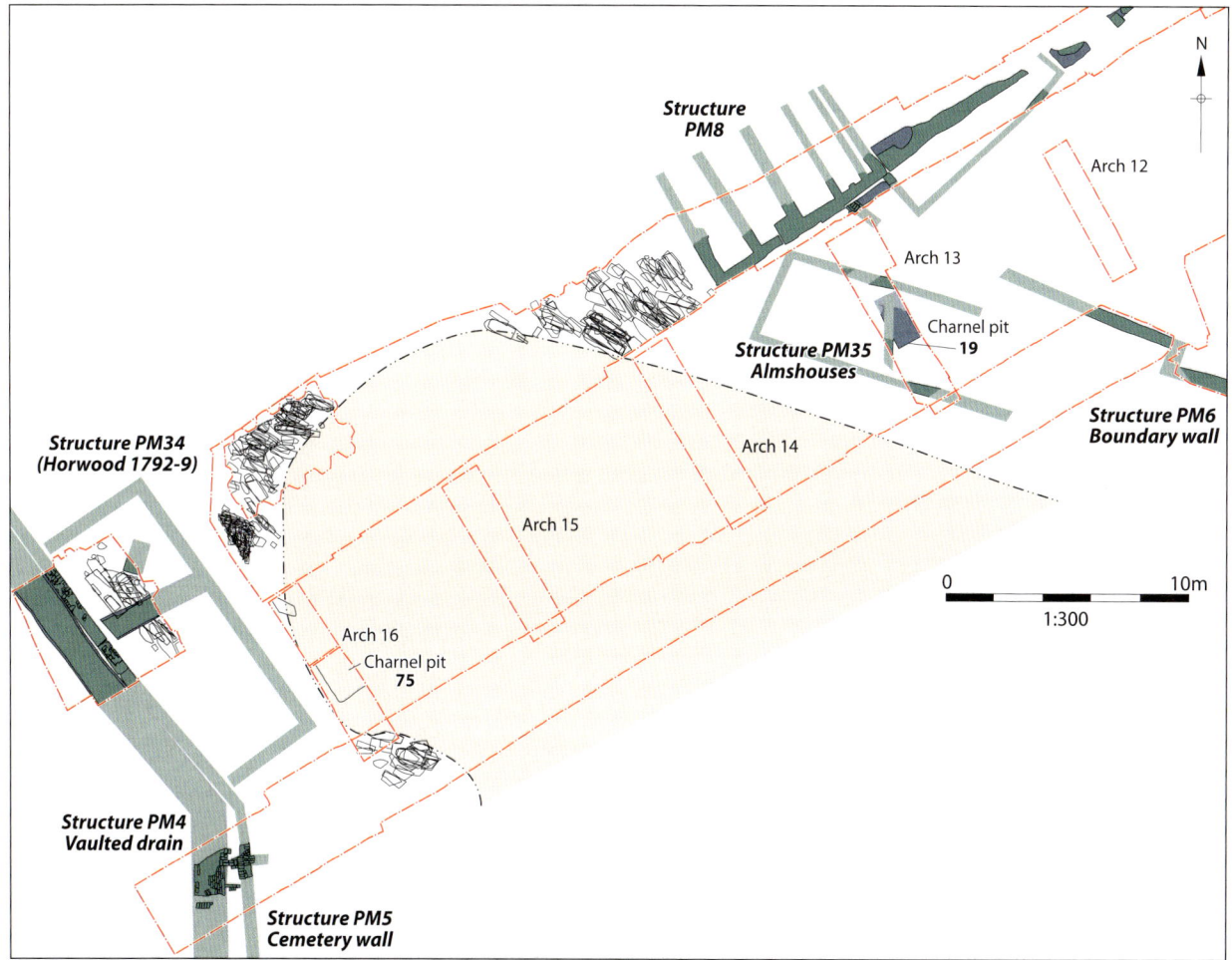

Fig. 3.3 The cemetery and associated structures

Burials that were demonstrably interred during an early phase of cemetery use were found in Pile Cap C. These burials were overlain by an almshouse building identified on maps as constructed by 1799 (Chapter 2). The burials in Pile Cap C respected the boundary marked by cemetery wall [4065] Structure PM5 (Fig. 3.3), dated to the mid-18th to 19th century (see below), but it should be borne in mind that an earlier boundary feature may have been removed by the construction of this wall. These burials have been assigned to Phase 2a.

The burial in 1816 of William Pope ([2280]) in the eastern part of Pile Cap E-H (Fig. 3.2) demonstrates that burial was taking place in this location at the eastern edge of the cemetery at least until that date. Pope's grave and stratigraphically later burials have been assigned to Phase 2b.

The use of artefacts for phasing was restricted by the general absence of objects associated with the individuals. Clothing did not survive, and coffin fittings were of limited value for dating burials except in the most general terms. Only the single dated coffin plate mentioned above was recovered, so even sequences of burials could be dated only in relative terms within the ranges shown in Table 3.1.

Pottery from pre-cemetery-soil deposits in Pile Cap E-H gives a *terminus post quem* of c 1600 for the burials in this area. Otherwise, none of the pre-cemetery deposits produced dating evidence that narrows the date range of the burials. The cemetery soils themselves contained mixed finds of mainly 18th- to mid-19th-century date. These soils would have been reworked through the life of the cemetery, and the finds from these deposits do not assist in dating the burials more closely.

Phase 2a
Thirty-nine graves containing the same number of individuals belonged to Phase 2a. Burials in Pile Cap C were assigned to Phase 2a on the evidence of map regression, which shows that by 1799 a building had been constructed in this area. The pre-1799 burials were bounded to the west by wall Structure PM5. There was a gap of 0.8m between Structure PM5 and the westernmost of the burials, and beyond that point the graves were aligned on the same NW-SE orienta-

tion as the wall. The earliest burials were well spaced and consistently aligned.

Although most of the Phase 2a burials were associated with the remains of coffins, it was not possible to date any of the graves on the evidence of artefacts, and no clothing, jewellery or personal items were recovered from them. Levels taken for all individual burials were found to be in the range 3.14m OD to 2.27m OD. The graves were heavily intercutting, and severe disturbance had largely obscured the stratigraphic relationships. The result was partial survival of the skeletons, and there was frequent redeposition of disarticulated skeletal elements within the surrounding cemetery soils. Decomposition of the remains had resulted in slumping, and grave fills were for the most part indistinguishable from the surrounding cemetery soil, so grave cuts were not always recorded.

The graves were all simple earth-cut features and there was no evidence for grave markers such as headstones, footstones or settings for them. It was unclear whether most were single or multiple interments as the grave cuts were not always visible, but definite vertical stacks were identified for this phase. Where visible, coffin remains consisted of heavily decayed wood surviving as only a fibrous brown stain. Where coffin outlines were clear they were of elongated hexagonal shape, or single-break style (see Chapter 5). The edges of some coffins were marked by lines of copper alloy studs, and a few fragments of breast plates, grips and grip plates survived in a heavily corroded and fragmentary condition.

The western extent of the Phase 2a burials was defined by Structure PM5, the western cemetery wall, and they were orientated approximately NW-SE on its alignment. The limit of burial activity in other directions was not defined. Burials from Pile Caps D, C1–G1 and E–H may also have been interred during this period but the stratigraphic evidence was insufficient to allow any other burials to be precisely attributed to this sub-phase. There was some variation in orientation, most notably in that of two of the later graves, [4046] and [4052], which were aligned WSW-ENE. The earliest burials in this area may have been more evenly spaced, but extensive cutting in of later graves during this period and the restricted excavation area meant that the evidence was not conclusive. However, there is an obvious gap between the burials and cemetery wall, indicating that this space was not used for burial by the end of this phase.

Phase 2b
The closely dated burial of William Pope [2280] and those that are stratigraphically later are assigned to Phase 2b. Pope's grave was located in the north-eastern part of Pile Cap E–H, and toward the middle of a sequence of intercutting burials in this area (Figs. 3.2 and 3.6). An associated breastplate fragment showed part of the name and a burial date (probably '1816'). This evidence places this and six later burials in the same sequence within Phase 2b. This group includes skeletons [2215], [2201], [2199], [2097], [2107] and [2127]. Skeletons [2201] and [2199] lay within a single grave cut.

All of these burials were located in the north-eastern part of Pile Cap E–H and were on a NW-SE orientation. All were plain earth-cut graves filled with similar dark grey soil that incorporated CBM and mortar fragments, oyster shell, and occasional disarticulated human bone. Grave [2285] (skeleton [2280]) was the earliest that could be assigned to this phase, and was at a depth of 2.49m OD. The two stratigraphically latest burials were [2199] and [2107], at levels of 2.77m OD and 2.95m OD respectively.

Some 30 sherds of pottery recovered from the fill of grave [2203] date to 1780–1830. A copper alloy drawn wire, pin and a simple unornamented ring found in the grave fill were unlikely to have been associated with the individual. All but one of the burials were accompanied by coffin remains, mostly consisting of stains or small fragments of wood.

Phase 2 (general)
The remaining 261 burials in Pile Caps D, C1–G1 and E–H cannot be closely dated. The skeletal remains were in various states of completeness, and some coffin remains were present, preserved only as fragments of wood or fibrous stains. Otherwise, fittings such as breastplates, studs, nails, grips and grip plates indicated the presence of coffins. A few buttons and a pin recovered from the mixed grave fills could not be linked to any specific burial. Small quantities of pottery recovered from grave fills included sherds with broad dates of 1750–1850, consistent with pottery from the surrounding cemetery soils.

Grave fills resembled the general cemetery soil, dark grey-brown sandy silts with inclusions of pottery, stone and CBM fragments, chalk and mortar fragments, and disarticulated human bone. In common with the Phase 2a and 2b grave cuts, those ascribed to Phase 2 in general were difficult to distinguish from the soil into which they were cut.

Phase 3

Cure's College was remodelled and the burial ground reduced in size in 1831 (see Chapter 2). During the 1860s, the area of the burial ground still in use was cleared of burials. No burials were found in the BVB10 site, which would have been within the reduced cemetery boundaries, apart from a set of lower legs and a charnel pit in the Arch 16 area, presumably missed during the removal and re-interment programme. In the north-eastern part of Pile Cap C1–G1, the clearance of the 1860s was evidenced by a disturbed mixed soil ([3001]) containing late-18th-century and early-19th-century material, which continued below the impact level of 2.3m OD. Three sondages were excavated through this deposit, down to a level of 1.48–1.60m OD, but no evidence for burials was found.

In all areas, the cemetery was truncated by later features, including drains, walls and pits of later 19th-century date. The drains and associated features probably served houses on Park Street to the north. Part of a cellar that post-dated the construction of the viaduct was found in the eastern part of Pile Cap C1–G1, and a cellared structure of similar construction was found in the western part of Pile Cap C1–G1.

Multiple burials

Some 21 of the recorded graves contained multiple burials or 'stacks'. These represent multiple burials that may have been inserted in a grave that was left open and filled over a relatively short space of time but there was no clear evidence of this. Some may represent family plots, but this could not be confirmed in any examples. Most of the graves containing multiple burials were in Pile Caps E–H. Here there were 10 double burials, four triple burials, one burial of four individuals, one burial of six individuals, and two burials of nine individuals. Mass grave [969] in Pile Cap D contained 36 individuals. In Pile Cap C1–G1 there was one grave that contained nine individuals. There were apparently no multiple burials in Pile Cap C, an area where burial activity began before 1799.

The distribution of multiple burials may reflect changes in burial tradition over time and within different parts of the cemetery. For instance, the lack of multiple burials in Pile Cap C could indicate that during Phase 2a multiple burial was unnecessary as space within the cemetery was not under pressure. Later, as other areas of the cemetery were used, a more efficient use of limited space may have necessitated multiple interment. Details of the multiple burials are set out in Table 3.2, apart from burial [969] which is presented separately in Table 3.3.

Table 3.2: Multiple burials (omitting mass burial [969])

Grave	Pile Cap	Skeleton	Sex	Age	Coffin remains
3078	C1–G1	3070	M	Young Adult	none
		3067	?	Adult	none
		3071	?	Older Child	none
		3068	?	Adolescent	none
		3063	?	Older Child	none
		3006	?	?	none
		3069	F	Young Adult	none
		3065	F	Adolescent	none
971	D	703	?	Adult	Decayed wood, studs, nails
		697	?	Adult	Decayed wood, studs, nails
2084	E–H	2077	M	Young Adult	Decayed wood, nail
		2070	?	Adolescent	Decayed wood
2247	E–H	2234	F	Prime Adult	Decayed wood
		2193	M	Prime Adult	Decayed wood
2142	E–H	2125	F	Older Adult	Decayed wood, footplate
		2079	M	Young Adult	Decayed wood, nails
2439	E–H	2268	F	Mature Adult	none
		2254	M	Prime Adult	none
		2236	?	Young Child	none
		2191	F	Older Adult	none
		2160	F	Adult	none
		2158	M	Mature Adult	Coffin base fragments
		2149	?	Adult	none
		2137	M	Prime Adult	stain
2468	E–H	2256	?	Adult	Decayed wood
		2217	M	Adult	Decayed wood
2441	E–H	2376	M	Young Adult	Stain
		2362	F	Young Adult	Decayed wood
		2364	?	Young Adult	Decayed wood
		2343	F	Young Adult	none
2112	E–H	2119	M	Older Adult	none
		2110	F	Mature Adult	none
2203	E–H	2201	M	Mature Adult	Decayed wood

Table 3.2 (continued)

Grave	Pile Cap	Skeleton	Sex	Age	Coffin remains
		2199	F	Mature Adult	Decayed wood
2436	E–H	2310	?	Adolescent	None
		2282	M	Mature Adult	Decayed wood, nails
		2270	F	Prime Adult	none
2426	E–H	2423	M	Mature Adult	Decayed wood
		2421	F	Mature Adult	Decayed wood
		2419	M	Prime Adult	Decayed wood
		2417	F	Young Adult	Decayed wood
		2415	M	Mature Adult	Coffin base fragments
		2401	?	Adult	Wood fragments
2414	E–H	2412	?	Young Child	stain
		2410	M	Prime Adult	stain
		2408	M	Adolescent	Wood fragments, nails
		2406	M	Mature Adult	Wood fragments, nails
		2403	M	Mature Adult	Wood fragments
		2397	M	Young Adult	stain
		2380	?	Young Child	Wood fragments
		2378	?	Older Child	none
		2378	F	Adult	Wood fragments, nails
2384	E–H	2374	F	Prime Adult	Stain
		2360	F	Prime Adult	Stain
		2338	?	Infant	Stain
2228	E–H	2240	M	Adult	none
		2230	?	Adult	none
		2232	?	Adult	none
2204	E–H	2207	F	Adult	none
		2209	?	Young Child	none
2449	E–H	2188	M	Adult	Decayed wood
		2186	M	Adult	stain
2434	E–H	2317	M	Young Adult	none
		2300	M	Prime Adult	Decayed wood
2432	E–H	2266	M	Prime Adult	Decayed wood
		2264	M	Adult	Decayed wood
		2262	M	Mature Adult	Decayed wood
2447	E–H	2184	F	Older Adult	Decayed wood, breastplate
		2182	?	Young Adult	Decayed wood, breastplate

Grave [969] Pile Cap D

A large grave in Pile Cap D contained the remains of 36 individuals (Table 3.3). The western end of the grave lay beyond the limit of excavation but it was square or rectangular in shape, at least 2.3m long and 0.72m deep. The fill was a dark brown clayey silt with a few stones, CBM and chalk fragments, oyster shell, and disarticulated human bone. There was nothing noted in the fieldwork record to suggest the presence of soil accumulations or deposits separating any of the burials, which, if present could have indicated that the individuals were buried during separate events, or that earth was deposited between each burial.

The grave was cut through the pre-cemetery soil and did not truncate any earlier burials, but was cut by later burials. Only four of the burials had associated coffin traces, small fragments of wood and a few iron nails.

The burials were not neatly placed within the cut but varied in orientation; eight were laid out on the conventional NW-SE or E-W orientations, and another 15 aligned NE-SW or approximate to it. Of the remaining burials, six were aligned N-S and five on various other alignments. A possible explanation for this is that these burials had been moved from another area of the site and re-interred in this grave, although it is clear that this would have occurred well within the timespan of the use of the cemetery as more burials were made directly above it after this grave was full. Furthermore, had they been moved it would have been prior to full decomposition as the skeletons were articulated. Most were apparently uncoffined. The absence of coffins can be an indicator of poverty or of rapid burial. The burials could represent the rapid interment of individuals within a mass grave due to an event that led to a large number of deaths, such as an epidemic.

Grave [971] Pile Cap D

Grave [971] cut the eastern edge of grave [969], and so was clearly later. It contained two burials [703]

Table 3.3: Skeletons in mass burial [969]

Skeleton number	Sex	Age group	Level (upper) mOD	Level (lower) mOD	Coffin remains
958	M	Young Adult	1.58	1.50	None
956	M	Mature Adult	1.65	1.44	None
949	?	Older Child	1.55	1.38	Decayed wood, nails
947	M	Young Adult	1.60	1.56	None
934	M	Prime Adult	1.63	1.63	None
962	?	Adolescent	1.59	1.58	None
927	M	Prime Adult	1.71	1.69	None
925	M	Adult (Unspecified)	1.79	1.62	None
921	M	Adult (Unspecified)	1.74	1.69	None
911	M	Prime Adult	1.87	1.64	None
909	?	Older Child	1.82	1.60	None
897	M	Prime Adult	1.88	1.70	None
895	?	Older Child	1.86	1.81	None
893	?	Adolescent	2.02	1.79	None
880	?	Adult (Unspecified)	1.96	1.74	None
891	F	Young Adult	2.11	1.71	None
887	M	Adult (Unspecified)	1.94	1.74	None
873	?	Adult (Unspecified)	2.00	1.93	None
864	?	Older Child	2.02	1.85	Decayed wood, nails
862	M	Prime Adult	2.07	1.81	None
805	?	Adult (Unspecified)	2.28	2.28	None
860	?	Adolescent	1.94	1.89	None
845	?	Older Child	2.15	1.92	None
801	?	Adolescent	2.26	2.14	None
829	M	Prime Adult	2.22	1.93	None
839	M	Prime Adult	2.33	2.16	None
785	M	Prime Adult	2.28	2.04	None
765	?	Older Child	2.36	2.14	None
773	?	Older Child	2.21	2.11	None
827	F	Prime Adult	2.12	2.04	None
825	F	Young Adult	2.13	2.04	None
731	M	Prime Adult	2.38	2.08	None
729	?	Young Adult	2.28	2.03	None
719	M	Prime Adult	2.37	2.17	Decayed wood
733	M	Mature Adult	2.31	2.10	None
717	?	Infant	2.48	2.48	Decayed wood

and [697] on a NW-SE orientation, one above the other. The fill and inclusions resembled the cemetery soil and other grave fills. Decayed wood, iron nails and coffin studs indicated that the individuals, which were of uncertain sex, were interred in coffins.

Grave [3078] Pile Cap C1–G1

Grave [3078] was one of the earliest burials in Pile Cap C1–G1, and the only multiple burial identified in this area. It was cut directly into the pre-cemetery soil. The surviving part of the grave was sub-rectangular, all but the northern part removed by modern features. There were three stacks of burials within this grave, but these may have originally been in four individual features with indistinguishable cuts. All of the burials were oriented NW-SE. The fill incorporated CBM fragments and much disarticulated human bone, particularly near the base, but no coffin remains.

Multiple burials in Pile Cap E–H

Grave [2084]

Grave [2084] contained two burials [2077] and [2070]. The individuals were oriented NW-SE, one above the other. They were interred in coffins, but only decayed wood and a single nail survived.

Grave [2142]

This grave lay to the west of grave [2084] and also contained two burials, [2125] and [2079], of which only the eastern edges were clearly visible. Both burials were oriented NW-SE and coffined, but only decayed wood and a fragmented footplate survived.

Grave [2247]

Grave [2247] contained two burials, [2234] and [2193]. The burials were oriented NNW-SSE, a slight deviation to the surrounding graves, and were stacked one above the other. Decayed wood fragments attested to the presence of coffins.

Grave [2439]
Grave [2439] held a stack of eight burials of males and females. The grave was rectangular but the south-east end lay beyond the limit of excavation. All of the burials were aligned NW-SE and stacked one on top of the other. Only two individuals were clearly coffined, with small wood fragments or staining recorded.

Grave [2468]
This grave contained two burials, both aligned NW-SE, stacked one above the other, both within coffins, of which only traces of decayed wood survived.

Grave [2441]
Grave 2441 lay at the north-western edge of Pile Cap E-H, partly beyond this limit of excavation. It contained four stacked burials, [2376], [2362], [2364] and [2343]. It was the earliest feature in this area and cut the pre-cemetery soil. The burials were aligned NW-SE and stacked one above the other. Three had associated traces of coffin wood.

Grave [2112]
This double grave lay above grave [2441], and cut a single grave [2452] which separated the two stacked graves. The grave was aligned NW-SE. An older male adult [2119] was interred below a female mature adult [2110].

Grave [2203]
Grave [2203] lay above grave [2452] and contained two individuals, [2201] and [2199], both coffined, mature adults, the lower one male and upper one female. This rectangular grave was aligned NW-SE.

Grave [2436]
Grave [2436] was located at the far western edge of Pile Cap E-H. It was aligned NW-SE and contained three individuals. The top burial [2310] was an adolescent of indeterminate sex, apparently uncoffined. The second individual [2282] was a male of indeterminate age, but decayed wood and three coffin nails show that it was coffined. The bottom individual [2270] was an uncoffined female in the prime adult age range.

The following multiple graves were in a sequence, interspersed with occasional single burials, in the southern corner of Pile Cap E–H:

Grave [2426]
The grave was aligned NW-SE and contained six individuals, all associated with decayed fragments of wood and staining. Three of the individuals were female, two male, and one of indeterminate sex.

Grave [2414]
This grave was situated slightly to the north of grave [2426], which it cut. It contained nine individuals, all associated with coffin remains, mostly wood fragments and stains.

Grave [2384]
Grave [2414] was aligned NW-SE and separated by a

Fig. 3.4 Wall [4065] (Structure PM5) and excavation of adjacent burials (top of photograph)

single burial [2394] from triple burial [2384]. The three individuals had been coffined, but only wood staining survived. Two were female, the other of indeterminate sex.

Grave [2228]

Two individual graves, [2316] and [2302], interrupted the sequence, which continued with triple burial [2228]. The southern end of the grave lay beyond the limit of excavation, so was only partly excavated. The three individuals were aligned NW-SE, one was male, the others indeterminate. No coffin remains were observed.

Grave [2204]

Double burial [2204] was later than grave [2228]. The grave was aligned NW-SE but the dimensions were not recorded. Skeleton [2007], a female, lay nearest the base and unsexed skeleton [2209] above. No coffin remains were observed.

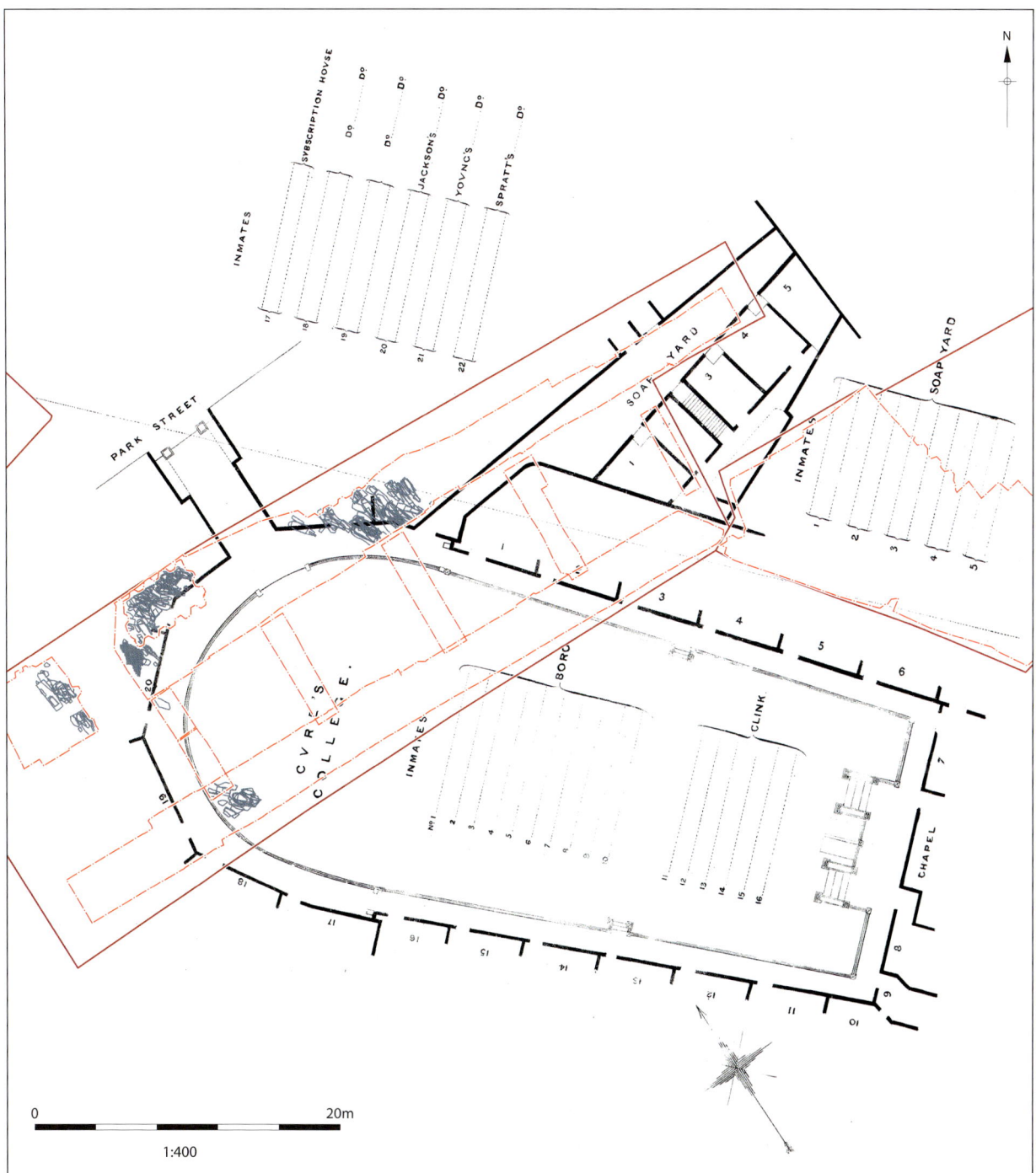

Fig. 3.5 Plan of excavated burials overlying Howe's 1844 plan of Cure's College

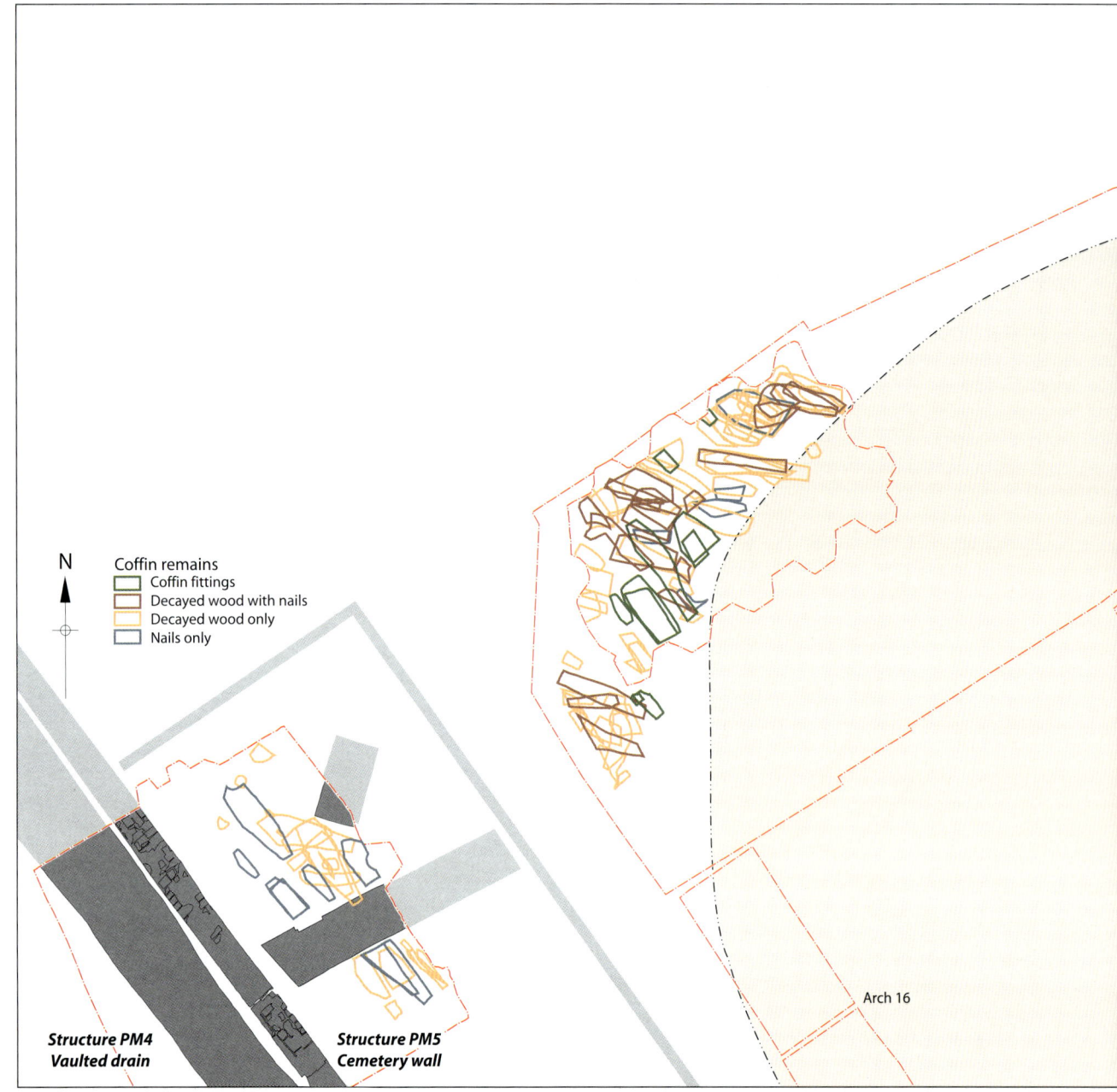

Fig. 3.6 Plan showing locations of preserved coffin remains and fittings (excluding Pile Cap C1–G1 – nails only)

Grave [2449]
Grave [2449] was aligned NW-SE and contained two burials. The lowest burial was skeleton [2188], and skeleton [2186] lay above it. Both were interred within coffins.

Grave [2434]
Grave [2434] was aligned E-W and contained two burials. The lower burial was skeleton [2317] and the upper [2300]. Only burial [2300] had coffin remains. Both were disturbed and the remains incomplete.

Grave [2432]
Grave [2432] was aligned NW-SE and contained three burials in a sequence from the lower [2266], then [2264], and [2262] uppermost. All three were disturbed and the remains partially intact. Traces of decayed wood associated with all three indicate that they were coffined.

Grave [2447]
Double grave [2447] was aligned NW-SE. The lower of the two unsexed individuals was [2184] and the upper was [2182]. Both skeletons were only partially intact due to later disturbance. Traces of decayed wood attest to coffins, and both burials produced fragments of breastplates.

Archaeological results

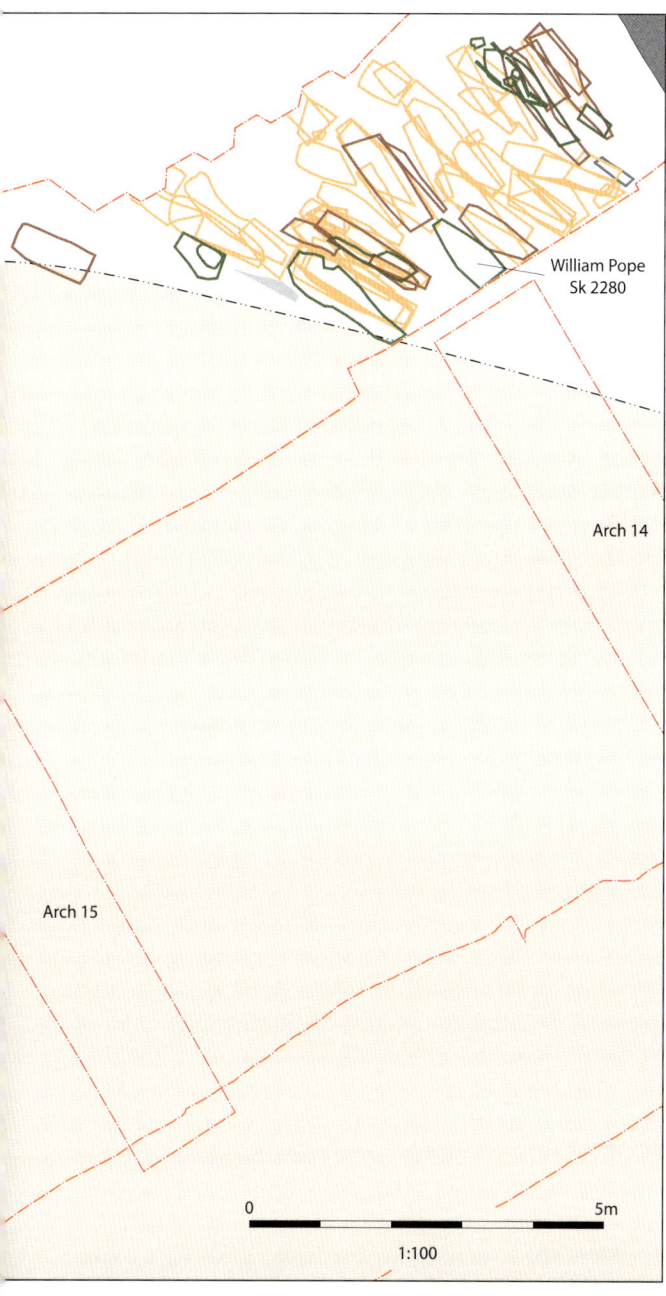

Structures bounding the burial ground

The western limit of the cemetery was defined during Phase 2a by brick wall [4065], Structure PM5 (Figs 3.3 and 3.4). The wall was constructed of unfrogged red brick with occasional purplish red stock brick, bonded with a soft light brown sandy mortar. It survived to a height of 0.65m and was 0.38m wide and extended for 5.8m along the western part of the excavation on a straight projection. A sample brick could be dated only broadly from about the mid-18th century to 1900, but the wall was certainly built during the earlier part of this date range, as it was overlain by a building, PM34, constructed by 1799 (see below). The position and alignment of the graves in Pile Cap C respected the line of the wall. Although no earlier features along this boundary line were identified it is possible that a boundary of some sort, perhaps an earlier wall or a ditch, predated this wall. As such, the date ascribed to the wall does not provide a *terminus post quem* for the burials.

This wall continued southwards on a N-S alignment as [3023], which was exposed in Pile Cap C1–G1. It apparently represented the same western cemetery boundary as [4065], and so is also numbered Structure PM5. It was, however, of different construction, utilising half bricks and patches of mortar, indicative of localised repair or remodelling. The wall survived to a height of 0.3m, with its top lying at a level of 2.66m OD. As the join between these two lengths of wall were not exposed in excavation it is not known whether they were contemporary.

Rocque's map of 1746 (Chapter 2, Fig. 2.6) shows that structure PM5 was standing by this date, by which time it defined the western side of Cure's College Yard. By 1792–9 Horwood's map (Chapter 2, Fig. 2.7) shows that further construction had taken place and the wall now formed the back wall of a building (Structure PM34), which extended eastwards (Fig. 3.3). This building was part of Cure's 'Almshouses'.

Wall [4025], which was aligned perpendicular to western wall Structure PM5 (Fig. 3.3) and truncated Phase 2a burials in Pile Cap C, appears to have belonged to building PM34, or a modification of that building. The construction of this building over the burials shows that the western boundary of the cemetery had moved eastwards by 1799, reducing the available burial area.

Sometime after this date a brick-built vaulted culvert [4014] Structure PM4 was constructed parallel to the western side of Structure PM5 (Fig. 3.3). It was constructed of dark orange frogged brick, suggesting a date of *c* post-1800, and was filled with soft organic soil containing pottery dated to *c* 1830–50 and clay pipes dated broadly to 1823–64. As the culvert was accumulating debris and dateable artefacts during this period until it went out of use when the viaduct was built, it seems it was not cleared out in the intervening years.

The north-eastern side of the cemetery was probably defined by Structures PM8 and PM35. Both structures can be seen on Gwilt's 1814 plan of the College, PM35 representing part of the College almshouses and PM8 being associated with Soap Yard (Fig. 2.8). Structure PM35 overlay a charnel pit containing large quantities of human bone; the backfill of this pit contained brick fragments dating to after *c* 1750. These buildings are described in detail in Thameslink Monograph 2. The other cemetery boundaries were not exposed within the excavated area.

Howe's plan of 1844 depicts Cure's College almshouses and grounds following the rebuild of 1831 (Chapter 2, Fig. 2.10). Figure 3.5 is an overlay on Howe's map of the excavated burials, showing that they lay outside the post-1831 boundary of the College burial ground.

Discussion

In summary, there was little apart from human bone found in the graves. No soft tissue, hair or textile survived. Apart from coffin wood and coffin furniture, artefacts were limited to a few copper alloy pins, a ring, buttons and clay pipe fragments, but these were not demonstrably associated with any individual. Coffin remains were limited to decayed wood fragments, upholstery studs, handles, nails, handle plate fragments, and breastplates (Fig. 3.6; see also Chapter 5). The metal objects were highly corroded and preservation was poor. Some *c* 200 burials were clearly coffined, but the coffin wood was in a very poor condition, in some cases no more than staining. Some groups of burials had no associated coffin material, suggesting that variation in survival was not purely a product of ground conditions and preservation.

Orientation
The available evidence indicates that all of the burials were supine and extended, and that most were on a NW–SE or closely approximate orientation. However, some burials deviated from this norm.

Two consecutive burials [4047] and [4053] in Pile Cap C were on a ENE-WSW alignment, suggesting that they were interred in rapid succession. Most of the burials in a stack within mass grave [2414] in Pile Cap E–H were oriented NW-SE, but the two nearest the top were on a SE-NW orientation. Both were child burials, and this may reflect the most efficient use of a small space at the top of the grave.

In Pile Cap D there were two divergent alignments. In the south-western part of the pile cap a NW-SE alignment was adhered to, but in the north-east area the burials were aligned WNW-ESE. It is possible that these two sectors represented two chronologically distinct phases of use.

Burial density and depth
Burial density varied across the site from 12 to 43 burials per square metre, with an average of approximately 22 per square metre. The deepest burial [703] was recorded at 1.32m OD, and the shallowest [661] at 3.43m OD, both in Pile Cap D. A correlation between burial depths and their location within the cemetery was investigated in order to ascertain whether burial depth could indicate spatial or chronological trends. No such correlation was observed.

The only concentration of particularly deep burials was mass grave [969], where 16 of the 29 burials lay at below 2m OD. The 58 shallowest burials were found in Pile Caps C and E–H because here the burial ground level sloped southwards. Additionally, the cemetery was affected by disturbance caused by centuries of intercutting of burials and construction of boundary walls, buildings, and drains, and some of the shallowest burials were likely to have been removed during these operations.

The earliest burials, which cut the pre-cemetery soils, were well spaced and probably aligned in rows. This spacing would have accommodated head and footstones and walking space between the graves. The existence of a passage way around the western edge of the burials during Phase 2a is suggested by an 0.8m gap between the burials and the western cemetery wall Structure PM5.

Burial status
Status could be indicated by the absence of a coffin, which can suggest poverty, and correspondingly by the presence of coffins, which can indicate higher status, especially when accompanied by fittings (Fig. 3.6). No coffin fittings other than nails were found in Pile Cap C1–G1, so it is possible that this area was reserved for poorer individuals. However, caution is needed here given the poor preservation of coffins and their fittings. Furthermore, changes in funeral customs over time means that the prevalence of coffins and coffin fittings relates to chronology as well as status (see Chapter 5).

Family plots
Some 21 of the grave cuts contained multiple burials or 'stacks' (see details above), which can suggest the burial over time of family groups. With very few surviving coffin plates bearing names, however, it was not possible to investigate this possibility for the Cure's College burial ground based on historical information. The age and sex of individuals within each multiple burial group are presented in Tables 3.2 and 3.3. These show that the larger group burials contain both males and females of different ages, but it is not possible on the archaeological evidence alone to determine whether these individuals were related. The osteological evidence was no more informative in this respect (See Chapter 4).

Four of the double and smaller group burials may represent married couples, perhaps with a child, but could equally be unrelated individuals who died within a short space of time. Although it is likely that there would have been family group burials in the cemetery, the evidence proved to be insufficient to demonstrate any clear cases.

Chapter 4

The people: scientific analyses of the human skeletons

by Louise Loe with Brian Dean, Mark Gibson, Rowena Henderson and Helen Webb

A total of 331 individuals, of whom 245 were adults and 86 were juveniles, were recovered during the excavations. All of the burials were interred during the Phase 2 period of burial activity (1587–1831). Of these, 39 could be assigned to the early phase of burial ground activity (Phase 2a), dated to 1587–1799. The closely dated burial of William Pope, who probably died in about 1816 (see Chapter 3) and six stratigraphically later burials were assigned to Phase 2b (1816–31). The remaining 285 burials were attributed broadly to Phase 2. This chapter describes the osteological and isotopic analyses of this assemblage.

OSTEOLOGICAL ANALYSIS

Osteological analysis of the skeletons was undertaken with the primary aim of developing a dataset that could be integrated with the archaeological and historical record to explore aspects of 16th–19th-century burial practice, attitudes towards the dead and the

Table 4.1: Definition of osteological and medical terms used in the text

Osteological/medical term	Definition
Acromegaly	Excess growth of body tissues after growth plates have fused due to the over production of growth hormone. May result in enlarged hands, feet and skull.
Aetiology	Cause or causes of a disease or condition
Ankylosis	Fusion of bones
Asymtomatic	A condition showing no symptoms
Bilateral	Involving right and left sides
Biogeographic	From biogeography: the distribution of species and ecosystems in geographic space and through (geological) time
Diastema	A space or gap between two teeth, most commonly the upper front teeth.
Dimorphic	Occurs in two distinct forms
Enthesial changes	Lesions at a site of enthesis, connective tissue between ligaments or tendons and bone
Exostoses	New bone on the surface of a bone (singular: exostosis)
Focal	Focussed in one particular area
Hypoplastic	Under developed or incompletely developed tissue
Interphalangeal joints	The joints between the finger bones
Lytic	Bone loss (resorption), for example porosity
Neoplastic	Cancerous
Osteomalacia	Disease causing the demineralisation of adult bone as a result of vitamin D deficiency ('rickets' in child bone)
Pathognomic	Characteristics which are specific to a particular disease or condition
Periapical	Around the apex (tip) of the tooth root
Seronegative spondyloarthropathies	A group of conditions characterised by a lack protein in the blood called rheumatoid factor. For example, reactive arthritis and ankylosing spondylitis, a type which causes the spine to fuse in a certain way.
Sesamoid bone	A bone which is formed within a tendon, typically where tendons pass over a joint. Found in the knee (the 'knee cap') and in the hands and feet
Symphalangism	Congenital condition in which fusion of the finger or toe bones occurs when the joint spaces fail to develop
Virilism	Female hormone disorder resulting in secondary male sexual characteristics such as a deep voice

Table 4.2: Comparative assemblages referred to in the present report

Site (authors)	Date range	Site type	No. adult skeletons	No. juvenile skeletons
St Hilda's, South Shields (McCarthy and Clough (2010)	17th to mid 19th century	Working class, industrial, port town	114	87
Littlemore Baptist Chapel, Oxford (McCarthy et al. 2010)	Late 19th century	Non-conformist, working and middle class, rural	15	15
Chelsea Old Church, London (Bekvalac and Kausmally 2008)	18th to mid 19th century	Upper-working to upper class, London suburb	165	33
St Martin's-in-the-Bull Ring, Birmingham (Brickley et al. 2006)	18th to 19th century	Working and middle class, industrial	352	153
St Marylebone, London (Miles et al. 2008)	Late 18th to mid 19th century	Upper class, London suburb	233	78
St Luke's, Islington, London (unnamed sample)* (Boyle 2005)	Late 18th to early mid 19th century	Largely working class, London suburb	550	102
St Luke's, Islington, London (named sample) (Boyle 2005)	Late 18th to early mid 19th century	Largely middle to upper classes, crypt/vault burials, London suburb	218	23
Newcastle Infirmary (Boulter 1998)	Mid 18th to mid 19th century	Infirmary, urban	191	19
St George's, Bloomsbury, London (named sample) (Boston et al. 2009)	19th century	Upper-middle class, crypt burials	67	5
Christ Church, Spitalfields, London (Molleson and Cox 1993)	18th to mid 19th century	Upper-middle class, crypt burials	623	251
Kingston upon Thames Quaker burial ground, Surrey (Bashford and Sibun 2007)	Late 17th to early 19th century	Non-conformist, middle class, urban	360 (total)	
New Bunhill Fields, Southwark (Miles and Connell 2012)	c 1821–1853	Private burial ground. Largely Non-conformist	157	357
Cross Bones, Southwark, London (Brickley et al. 1999)	Mid 19th century	St Saviour's burial ground Paupers, urban	45	103
St Pancras burial ground, (Emery et al. 2011) London**	Late 18th to mid 19th century	All social classes, urban / (incl. 'non-locals' & refugees of the French Revolution)	490	183
Bow Baptist Chapel, London (Henderson et al. 2013)	Early-mid 19th century	Non-conformist, ?working class, urban	182	169
St Benet Sherehog, London (Miles and White 2008)	17th to mid 19th century	Upper-working class, urban	165	65
West Butts Street Baptist Burial Ground, Poole (McKinley 2008)	18th century	Non-conformist, upper-working class, port town	72	28
Whitefriars Anabaptist Cemetery, Norwich (Caffell and Holst 2007)	18th to 19th century	Non-conformist, mostly urban working class	39	24

*3 skeletons in the St Luke's unnamed sample could not be identified as adult or juvenile, so the total number of individuals in this sample is 655.
**42 skeletons are of unknown sex and age

interaction between these former inhabitants of Southwark and their environment. Objectives were to reconstruct the mortality profile of the population and to explore evidence for physical attributes and health and disease. The skeletons were not generally analysed with reference to their phases because numbers were too small to allow meaningful observations. However, phasing is considered where it is considered to be most relevant and informative.

Terminology

This report employs standard osteological and medical terminology. Definitions of some of these terms are presented in Table 4.1. All other terms are defined in the relevant places in the text.

Methods

All articulated skeletons were fully analysed employing the guidelines prepared by Brickley and McKinley (2004). This report has been prepared in accordance with English Heritage guidelines (Mays *et al*. 2002).

All bones and teeth were analysed macroscopically with the application of radiography where required. Analysis involved recording condition and completeness, estimation of sex, age and stature, exploring other physical attributes (ancestry and bone physiology) and scoring non-metrical traits. This was in addition to palaeopathological observations relating to health and disease.

Palaeopathological and non-metrical data were analysed by calculating the crude prevalence rate (CPR) and the true prevalence rate (TPR). The former refers to the number of skeletons with a given condition or trait out of the number of skeletons present. The latter takes into account the variable preservation of the skeletons, and refers to the number of skeletal landmarks or elements with a condition or trait, relative to the total number that could be observed.

Where relevant, data were compared with that of a number of post-medieval assemblages, mainly deriving from London, but also from the north of England and the Midlands. Particularly relevant was comparison with the Cross Bones assemblage (Brickley *et al*. 1999), which was recovered from the same parish as Park Street. Details of the main comparative assemblages referred to, including the date range of the burials, numbers of individuals and type of population, are given in Table 4.2. Comparisons were also made with the data published for the post-medieval period in Roberts and Cox (2003), which has been synthesised from osteological reports on British assemblages dating between *c* 1550 and *c* 1850.

Results

Condition and completeness

Bone condition was scored with reference to McKinley (2004, 16) and by assigning each skeleton an overall score on a scale ranging from 0 (excellent) to 4 (poor). Likewise, skeletal completeness was scored on a scale of 1–4: 1 (< 25 %); 2 (25–50 %); 3 (50–75 %); and 4 (> 75 %).

The vast majority of skeletons, particularly adults, were not excavated in their entirety because they ran beyond the limits of the excavation trenches. As a result, almost 70% of the assemblage was approximately 50%, or less than 50% complete (Table 4.3; Fig. 4.1). Skeletons that were between 75% and 100% complete totalled 58 (17.5% of the assemblage).

Despite their incompleteness, the overall condition of the skeletons was good, with most having bone surfaces that showed little or no erosion and were only slightly or moderately fragmented (Tables 4.3–4.5; Figs 4.2–4.3). Thus, when present, the good condition of the bone permitted the majority of anthropological and palaeopathological observations that could be made.

Table 4.3: Completeness of skeletons

Completeness	%	No. of skeletons
0–25%	45.02	149
26–50%	23.56	78
51–75%	13.9	46
76–100%	17.52	58
Total	100	331

Table 4.4: Condition of skeletons

Condition grade (McKinley 2004)	%	No. of skeletons
Grade 0	0.3	1
Grade 1	70.09	232
Grade 2	25.68	85
Grade 3	3.32	11
Grade 4	0.6	2
Grade 5	0	0
Grade 5+	0	0
Total	100	331

Table 4.5: Fragmentation of skeletons

Fragmentation	%	No. of skeletons
Low	38.67	128
Medium	42.6	141
High	18.73	62
Total	100	331

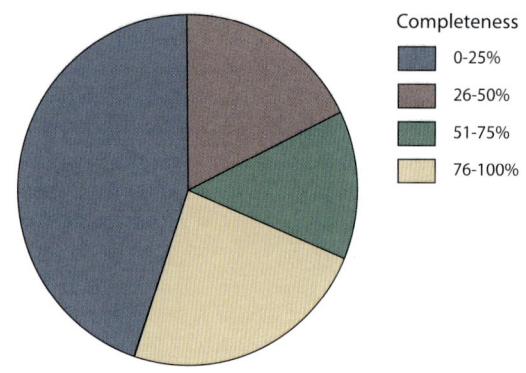

Fig. 4.1: Completeness of skeletons

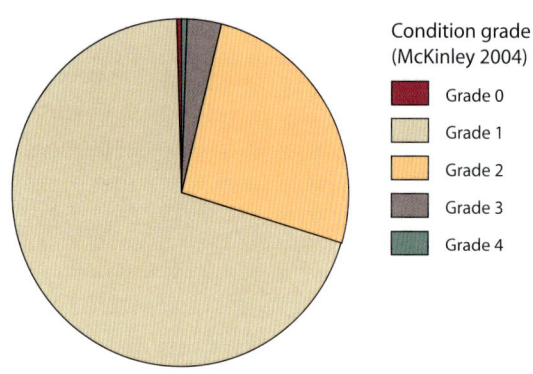

Fig. 4.2 Condition of skeletons

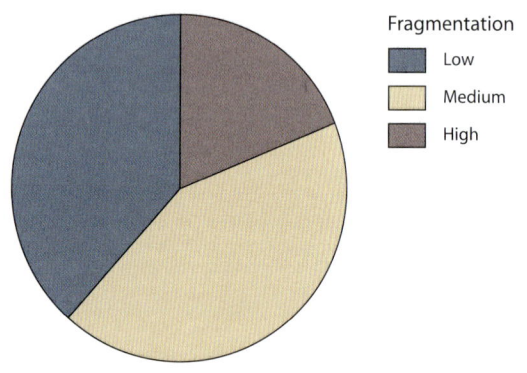

Fig. 4.3 Fragmentation of skeletons

Ancestry

Ancestry may be defined as '...the biogeographic population to which a particular individual belongs, by virtue of their genetic heritage' (Barker *et al.* 2008, 322). Ancestry was assessed for all adult skeletons with complete, intact skulls by visual assessment of craniofacial traits with reference to Buikstra and Ubelaker (1994) and Gill (1986; 2001). This method categorises skulls as being either of 'white', 'black', 'east Asian', 'American Indian' [sic], or of 'mixed' ancestry. The ancestry of the juveniles was not assessed because there are currently no accepted methods for this (Barker *et al.* 2008).

Ancestry was also explored by employing metrical analysis applied to the formula and associated software programme CRANID (Wright 2008). The CRANID package achieves broad geographic classifications for crania (for example, European and east Mediterranean) by automated multivariate comparison of 29 measurements with those of some 3000 crania from around the world (Wright 2008).

Assessment of ancestry was hindered by the limited survival of intact, complete skulls. Of those that could be visually assessed (48 skeletons), all had features that are typical among individuals of white ancestry, with the single exception of [4050], who had mixed features. Most notable traits in this individual included round orbits and a nasal bone that was broad and lacked a nasal sill, features that are consistent with black ancestry. Others included a prominent chin and simple cranial sutures (characteristic of whites), a medium to broad cranial form (an American Indian characteristic), and a high globular sagittal outline (common among east Asian populations). This result, while interesting, must not be regarded as a true reflection of the ancestry of the population, because the visual assessment oversimplifies the relationship between biological expression and genetic affinity. No distinct skeletal characteristics correspond perfectly to a specific ancestral group, and therefore the method is very subjective. Rather, the method is a means of characterising populations in terms of their degree of homogeneity. It serves to highlight individuals for further consideration by the application of other scientific techniques, such as metrical or DNA haplotype analysis.

Unfortunately, metrical analysis applied to CRANID could not be performed on [4050], whose condition did not allow for all of the measurements to be taken. However, seven skeletons determined to be 'white' based on visual assessment had crania that were sufficiently preserved for this, including [623], [637], [701], [709], [837], [2406] and [4068]. Overall, the results revealed individuals whose measurements were most closely affiliated to European (British and southern and northern European) populations.

Demography

Sexually dimorphic features of the pelvis and cranium were employed to estimate osteological sex of adult skeletons based on standards set out in Buikstra and Ubelaker (1994) and Schwartz (1995). No attempt was made to estimate the sex of juvenile skeletons because there are currently no accepted methods available (Brickley and McKinley 2004).

The people 45

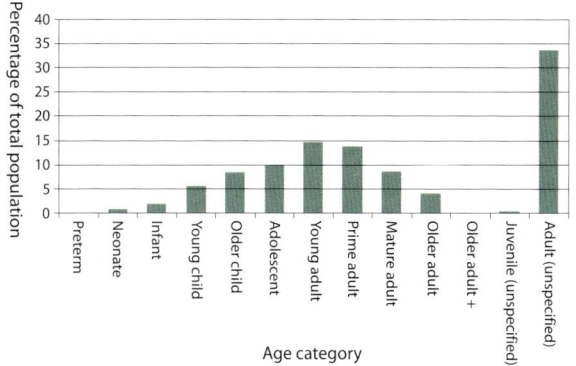

Fig. 4.4 Age distribution of the total assemblage (n=331)

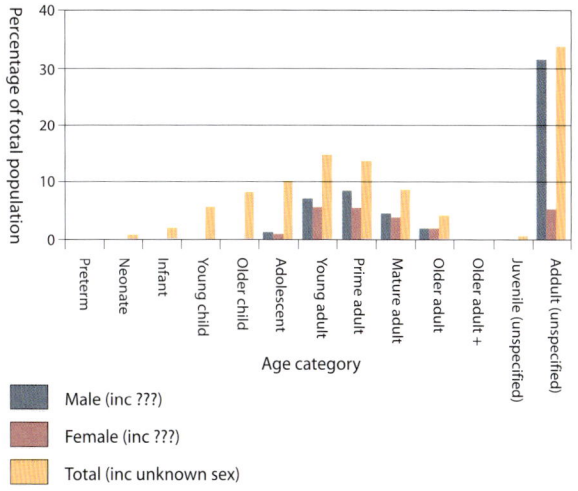

Fig. 4.5 Age/sex distribution of the total assemblage (n=331)

Skeletons were assigned as either: possible male, probable male, definite male, possible female, probable female, definite female or unsexed. These are entered as such in the archive, but for the purposes of the present report all possible and probable males and females have been counted as definite males and females Figs 4.4–4.6).

All individuals were assigned to one of the age categories set out in Table 4.6. Diaphyseal long bone lengths were used as the basis for ageing foetuses and neonates using methods developed by Fazekas and Kósa (as adapted in Scheuer and Black 2000). Juveniles were otherwise aged by the stage of dental eruption (Moorrees et al. 1963a and b), stage of epiphyseal fusion (Scheuer and Black 2000) and diaphyseal length of the major long bones (Maresh 1970).

The adult skeletons were aged by employing methods that refer to degeneration of the auricular surface of the pelvis (Buckberry and Chamberlain 2002, Lovejoy et al. 1985), the sternal ends of the ribs (İşcan and Loth 1998) and the pubic symphysis (Brooks and Suchey 1990), late fusing epiphyses

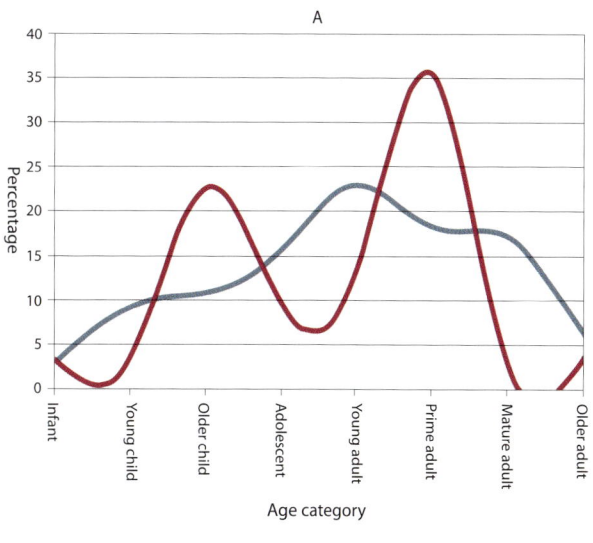

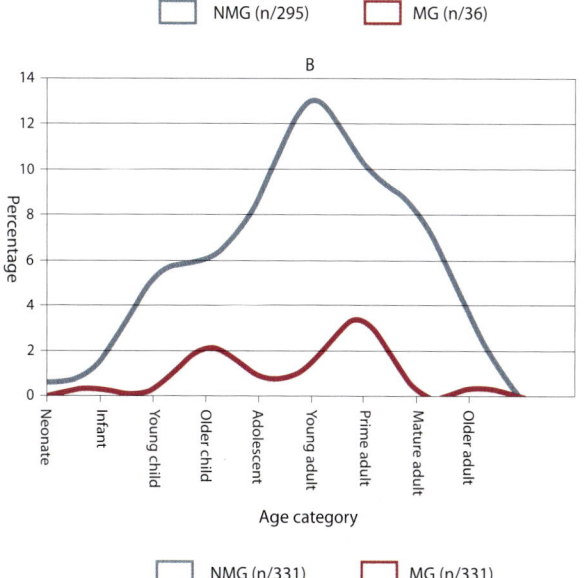

Fig. 4.6 Mass grave (MG) and non-mass grave (NMG) mortality profiles compared A: as a percentage of each sample; B: as a percentage of the total assemblage

Table 4.6: Numbers of skeletons in each age category

Age group	Age range	%	No. of skeletons
Pre-term	<37 weeks gestation	0	0
Neonate	Birth–1 month	0.60	2
Infant	1–12 months	1.81	6
Young child	1–5 years	5.44	18
Older child	6–12 years	8.16	27
Adolescent	13–17 years	9.67	32
Young adult	18–25 years	15.50	48
Prime adult	26–35 years	13.60	45
Mature adult	36–45 years	8.46	28
Older adult	> 45 years	3.93	13
Older adult+	> 60 years	0.00	0
Child	2–12 years	0.00	0
Juvenile	< 18 years	0.30	1
Adult	> 18 years	33.53	111
Total		100.00	331

(Scheuer and Black 2000), and dental attrition (Miles 1962).

It was possible to estimate the sex of 177 skeletons. A total of 104 were definite, possible or probable males and 73 were definite, possible or probable females. Among them were seven adolescents, four males and three females, whose innominate bones had fused and could therefore be observed for distinctive male or female traits, and/or whose measurements fell well into the male or female range. The remaining 170 skeletons were all adults.

These estimations give a male to female ratio of 1.42:1. This may reflect a bias towards identifying males in skeletal assemblages (Waldron 1998, 36). The same pattern has been observed in male to female ratios at broadly contemporary populations of similar socio-economic background, including St Marylebone (1.2:1), St Luke's (1.3:1), and St Martin's-in-the-Bull Ring, Birmingham (1.3:1), but not at St Pancras, where the ratio was 1:1 (White 2011, 112). Thus, other factors, cultural and genetic, should be considered.

Age estimations placed most of the juveniles in the adolescent age category (32 individuals), followed by the older child (27 individuals), and then the young child (18 individuals) age categories. Two and six individuals were estimated to have been neonates and infants respectively, and there were no pre-term infants. It was not possible to assign one of the juveniles to an age category owing to incompleteness.

Data analysed from the Bills of Mortality for London between 1728 and the 1840s suggests that approximately 40% of deaths were among those aged five years and under, and between 6–7% of deaths were among those aged between 6 and 20 years (Roberts and Cox 2003, 304). This pattern – a high proportion of deaths among individuals aged 5 years and below – is reflected in data collected from several London assemblages (Table 4.6), but not among the Park Street burials where only a small proportion of individuals (7.9%) fall into this group, as at Spitalfields where socio-economic factors are known to have been influential in the choice of burial place (Molleson and Cox 1993).

A total of 134 adults could be assigned to an age category (Table 4.6). Of these, 69% were estimated to have been 18–25 (48 individuals) or 26–35 (45 individuals) years when they died. Very few (3.9%) were 45+ years of age and none were estimated to have been over the age of 60 years. One hundred and eleven adults could not be assigned to an age category owing

Table 4.7: Park Street mortality patterns compared with other post-medieval assemblages (adapted from Bekvalac and Kausmally 2008, 43)

	Total number of individuals	Total number of juveniles (%)	Juveniles <5 years (%)	Juveniles 6–<18 years (%)	Total number of adults (%)
Park Street, Southwark	331	86 (26)	7.9	17.8	245 (74.0)
Cross Bones burial ground	148	103 * (69.6)	66.2	3.4	45 (30.4)
New Bunhill Fields	514	357 (69.5)	64.4	5.1	157 (30.5)
Chelsea Old Church	198	33 (16.7)	11.1	4.0	165 (83.3)
St Bride's crypt	131	21 (16.0)	10.7	5.3	110 (84.0)
Christ Church, Spitalfields	968	215 (22.2)	-	-	660 (68.2)
St Marylebone	301	78* (25.9)	22.3	3.3	223 (74.1)
St Pancras	715	183 (25.6)	19.7	5.9	532 (74.4)
The New Churchyard, Broadgate	388	122 (31.4)	15.7	15.7	266 (68.6)
St Benet Sherehog	230	65 (28.3)	18.7	9.6	165 (71.7)
St Bride's lower Churchyard	533	193 (36.2)	-	-	340 (63.8)

* includes unaged sub-adults

Table 4.8: Park Street male and female mortality patterns compared with other post-medieval assemblages

Site	16–25/18–25 yrs			26–35 yrs			
	M (%)	F (%)	? (%)	M (%)	F (%)	? (%)	M (%)
Park Street, Southwark	23 (9.4)	18 (7.3)	7 (2.9)	28 (11.4)	17 (6.9)	0	14 (5.7)
New Bunhill Fields	10 (2.0)	14 (2.7)	0	15 (2.9)	17 (3.3)	0	26 (5.0)
Cross Bones	2 (4.4)	1 (2.2)	0	3 (1.2)	5 (11.1)	0	5 (11.1)
Chelsea old church*	(3.0)	9 (5.5)	0	9 (5.5)	7 (4.2)	1 (0.6)	26 (15.8)
St Marylebone*	8 (3.5)	11 (4.9)	1 (0.4)	15 (6.7)	20 (9.0)	7 (3.1)	44 (19.7)
St Brides lower churchyard*	5 (1.4)	4 (1.1)	1 (0.3)	22 (6.0)	21 (5.7)	1 (0.3)	54 (14.6)
St Pancras**	48 (9.8)	55 (11.2)	19 (3.9)	109 (22.2)	81 (16.5)	11 (2.2)	-

* Data provided by the Museum of London online at:
http://www.museumoflondon.org.uk/Collections-Research/LAARC/Centre-for-Human-Bioarchaeology/Database/Post-medieval+cemeteries/
**individuals in the 26–35year column are 26–45 years from this site

to missing elements. These results could be a product of the methods that have been used to age the assemblage and which are believed to over age the young and under age the old (Cox 2000). However, this is unlikely because the same methods employed in the present analysis have been employed in the analysis of other assemblages from London and beyond and these do not show such a marked absence of older individuals (Table 4.7).

Male deaths were more numerous in all adult and the adolescent age categories, than female deaths. This is with the exception of those in the 45+ years category, to which an equal number of females and males (six each) were assigned. The slight increase in the number of females in the 25–35 year category may be explained by increased mortality as a result of childbirth. In no age category, however, did female deaths exceed male deaths, unlike other contemporary assemblages from London and elsewhere (Table 4.8).

Pile Cap D mass grave demography
A total of 36 skeletons were from a mass grave in Pile Cap D (Table 4.9). The group comprised 12 juveniles and 16 male, four female and four unsexed adults. Ages at death were highest among older children and prime adults, in marked contrast to the mortality profile of the non-mass grave group (Fig. 4.6). In addition, the ratio of males to females was higher among the mass grave group (4.7:1) than the non-mass grave group

Table 4.9: Age and sex distribution: Pile Cap D mass grave

	?	M	F	Total (%)
Neonate				
Infant	1 (2.8)			1 (2.8)
young child	1 (2.8)			1 (2.8)
older child	7 (19.4)			7 (19.4)
adolescent	3 (8.3)			3 (8.3)
young adult	1 (2.8)	2 (5.6)	2 (5.6)	5 (13.9)
prime adult		10 (27.8)	1 (2.8)	11 (30.6)
mature adult		1 (2.8)	1 (2.8)	
older adult		1 (2.8)		1 (2.8)
adult	3	2 (5.6)	1 (2.8)	6 (16.7)
Total (%)	16 (44.4)	16 (44.4)	4 (11.1)	36

(1.1:1). The high number of juveniles and high male to female ratio observed in the mass grave group from Park Street is in keeping with the mortality profile of known plague victims from East Smithfield, and shares some similarities with mass grave assemblages from St Mary, Spital (Table 4.10). This is considered further below (and see Chapter 6).

Physical attributes

Stature
The maximum lengths of major long bones were measured in order to calculate statures, which were estimated by employing the method for Caucasians developed by Trotter and Gleser (1952; 1958), and

Table 4.10: Comparison between Park Street non-mass grave and mass grave demographic trends with other assemblages associated with plague/epidemic

Assemblage	Juvenile trends	Male to female ratio
Park Street non-mass grave	39.8% (73/183) = juveniles; neonates and young infants almost entirely absent	M :F ratio 1.1:1
Park Street mass grave	40% (12/30) = juveniles; neonates and young infants almost entirely absent	M:F ratio 4.7:1
East Smithfield Black Death (1348–50) assemblage (Cowal *et al.* 2008)	40.5% = juveniles; neonates and young infants almost entirely absent	M:F ratio 1.98:1
St Mary Spital (1400–1539) (Connell *et al.* 2012)	23.4% (29/124) = juveniles; neonates and young infants almost entirely absent	M:F ratio 1.1:1

36–45 yrs F (%)	? (%)	M (%)	45+ F (%)	? (%)	Adult M (%)	F (%)	? (%)	Total
12 (4.9)	2 (0.8)	6 (2.4)	6 (2.4)	1 (0.4)	29 (11.8)	17 (6.9)	65 (26.5)	245
15 (2.9)	0	32 (6.2)	23 (4.5)	0	2 (0.4)	3 (0.6)	0	514
2 (4.4)	0	11 (24.4)	12 (26.7)	1 (2.2)	0	0	3 (1.2)	45
17 (10.3)	3 (1.8)	35 (21.2)	36 (21.8)	1 (0.6)	3 (1.8)	5 (3.0)	8 (4.8)	165
22 (9.9)	3 (1.3)	25 (11.2)	25 (11.2)	2 (0.9)	14 (6.3)	8 (3.6)	18 (8.1)	223
30 (8.1)	4 (1.1)	88 (23.8)	64 (17.3)	10 (2.7)	25 (6.8)	6 (1.6)	34 (9.2)	369
-	-	54 (11.0)	66 (13.5)	5 (1.0)	20 (4.1)	22 (4.5)	-	490

revised by Trotter (Trotter 1970). Combined measurements of the femur and tibia were utilised wherever possible, and in the absence of one of these bones the femur and then the tibia was used. The major bones of the upper limb were used if no lower limb bones were present. The left side was used preferentially, in keeping with standard osteological practice (Buikstra and Ubelaker 1994).

It was possible to estimate the statures of 44 males and 30 females. Male statures ranged from 157.32–182.87cm, with an average of 168.88cm (*c* 5' 6"). Female statures ranged from 143.51–165.25cm, with an average of 158.47cm (*c* 5' 2"). However, 34 of these calculations were performed using measurements taken from the least reliable bone for estimating stature, the humerus (Trotter 1970). Calculations using this bone have an error margin of plus or minus 4.05cm, compared to those that use the femur, one of the most reliable bones, which gives an error margin of plus or minus 3.27cm (Trotter 1970). It was possible to employ the length of the femur in stature calculations for 24 males and 15 females, giving a male range of 160.42–180.17cm, with an average of 167.27cm (*c* 5' 5"), and a female range of 143.51–165.25 cm, with an average of 156.93cm (*c* 5' 1"). The stature of one female was estimated by employing the maximum length of the fibula, which has an error margin of 3.57cm (Trotter 1970).

Comparison with other contemporary assemblages shows that the mean male and female statures (estimated using any available long bone) from Park Street are the same as those estimated for males and females from Cross Bones, which are among the lowest of all assemblages (Table 4.11). However, overall, the individuals from both sites do not appear to be significantly shorter than other contemporary populations.

Child growth

Child growth was explored by comparing age estimated from dental development (after Moorees *et al.* 1963a and b) with that estimated from diaphyseal femur lengths. Femur lengths, as opposed to any other long bone length, were employed in this analysis because the femur shows the most rapid growth and is therefore considered to reflect growth disruption better (Mays *et al.* 2008). The results are shown in Table 4.12.

Indices

Besides stature, and where preservation permitted, bones were also measured to calculate skeletal indices. Skeletal indices are used to explore general bone physiology and proportions, and include the cephalic index (cranial shape) and the platymeric (degree of flattening of the femur, front to back), and platycnemic (degree of transverse flattening of the tibia) indices.

The cranial index, which calculates variation in skull shape between populations, could be estimated for 21 individuals, seven females and 14 males. Six individuals (all males) were classified as dolichocranic ('long-headed') and four (three females and one male) were classified as bracycranic ('round-headed'). The majority, however, were of average dimensions, or mesocranic (11 individuals, four females and seven males), which is the most common shape seen among post-medieval populations (Molleson and Cox 1993, 31). This contrasts with medieval populations from London and elsewhere in Britain, whose skull shapes

Table 4.11: Comparison of statures

Site	Males				Females			
	Mean (m)	Range (m)	V	n	Mean (m)	Range (m)	V	n
Park Street, Southwark	1.69	1.57–1.83	3.7	44	1.58	1.44–1.65	3.1	30
Redearth Primitive Methodist Chapel, Darwen	1.68	1.62–1.77	2.9	10	1.55	1.49–1.68	3.6	17
New Bunhill Fields	1.68	1.56–1.81	3.5	52	1.61	1.52–1.73	3.0	48
Cross Bones, Southwark	1.69	1.53–1.80	-	16	1.58	1.42–1.72	-	19
St Hilda's, South Shields	1.71	1.49–1.81	-	49	1.59	1.49–1.74	-	44
Littlemore Baptist Chapel, Oxford	1.66	1.60–1.69	-	3	1.58	1.47–1.61	-	7
Chelsea Old Church	1.70	1.58–1.80	-	37	1.60	1.52–1.69	-	35
St Martin's-in-the-Bull Ring, Birmingham	1.72	1.56–1.85	3.3	173	1.59	1.39–1.71	3.6	124
St Marylebone, London	1.70	1.54–1.82	3.3	76	1.59	1.45–1.69	3.4	62
St Luke's, Islington (unnamed sample)	1.71	1.49–1.94	-	295	1.58	1.39–1.74	-	238
St Luke's, Islington (named sample)	1.70	1.55–1.93	-	-	1.58	1.49–1.72	-	-
Newcastle Infirmary	1.71	1.60–1.83	-	-	1.60	1.50–1.76	-	-
St George's, Bloomsbury (named sample)	1.72	1.52–1.85	-	15	1.60	1.48–1.79	-	20
Christchurch, Spitalfields	1.69	1.68–1.70	3.7	211	1.57	1.54–1.59	4.5	206
Kingston-upon-Thames, Surrey	1.69	1.55–1.90	-	-	1.60	1.40–1.75	-	-
St Pancras burial ground	1.71	1.50–1.88	-	168	1.57	1.43–1.77	-	138

V = Coefficient of variation; n=number of skeletons

Table 4.12: Juvenile femur age (Scheuer and Black 2000) compared with dental age (Moorees et al. 1963a and b)

Skeleton number	Femur diaphyseal length (mm)	Femur length age	Dental age	Assigned age range
949	325	8.5–9 yrs	11.5–12.5 yrs	11–13 yrs
705B	332	9–9.5 yrs	no data	9–10.5 yrs
721	394	10–11 yrs	no data	12–16 yrs
771	279	6–7 yrs	10.5–13.5 yrs	6–12 yrs
797	276	6–6.5 yrs	6–7 yrs	6–7 yrs
835	354	9–10.5 yrs	12–15 yrs	11–12 yrs
843	301	7.5–8 yrs	12.5–13.5 yrs	12.5–13.5 yrs
858	72	38–40 weeks gestation	1.5–4 mths	1.5–4 mths
2215	181	2 yrs	no data	1.5–3 yrs
2236	256	5–5.5 yrs	no data	4–6 yrs
2338	127	0.5–1 yr	no data	1–12 mths
2352	430	12–14.5 yrs	13–20 yrs	13–14.5 yrs
2378A	293	7–7.5 yrs	No data	7–8 yrs
2380	147	1–1.5 yrs	10.5 mths–1.5 years	1–1.5 yrs
3063	248	5–5.5yrs	No data	6–11 yrs
3071	331	9–9.5 yrs	No data	8–9.5 yrs
4019	204	3–3.5 yrs	No data	6–8 yrs
4022	72	38–40 wks	No data	38–40 wks

tended to be bracycranic (White 2011). Whether a change in cranial form reflects genetic influence from immigrant populations or changes in the environment (for example a shift to cooler temperatures and a softer diet) has long been debated (Mays 1998). Re-analysis by Gravlee et al. (2003) of cranial data captured from early 20th-century first generation immigrants in New York has emphasised the influence of the environment; perhaps this was also a significant factor in the change in cranial form between medieval and post-medieval populations.

Calculation of the femoral shaft index (platymeric index) indicates an overall tendency in the assemblage towards a rounded, rather than a flattened (anterior to posterior) femoral shaft (Table 4.13). Males showed a tendency to have more rounded shafts than females, a finding that has also been observed for the post-medieval sample excavated from St Peter's Barton-Upon-Humber, Lincolnshire (Waldron 2007, 46–7). Among the skeletons examined from St Pancras, London, there was no significant difference between the sexes, with both showing a roughly equal tendency towards rounding of the shaft (White 2011, 113).

Over time, the femoral shaft has become more rounded, meaning that the index has increased (Waldron 2007). The reason for this is not clear, but it may be an adaptive response to increased mechanical stress as a result of mechanical work (Brothwell 1981; Wells 1964, 32). Squatting, and mineral and vitamin deficiency are other possible factors (Waldron 2007).

Finally, the calculated tibial shaft indices, which reflect the degree of medio-lateral flattening of the shaft (platycnemic index), showed a tendency toward little or no flattening in the group (Table 4.14). As with the femur, squatting, mechanical stress and pathology have all been suggested as factors that cause the flattening (Brothwell 1981). Most of the Park Street sample had values that were over 70, whereas values less than 62.9 indicate medio-lateral flattening. This result is consistent with other post-medieval assemblages from London (for example, St Pancras) and elsewhere in Britain (for example, St Peter's, Barton-Upon-Humber, Lincolnshire) (White 2011, 113; Waldron 2007, 47).

Enthesial changes
Enthesial changes are reactions which occur at the sites of muscle, tendon and ligament attachments (the entheses) and are considered in the context of activity-related stress markers (eg Henderson and Cardoso 2013), though this interpretation is contested (Jurmain et al. 2012). They may be identified as lytic defects with

Table 4.13: Femoral shaft index

		60-	70-	80-	90+
Male	n	0	12	17	25
	%	0	22.22	31.48	46.3
Female	n	1	13	15	8
	%	2.7	35.14	40.54	21.62

Table 4.14: Tibial shaft index

		60-	70-	80-	90+
Male	n	8	14	6	1
	%	27.59	48.28	20.69	3.45
Female	n	4	15	2	2
	%	17.39	65.22	8.7	8.7

Table 4.15: Age and sex distribution of skeletons with pronounced muscle/ligament/tendon sites

Age category	Male	Female	Unsexed	Total
Older child			1	1
Adolescent	4		5	9
Young adult	6	3	2	11
Prime adult	9	3	0	12
Older adult	5	3	0	8
Mature adult	3	2	0	5
Adult unspecified	13	2	6	21
Total	40	13	14	67

pitting and/or furrowing; areas of robusticity (for example, sharp ridges and crests of bone) and areas of bone forming and production (ossification exostoses) (Henderson *et al.* 2013, 153).

A total of 57 adults and 10 juveniles (four males and six unsexed) had enthesial changes (Table 4.15). They were more frequent among males (36) than females (13) and involved upper limbs (56/61 individuals with defects; 92%) more commonly than lower limbs (25/54 individuals with defects; 46.3%; see Table 4.16). The majority of upper limb changes were defects at the insertion site for the costo-clavicular ligament on the medial clavicle.

Enthesial changes, or more specifically, ossification exostoses can be pathological. For example, they are typical among individuals who have bone forming diseases such as diffuse idiopathic skeletal hyperostosis and seronegative spondyloarthropathies. When the lesions are diffuse they show a particular pattern of skeletal involvement and are (usually) in association with osteophytosis (Rogers and Waldron 2001). However, no such examples were observed in the present assemblage.

Non-metrical analysis

Non-metric traits, or morphological, non-pathological variations in the skeleton, were scored on a presence/absence basis with reference to those listed in Brickley and McKinley (2004). Cranial traits in particular have a strong genetic component in their aetiology, and in a burial context may be used to explore relatedness between individuals. Inheritance is thought to play a lesser role in the aetiology of post-cranial traits and, as such, these may refer to activity-related patterns.

Cranial non-metric traits

The most frequent non-metric cranial traits were mastoid foramen (extrasutural), lambdoid ossicles, supra-orbital foramen and parietal foramen (Table 4.17). The origin of these traits is probably genetic, and as such they may be used to explore the identification of family burial plots by examining the burial locations of those sharing the same traits (Tyrell 2000). However, such analysis applied to the Cross Bones skeletons did not identify individuals who shared the same distribution of traits, although calculated trait frequencies were too low to explore in any detail (Brickley *et al.* 1999). Shared traits among the Park Street skeletons are considered further below.

Post-cranial non-metric traits

The most frequent post-cranial traits were calcaneus double anterior facets, acromial articular facets on the scapulae, talus double inferior facets and tibial lateral squatting facets (Table 4.18). These, and the other post-cranial traits that were observed, are believed to be under greater influence from mechanical stresses, than genetics (Tyrell 2000). For example, squatting facets on the tibia are thought to arise as a result of extended periods of time spent with the legs hypodorsiflexed, such as when squatting (Boulle 2001).

Spatial analysis for shared traits

Twenty-one graves were investigated as possible family burial plots, because they comprised more than one individual buried in the same grave (see Chapter 3). All of these group burials were considered for

Table 4.16: Prevalence of pronounced sites by sex and skeletal region

Age category	Male Upper limb (n/N)	Male Lower limb (n/N)	Female Upper limb (n/N)	Female Lower limb (n/N)	Unsexed Upper limb (n/N)	Unsexed Lower limb (n/N)
Older child	0	0			1/1	0/1
Adolescent	4/4	0/4			5/6	0/5
Young adult	5/5	4/5	3/3	1/2	1/2	1/2
Prime adult	9/9	4/11	2/3	2/4	0	0
Older adult	5/5	1/5	3/3	1/3	0	0
Mature adult	3/3	2/3	1/2	1/2	0	0
Adult unspecified	11/12	2/4	2/2	0/1	1/1	5/5
Total	37/38 97%	13/32 41%	11/13 85%	5/12 42%	8/10 80%	6/13 46%

Table 4.17: Prevalence of cranial non-metric traits

Cranial trait	R/L/Central	No. observable	No. with trait	TPR %
Ossicle at lambda	C	46	5	10.87
Bregmatic bone	C	49	0	0
Lambdoid ossicle	R	41	12	29.27
	L	38	11	28.95
Coronal ossicle	R	42	0	0
	L	44	0	0
Ossicle at asterion	R	30	1	3.33
	L	30	3	10
Epipteric bone	R	25	2	8
	L	26	1	3.85
Parietal notch bone	R	29	2	6.9
	L	30	2	6.67
Fronto-temporal articulation	R	25	1	4
	L	28	1	3.57
Metopism	C	67	7	10.45
Palatine torus	C	53	1	1.89
Maxillary torus	R	60	0	0
	L	57	0	0
Mandibular torus	R	68	1	1.47
	L	63	2	3.17
Auditory torus	R	72	0	0
	L	69	0	0
Highest nuchal line	C	61	0	0
Parietal foramen	R	67	15	22.39
	L	67	13	19.4
Access. Infraorb. For.	R	44	4	9.09
	L	42	4	9.52
Absent zygo-facial For.	R	56	6	10.71
	L	57	8	14.04
Supraorb. Foramen	R	60	16	26.67
	L	61	20	32.79
Access. Supraorb. For.	R	57	11	19.3
	L	58	5	8.62
Mastoid for. Extrasutural	R	40	20	50
	L	40	18	45
Mastoid foramen absent	R	55	5	9.09
	L	54	4	7.41
Double condylar facet	R	41	1	2.44
	L	41	1	2.44
Precondylar tubercle	R	37	2	5.41
	L	37	2	5.41

shared non-metric cranial traits in addition to any other shared traits/conditions that have a strong genetic component in their aetiology, including pathological conditions that are familial, non-metric post-cranial traits and dental traits.

Three grave stacks in particular stood out in this respect. The first comprised six individuals within grave [2426] in Pile Cap E–H, including mature adult female [2423], mature adult female [2421], prime adult male [2419], young adult female [2417], mature adult male [2415], and unsexed adult [2401]. Shared traits/conditions within this group included the following: a congenital abnormality (fusion of interphalangeal joints in both feet, or symphalangism on [2419] and [2415]), two cranial non-metric traits (an ossicle at Lambda on [2421] and [2417] and absent mastoid foramen on [2423] and [2419]), and one post-cranial non-metric trait (a double anterior facet on the calcaneus on [2421], [2417], and [2415]). The second group was within grave [2414], Pile Cap E–H, and comprised young child [2412], prime adult male [2410], adolescent [2408], mature adult female [2406], mature adult male [2403], young adult male [2397], young child [2380], older child [2378A], and adult female [2378B]. Shared traits/conditions in this group included defects in the axial skeleton in [2408] (vertebral border shifting), [2403] (spondylolisis) and [2378A] (bifurcated fifth lumbar vertebral arch). In addition, shared cranial non-metric traits were observed in the form of extra-sutural mastoid foramen [2406] and [2378B] and supra-orbital foramen in [2410] and [2378B].

Apart from these graves, the only other grave with individuals with shared traits/conditions was [2203], Pile Cap E–H, which contained mature adult male [2201] and mature adult female [2199].

Table 4.18: Prevalence of post-cranial non-metric traits

Cranial trait	R/L/Central	No. observable	No. with trait	TPR %
Atlas – double facet	R	64	8	12.5
	L	64	6	9.38
Atlas – lateral bridge	R	61	0	0
	L	59	2	3.39
Atlas – posterior bridge	R	60	3	5
	L	58	1	1.72
Atlas – bipartite transverse foramen	R	53	0	0
	L	56	0	0
Supra-scapular foramen	R	38	0	0
	L	32	0	0
Scapula – acromial articular facet	R	36	8	22.22
	L	31	5	16.13
Sternal foramen	C	70	1	1.43
Humerus – septal aperture	R	76	3	3.95
	L	79	4	5.06
Humerus – supra-condyloid process	R	84	0	0
	L	85	0	0
Accessory sacral facets	R	64	1	1.56
	L	62	1	1.61
Acetabular crease	R	80	4	5
	L	83	2	2.41
Femur – Allen's fossa	R	77	0	0
	L	85	3	3.53
Femur – Poirier's facet	R	76	5	6.58
	L	83	5	6.02
Femur – plaque formation	R	75	0	0
	L	81	1	1.23
Femur – third trochanter	R	77	4	5.19
	L	80	6	7.5
Femur – hypotrochanteric fossa	R	82	3	3.66
	L	81	3	3.7
Femur – exostosis in trochanteric fossa	R	78	0	0
	L	79	0	0
Emarginate patella	R	41	0	0
	L	50	2	4
Patella – vastus notch	R	41	3	7.32
	L	49	4	8.16
Patella – vastus fossa	R	41	0	0
	L	49	0	0
Tibia – medial squatting facet	R	62	1	1.61
	L	64	3	4.69
Tibia – lateral squatting facet	R	61	10	16.39
	L	66	8	12.12
Talus – os trigonum	R	58	2	3.45
	L	63	2	3.17
Talus – double inferior facet	R	59	10	16.95
	L	60	9	15
Lateral talar extension	R	59	3	5.08
	L	62	5	8.06
Medial talar facet	R	59	0	0
	L	62	0	0
Calcaneus – anterior facet absent	R	72	1	1.39
	L	62	0	0
Calcaneus – double anterior facet	R	70	24	34.29
	L	63	19	30.16
Calcaneus – peroneal tubercle	R	68	0	0
	L	60	0	0

Both of these individuals shared the non-metric cranial trait, supra-orbital foramen, but they also had other non-metric traits that they did not share.

The shared conditions/traits observed in these three graves may be because the individuals were related, but overall numbers are low and therefore this could simply be chance. A similar analysis was performed on the Cross Bones skeletons, but did not identify any individuals who shared the same distribution of traits, although calculated trait frequencies were too low to explore in any detail (Brickley *et al.* 1999).

Dental status

A total of 136 dentitions were available for examination, including 92 from the adults and 44 from the juveniles. Dental pathology was identified in accordance with Hillson (2003) and Ortner (2003). Dental calculus was recorded according to Brothwell's methods (1981), and dental enamel hypoplasia, according to Hillson (2003). The location on the tooth and severity of carious lesions were also described in the primary record.

Adult dentitions

Just over 37% (92/246) of the adults had dentitions that could be observed, including those with teeth only, those with teeth and sockets, and one individual who had sockets only. Out of the expected total number of 2944 teeth and sockets (92 individuals x 32 teeth each) there were 1726 teeth and 1969 tooth sockets present. The shortfall in these figures is accounted for by the fact that a total of 228 teeth had been lost post-mortem and a further 257 teeth had been lost ante-mortem. Twenty-nine teeth (all third molars) were missing due to agenesis. In addition, a further five teeth (all third molars) were missing, but it was not possible to say, without radiography, whether this was also due to agenesis, or whether the teeth had not erupted. A total of 699 teeth are unaccounted for because of missing jaws.

Ante-mortem tooth loss

The loss of a tooth or teeth before death may be the result of a number of disease processes. For example, dental tissues may become irritated by calculus, which can weaken the periodontal ligament and cause resorption of the alveolar bone (periodontal disease), followed eventually by ante-mortem tooth loss (AMTL). In addition, periapical abscesses developing from the exposure of the underlying pulp cavity as a result of caries or severe attrition may result in the death of a tooth root and subsequent loss. Trauma and intentional extraction are other factors that may result in AMTL (Ortner 2003).

In the present sample, a total of 60 (65.2%) adults with surviving dentitions, or 257 sockets (13.1%) had AMTL. The condition involved a higher proportion of females (69.4%; 25/36) than males (65.4%; 34/52), but there were marginally more tooth spaces affected among males (13.9%; 157/1131), than among females (12.4%; 94/761). Individuals had lost between one and 26 teeth ante mortem.

Overall, the TPR for Park Street was the lowest compared with other contemporary assemblages (Table 4.19). It is generally considered that AMTL is a degenerative disease process, positively associated with increasing age (Hillson 1996, 198). This observation is reflected in the fact that there is a sharp increase in the prevalence of AMTL among the older age categories at Park Street (Fig. 4.7). This result is therefore consistent with the demographic profile of the sample, which shows a distinct lack of older adults and a higher than expected number of young individuals (see above).

Dental caries

Dental caries, or cavities, are the result of a disease process in which there is focal demineralisation and destruction of the hard tissues and organic matter of teeth (Hillson 1996, 290). This infectious condition is brought about by dietary sucrose in association with acid-producing bacteria (Hillson 1996, 282), but there are other contributory factors, such as dental wear and the presence of other dental diseases (Roberts and Manchester 1995, 47).

Caries were observed on a total of 249 teeth, giving a TPR of 14.4% (249/1726). In total they affected 71 individuals, 77.2% (71/91) of all skeletons with teeth. This result exceeds the prevalence of 49% calculated for a range of assemblages for the period (Roberts and Cox 2003, 326). When the Park Street TPR is considered alongside other sites (Table 4.19), however, they do not appear to be that high, being at the lower end of the range, which is between 9.74% (St Luke's, Islington, London) and 40.58% (Littlemore Baptist chapel, Oxford). Thus, although caries affected a large proportion of the Park Street individuals, the number of teeth affected was relatively small.

Rates were similar to those calculated for nearby New Bunhill Fields (11.63%), the upper-working- to middle-class assemblage from Chelsea Old Church, London (11.06%), the working- and middle-class,

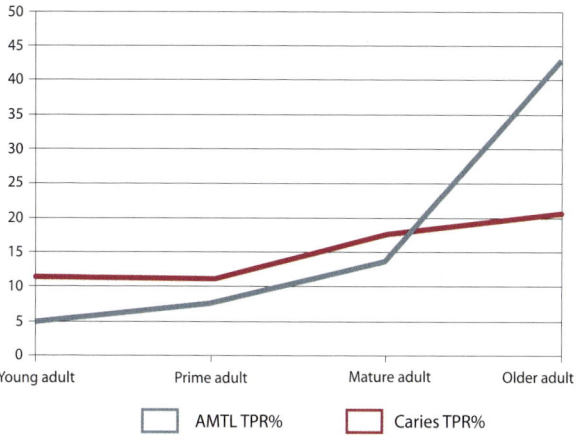

Fig. 4.7 Prevalence of ATML and caries

industrial assemblage from St Martin's-in-the-Bull Ring, Birmingham (11.1%), and the upper-middle-class assemblage from St George's, Bloomsbury (13.4%). Interestingly, rates calculated for the assemblage from the nearby Cross Bones burial ground were almost twice as high as Park Street at 25.9%, compared with 14.4%.

When considered by sex, caries was more prevalent among females than males. They were observed on 20.2% (130/643) of all female teeth, or 85.7% (30/35) of all females, and on 11.4% (115/1007) of all male teeth, or 71.6% (37/52) of all males. The difference in the number of affected female and male teeth was extremely statistically significant (X^2=24.0022, P=<0.0001, d.f1).

When considered alongside age, the true prevalence of caries shows a positive correlation, as with AMTL (Fig. 4.7). However, unlike AMTL, there is a sharp drop off in the number of cases in the older adult age category. This is likely to be a result of the high number of teeth lost AMTL among this age group, and thus a lower number of teeth to observe for cavities.

Calculus

When micro-organisms, embedded in a matrix of saliva and protein, adhere to teeth they may mineralise resulting in dental calculus or 'plaque' (Hillson 1996, 300). Levels of calculus in archaeological populations are an indication of oral hygiene and diet, being associated with diets that are high in protein and/or carbohydrates. Prevalence rates determined for archaeological populations are difficult to interpret, however, because calculus is easily destroyed when remains are handled. They should, therefore, be regarded as a minimal reflection of the true extent in a once living population.

In the present sample, 1085 teeth had calculus deposits, observed as flecks, or as slight, moderate or considerable deposits (after Brothwell 1981), that is 62.9% (1085/1726) of all observable teeth. This latter rate is lower than that which has been calculated for other London assemblages, including New Bunhill Fields (72.88%), Chelsea Old Church (69.29%), St Marylebone (70.7%) and St George's, Bloomsbury (70.9%), in addition to assemblages from further afield, such as St Martin's-in-the-Bull Ring, Birmingham (68.7%). However, it is similar to the rate calculated for the sample from St Hilda's, South Shields (61.1%).

Calculus deposits among the Park Street skeletons involved 87 out of 91 dentitions (95.6%, discounting one female endentulous dentition), or 33 female (94.3%; 33/35, one endentulous dentition discounted) and 51 (98.1%; 51/52) male dentitions. The TPR for females was 55.8% (359/643), and the TPR for males was 66.4% (669/1007).

Periodontal disease

This refers to chronic inflammation of the gums, periodontal ligament and alveolar bone. Although there are several factors that may lead to the disease (for example, genetics, diet and oral hygiene), the accumulation of calculus around the tooth sockets is the most widely cited cause. This can result in retraction of the gums and alveolar bone, leading ultimately to tooth loss.

The disease was present in 34.8% (32/92) of all observable dentitions, and involved 8.4% (165/1969) of all observable sockets. The TPR correlates well with that calculated for St Marylebone (8.0%), which is much lower than all other contemporary assemblages for which data were available (Table 4.19).

Female rates exceeded male rates, in terms of CPRs – 38.9% (14/36) compared with 34.6% (18/52) – and TPRs – 10.5% (80/761) compared with 7.5% (85/1131), the difference between the TPRs being statistically significant (X^2=5.133, P=0.0235, d.f1). Periodontal disease is positively associated with increasing age in archaeological and modern populations. However, this does not explain the observed differences between male and female rates, because older females were not more numerous than older males. Instead, the results may refer to differences in oral hygiene or diet between men and women.

Table 4.19: Comparison of adult dental status

Site	AMTL TPR% (n/N)	Caries TPR% (n/N)
Park Street, Southwark	13.05 (257/1969)	14.43 (249/1726)
New Bunhill Fields, Southwark	29.11 (1317/4524)	11.63 (319/2743)
Redearth Primitive Methodist Chapel, Darwen	37.10 (351/946)	27.44 (208/758)
St Hilda's, South Shields	39.4 (1000/2536)	19.67 (273/1388)
Littlemore Baptist Chapel, Oxford	57.31 (247/431)	40.58 (56/138)
Chelsea Old Church	34.35 (903/2629)	11.06 (166/1501)
St Martin's-in-the-Bull Ring, Birmingham	29.20 (2481/8495)	11.07 (468/4227)
St Marylebone, London	34.57 (1492/4316)	23.07 (510/2211)
St Luke's, Islington (named sample)	35.35 (1726/4883)	9.74 (219/2249)
Newcastle Infirmary	16.94 (969/5720)	12.27 (339/2762)
St George's, Bloomsbury (named)	40.99 (669/1632)	13.39 (110/844)
St Pancras, London	No data	9.79 (583/5956)
Cross Bones, Southwark	No data	25.92 (161/621)

Periapical cavities

These are identified as openings or holes in the periapical bone of the mandible or maxilla at the apex of the tooth root. They arise as a result of inflammation of the dental pulp that can occur as a result of trauma, caries or attrition. Depending on severity, these cavities may contain granulation tissue (a 'granuloma'), a fluid-filled sac (a 'periapical cyst') or a pus-filled sac (an 'abscess'). Granulomas and periapical cysts are usually asymptomatic, but abscesses may result in a persistent fever and a general feeling of being unwell (Tayles 1997). Acute abscesses may lead to osteomyelitis (bone infection) which in turn may be fatal causing, for example, septicaemia (Tayles 1997).

In total, there were 28 (1.4%; 28/1969) sockets with one or more periapical cavities. These were present on 20 out of 92 adults (21.7%) with dentitions that could be examined. They were more prevalent among males (23.1%; 12/52) than females (19.4%; 7/36), but affected slightly more female sockets (1.3%; 10/761) than male sockets (1.2%; 13/1131). It was rarely possible to say whether the observed cavities were the result of a dental abscess rather than a cyst or granuloma. Exceptions include [911], a prime adult male, who had a large cavity associated with the right maxillary first molar that drained externally and internally into the hard palate (Fig. 4.8). The first molar had gross caries and there was heavy dental calculus. In addition, [3011] had an externally draining abscess at the apex of the buccal/distal root of the right mandibular first molar and associated heavy calculus. In both skeletons the lesions were associated with bony channels through which pus would have been discharged and are indicative of a chronic abscess (Dias and Tayles 1997, 551).

When compared with contemporary assemblages, the TPR for Park Street is second to lowest after the Newcastle Infirmary (Table 4.19). There is almost a 2% difference between the TPR for Park Street and the TPR for St Marylebone, which has the highest TPR (3.3%) of those assemblages analysed.

Dental enamel hypoplasia

Dental enamel hypoplasia (DEH) is observed as lines, furrows, pits or grooves of depressed enamel, most commonly on the cervico-middle region of canine and incisor crowns (Hillson 1986). The condition affected 6.53% of all available teeth (105/1607) and 33 dentitions (one dentition with no surviving teeth excluded), or 36.26% (33/91) of all dentitions that could be observed. Males had more than twice as many teeth affected than females, with a TPR of 7.65% (77/1007), compared with 3.89% (25/643), and this

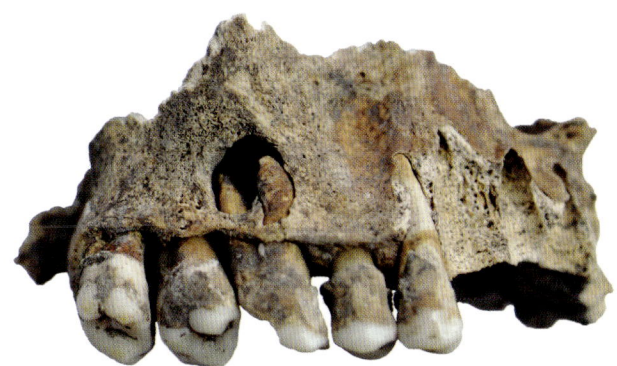 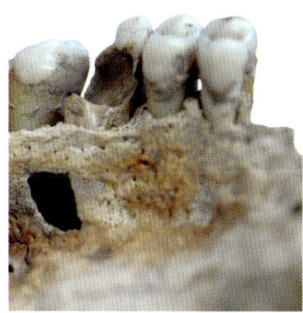

Fig. 4.8 SK [911] Prime adult male. Large internally (right) and externally (left) draining cavity associated with the right maxillary first molar

Periapical cavities TPR% (n/N)	Calculus TPR% (n/N)	Periodontitis TPR% (n/N)	DEH TPR% (n/N)
1.42 (28/1969)	62.86 (1085/1726)	8.38 (165/1969)	6.53 (105/1607)
1.95 (88/4524)	72.88 (1999/2743)	No data	6.02 (165/2743)
1.90 (18/946)	44.06 (334/758)	20.08 (190/946)	15.08 (108/716)
2.05 (52/2536)	61.10 (848/1388)	9.83 (151/1536)	19.40 (250/1289)
2.6 (11/431)	52.90 (73/138)	16.71 (72/431)	22.02 (24/109)
1.56 (41/2629)	69.29 (1040/1501)	46.44 (1221/2629)	16.92 (254/1501)
2.86 (213/7445)	68.69 (3489/5079)	No data	29.75 (1353/4548)
3.27 (141/4316)	70.65 (1562/2211)	8.02 (346/4316)	20.08 (444/2211)
1.78 (87/4883)	46.33 (1042/2249)	No data	10.27 (231/2249)
0.65 (37/5720)	58.66 (1551/2644)	No data	18.00 (476/2644)
2.82 (46/1632)	70.85 (592/844)	No data	16.35 (138/844)
No data	No data	No data	15.09 (899/5956)
No data	No data	No data	No data

was very statistically significant ($X^2=9.558$, $P=0.0020$, d.f1). Defects were most commonly seen as lines, but pits and grooves were also recorded.

The TPR for DEH at Park Street is the second lowest after New Bunhill Fields when compared with other contemporary British assemblages listed in Table 4.19, from London and beyond. The rate is over 15% lower than the highest TPR of 22.02%, for Littlemore Baptist Chapel.

Enamel hypoplasia occurs during the development of the teeth and is caused by disruption to amenoblastic matrix formation (Sarnat and Schour 1941). Inheritance and trauma can cause the condition, but systemic metabolic disruption is believed to account for most cases seen in archaeological and modern populations (Goodman and Armelagos 1985). The specific aetiology of systemic DEH is unknown, but studies on living populations and experiments conducted on animals have identified numerous factors, broadly categorised as those relating to childhood illness (eg measles) and those that relate to nutritional deficiency (Hillson 1986; Pindborg 1982). Based on this work, it is generally concluded that DEH is a non-specific indicator of physiological stress lasting from anything between a few weeks to months (Condon 1981; Goodman and Armelagos 1985). Whether DEH represents individuals who were physiologically compromised or, because DEH indicates recovery, individuals who had a good immune response, is an ongoing debate (Duray 1996; Lewis and Roberts 1997).

The position of the defects on the Park Street teeth suggest that they were appearing in the individuals from as young as a few months old to up to about 14 years, with most in the first five years. The low prevalence of DEH compared to other sites may suggest that the population had poor or good health, depending on whether or not they are considered to have been physiologically compromised.

Dental anomalies/general observations

It was noted that many of the dentitions exhibited low levels of occlusal wear, a pattern that is typical of post-medieval skeletal populations and which may refer to a softer diet, than earlier periods for which dental wear patterns are, by contrast, heavier. For this reason, dental attrition has not been employed to age the individuals in this assemblage, but any unusual patterns were noted.

One such pattern was attributed to pipe smoking and was observed on the dentitions of two individuals. Nine further individuals were noted for having unusual wear patterns that may be attributed to the habitual use of the teeth as tools (a 'third hand') to perform specialised tasks in life. For example, prime adult male [841] (Fig. 4.9) had extreme levels of attrition (considering the age of the individual) in

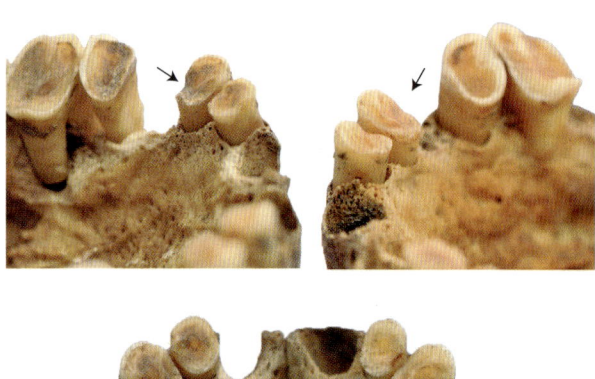

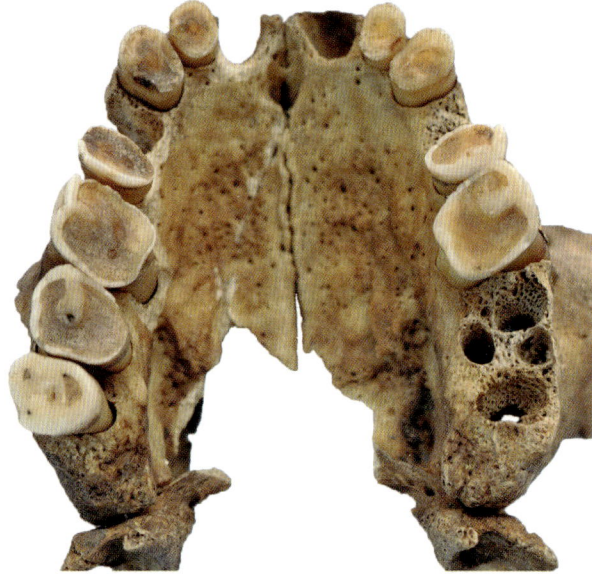

Fig. 4.9 SK [841] prime adult male with extreme dental attrition and grooves on the occlusal surfaces of maxillary teeth (arrowed)

addition to oblique grooves on the occlusal surfaces of the maxillary lateral incisors and canines. The extent to which this pattern has been influenced by diet, physiology and activity is unclear.

Other dental anomalies were relatively minor and include overcrowding/malalignment (four skeletons) (Fig. 4.10), supernumerary teeth (two skeletons), shovelling (one individual), cusp variation (two individuals), under-developed (peg) teeth (one individual),

Fig. 4.10 Dental overcrowding, SK [2352]

diastema (one individual) and retained deciduous teeth (two individuals). In addition, the right maxillary first molar of adult female [885] had a possible hypoplastic groove, possibly a mulberry molar caused by congenital syphilis, which demarcated the lingual sides of the lingual cusps. The changes were obscured by attrition, such that it was not possible to say whether other cuspal hypoplastic defects had been present, but were no longer visible.

Juvenile dentitions

There were a total of 44 juvenile skeletons with surviving dentitions, 40 with sockets and teeth and four that comprised loose teeth only. In total, there were 210 deciduous and 725 permanent teeth. However, these figures include unerupted teeth that were only partially visible in the jaw bones, but could not be fully observed for pathology. Deciduous and permanent teeth that could be fully examined were 170 and 654 respectively. Seventy-three teeth had been lost post-mortem and three (two deciduous and one permanent) teeth had been lost ante-mortem. The number of tooth spaces that survived was 855.

Calculus, caries, DEH, peri-apical cavities and dental anomalies were all observed, and these are detailed below. Comparisons have been made with contemporary assemblages, but these are limited to general observations because detailed data are not available.

Ante-mortem tooth loss

Two individuals had lost teeth before death. An older child [864] (10.5–11.5 years) had lost both mandibular deciduous first molars and adolescent [3068] had lost one mandibular permanent right first molar. The adolescent was estimated to have been between 13 and 16 years at death which, given the eruption age of the right first permanent molar (c 6 years), means that they had not had this tooth for long before it was lost.

There was no indication, whether trauma or disease, why the teeth from these individuals had been lost, although calculus and caries were observed on the rest of their dentitions, indicating overall poor oral health.

Dental caries

Out of the 44 individuals with dentitions, a total of 21 (47.73%), had as few as one and as many as six teeth with caries. In total 2.35% (4/170) of all deciduous and 8.1% (53/654) of all permanent teeth were affected.

Calculus

Calculus was observed on 4.71% (8/170) of all deciduous and 40.37% (264/654) of all permanent teeth, and involved a total of 25 individuals with teeth, or 56.82% (25/44).

Periapical cavities

Four individuals, all adolescents, had five periapical cavities between them, giving a CPR of 10% (4/40) and a TPR of 0.58% (5/855).

Dental enamel hypoplasia

A total of 11 individuals had DEH, or 25% (11/44) of all those with teeth that could be observed. The TPR for deciduous teeth was 0.59% (1/170) and for permanent teeth was 11.47% (75/654).

Defects were most commonly present as lines, but pits were also seen. Their locations on the crowns suggested that they occurred between as young as c 5 months and up to c 7.5 years, with the majority occurring in the first three to four years of life.

Dental anomalies

These included overcrowding/malalignment (three individuals), shovelling (two individuals), bifid roots (one individual), abnormal morphology (one individual), retained deciduous teeth (two individuals) and anomalies in eruption timing (two individuals). These are detailed in the archive.

Skeletal pathology

Skeletal pathology was encountered only infrequently overall. Where observed, it was described and differential diagnoses explored with reference to standard palaeopathology texts, such as Ortner (2003) and Aufderheide and Rodríguez-Martín (1998). They are discussed here according to their primary aetiology, broadly classified as infectious, metabolic, congenital and developmental, joint, vertebral, circulatory, neoplastic and miscellaneous disease. Data are presented with reference to the crude prevalence rate and the true prevalence rate. The former refers to the number of skeletons with a given condition or trait out of the total number of skeletons present. The latter takes into account the variable preservation of the skeletons, and refers to the number of skeletal landmarks or elements with a condition or trait, relative to the total number that could be observed.

Infection

Infection manifests on bone as inflammation and may involve the entire bone ('osteomyelitis'), the cortical bone ('osteitis'), or the fibrous sheath that covers the bone ('periostitis'). These changes may be observed as a result of tuberculosis, leprosy and syphilis (among others) or, where the pattern of change is non-diagnostic and the pathogen is unknown, non-specific infection.

Infection may arise when pathogens spread from an adjacent lesion via the blood stream, for example, as seen in trauma, chronic skin ulceration, paranasal sinusitis, middle ear cavity infection, a dental abscess and visceral rib surface inflammation. Infection may also arise as a result of direct implantation into bone, as for example seen in puncture and penetrating injuries.

Periostitis

Periostitis is the most commonly observed lesion in this category, in archaeological populations. This surface inflammation may be identified on dry bone, most often long bones, as fine pitting, longitudinal striations, swelling and/or plaque-like new bone formation on the original bone surface. These changes may occur as a result of infection, or they may accompany other conditions of a metabolic (for example, scurvy) neoplastic or traumatic nature (Resnick and Niwayama 1995).

When surface inflammation affects the cranium the term 'periostitis' does not apply, owing to a difference in anatomy. As with periostitis, there are numerous conditions that may cause this, scurvy, chronic meningitis, trauma, anaemia, neoplasia, venous drainage disorders and tuberculosis being among them (Lewis 2004; Ortner and Erikson 1997). The level of surface inflammation in a population is generally regarded as an indicator of adaptation or mal-adaptation to environmental conditions, or more specifically malnutrition, poor sanitation and generalised health stress (Roberts and Manchester 1995).

In the present sample, 40 adults (16.33%; 40/245) and seven juveniles (8.14%; 7/86) had periostitis and/or cranial surface inflammation involving one or more bones (eg Fig. 4.11), giving a crude prevalence rate of 14.20% (47/331) for the population. The crude prevalence rate for several contemporary assemblages (Table 4.20) ranges from between 3.70% for New Bunhill Fields and 37.50% for St George's, Bloomsbury, and therefore the rate for Park Street is one of the lowest. When the juvenile CPR (8.14%) is considered, it sits in the middle of the range of several comparative assemblages (Table 4.20), although this analysis is

Fig. 4.11 Inflammation, left parietal bone (copper staining on left), SK [4038]. Young child (considered for porotic hyperostosis but discounted based on radiography)

hindered by the fact that fewer reports present data for this. The adult CPR (16.33%) is among the lowest of all comparative assemblages, which range from 11.54% for St Marylebone to 40.30% for St George's, Bloomsbury.

Among the adults the most frequently affected bone was the tibia (TPR, 16.29%), followed by the mandible (TPR, 12.64%), then the ecto-cranium (TPR, 7.32%). Among the juveniles, the most frequently affected bone was the sphenoid (TPR, 5.26%), followed by the maxilla (3.57%), then the tibia (3.33%) (Fig. 4.12).

It is usual to observe a higher frequency of tibial periostitis compared with other bones in archaeological skeletal assemblages. This is because the tibia is more easily affected by mild trauma than other bones in the rest of the skeleton (Roberts and Manchester 1995, 130). However, several (6/30) of the skeletons with tibial periostitis had bilateral involvement (a further nine had unilateral lesions and a further 10 only had one tibia surviving). Further, the plotted distribution of element involvement indicates that at least eight of the affected individuals had changes that

Table 4.20: Inter-site comparison of crude prevalence rates for periostitis/surface inflammation

Site	Adult CPR% (n/N)	Juvenile CPR% (n/N)	Total CPR% (n/N)
Park Street, Southwark	16.33 (40/245)	8.14 (7/86)	14.20 (76/331)
New Bunhill Fields, Southwark	7.64 (12/157)	1.96 (7/357)	3.70 (19/514)
Cross Bones, Southwark	13.0 (6/45)	38.0 (39/103)	30.41 (45/148)
Redearth Primitive Methodist Chapel, Darwen	32.14 (18/56)	18.60 (16/86)	23.94 (34/142)
St Hilda's, South Shields	23.08 (27/117)	1.15 (1/87)	13.73 (28/204)
Littlemore Baptist Chapel, Oxford	33.33 (5/15)	0.00 (0/15)	16.67 (5/30)
Chelsea Old Church	No data	No data	19.19 (38/198)
St Martin's-in-the-Bull Ring, Birmingham	26.14 (92/352)	13.89* (20/144)	22.58 (112/496)
St Marylebone, London	9.87 (22/223)	6.41 (5/78)	8.97 (27/301)
Bow Baptist Chapel, London	11.54 (21/182)	0.00 (0/169)	5.98 (21/351)
St George's, Bloomsbury (named)	40.30 (27/67)	0.00 (0/5)	37.50 (27/72)

* The total number of juveniles for St Martin's does not include foetuses (9 individuals)

Table 4.21: Adult and juvenile TPR for periostitis/surface inflammation

(L+R combined)	No. obs Ad	No. affected Ad	Adult TPR %	No. obs Juv	No. affected Juv	Juvenile TPR%
Ectocranium	82	6	7.32	37	1	2.70
Orbit	133	0	0	42	1	2.38
Maxilla	66	0	0	56	2	3.57
Sphenoid	52	1	1.92	19	1	5.26
Mandible	87	11	12.64	69	1	1.45
Innominate	193	1	0.52		0	0
Clavicle	204	1	0.49	78	0	0
Manubrium	40	1	2.5	18	0	0
Humerus	201	4	1.99	85	0	0
Femur	210	8	3.81	88	0	0
Tibia	178	29	16.29	60	2	3.33
Fibula	167	3	1.8	60	1	1.67
Tarsal	801	2	0.25	162	0	0
Rib	1598	10	0.63	617	5	0.81

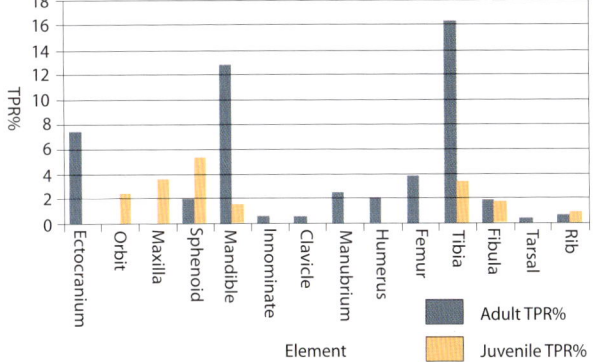

Fig. 4.12 Prevalence of periostitis by element

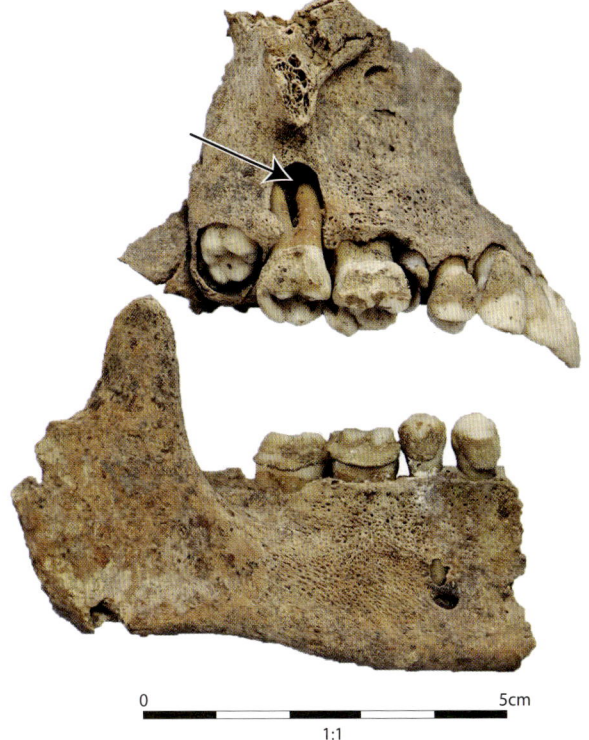

Fig. 4.13 Inflammation, right maxilla and mandible of SK [962]. Likely to be related to the maxilliary periapical cavity (arrowed)

involved more than one element (Table 4.21), this being a minimum number because the plot does not take into account observations that could not be made owing to preservation. This therefore suggests that something other than just mild trauma was causing periosteal reactions in the present sample.

Multiple element involvement was seen in a total of 12 adults (five females, three males and four unknown) and three juveniles, and is indicative of systemic disease, although most of the patterns of involvement in the present skeletons are not exclusive to any one particular disease process (Table 4.22). This is with the exception of Skeletons [833] and [4009], whose lesions are probably related to syphilis (see below), and [962] whose non-specific bone inflammation was associated with dental disease (Fig. 4.13). In addition, [775B] and [885] had inflammation involving their sphenoid bones, a pattern that is considered to be strong evidence for scurvy (Brickley and Ives 2008; Ortner and Erikson 1997), as discussed in the relevant section below.

Osteitis

Osteitis was observed in five skeletons, two juveniles [724] and [833] and three adults [703], [789] and [4009]). All of the adults were of unknown sex, with the exception of one who was a male [789]. In two of these [833] and [4009], the lesions were probably associated with other changes diagnostic of syphilis (see below). A further skeleton, prime adult male [789], had lesions involving the shaft of the left femur, which had also sustained a fracture to the neck and secondary osteoarthritis in the left hip (Fig. 4.17). Skeleton [703], an unsexed adult, showed involvement of the left tibia shaft, which was accompanied by osteoarthritis affecting the ankle, and gout in the toe of the same leg. The skeleton's right tibia also had periostitis. Osteitis

Table 4.22:
Distribution of elements with periostitis/surface inflammation (skeletons with multiple element involvement only)

Skeleton number	Age category	Sex	Endocranium	R Orbit	L Orbit	Sphenoid	R maxilla	L maxilla	R mandible	L mandible	Manubrium	R ribs
775B	Young child	?	X		X	X						
833	Older child	?										
962	Adolescent	?					X		X			
2350	Young adult	M										
2317	Young adult	M										
2360	Prime adult	F										
889	Prime adult	F	X									
2127	Mature adult	?										X
2272A	Mature adult	M										
2191	Older adult	F										
673	Adult	?										
885	Adult	F	X			X						
2160	Adult	F										
667	Adult	?										
4009	Adult	?									X	

affected the shafts of both fibulae of young child [724], but the skeleton had no associated pathology.

Osteomyelitis
No cases of osteomyelitis were identified in the assemblage with the exception of dental absesses (see above).

Maxillary sinusitis
Maxillary sinusitis is diagnosed based on the presence of new bone in the nasal sinuses. Upper respiratory tract infections, poor living conditions, environmental pollution, congenital abnormalities, dental disease and specific infectious diseases such as tuberculosis and leprosy are among the aetiological factors associated with this condition (Lewis 2002, 21).

Twelve skeletons had changes consistent with this condition, including four juveniles, three females and five males, giving an overall CPR of 3.6%. In one skeleton, adolescent male [2408], the inflammation was associated with a dental abscess that had perforated the nasal sinus. It was not possible to say what had caused the lesions in the other skeletons.

Compared with other assemblages the CPR is lower than St Martin's-in-the-Bull Ring (5%; Brickley and Ives 2006) and Christ Church, Spitalfields (18.02%; Roberts and Cox 2003). However, the calculated TPR for Park Street, 9.4% (12/128), is higher than the TPR of 5% reported for St Marylebone (Miles *et al.* 2008).

Specific inection
There were two probable cases of syphilis involving an older child [833] and an unsexed adult [4009]. Both tibiae belonging to the child displayed sharp anterior bowing (Fig. 4.14), thickening and periostitis. There was also periostitis on the left fibula shaft. Bowing deformity is seen in association with latent congenital syphilis, but it may also occur in rickets, advanced acquired syphilis and Paget's disease. In the present case, the two latter possibilities do not apply because of the age of the individual. Rickets is a possibility

Fig. 4.14 SK [833] Older child. Anteriorly bowed right and left tibiae with thickening and periostitis

because, in addition to bowing, thickening is seen in healed rickets (or a variant form). Unfortunately, the distal metaphyses of skeleton [833] were not present, so could not be examined for the porosity, flaring, fraying and cupping which are also associated with rickets (Brickley and Ives 2008, 97). Further, the skeleton could not be investigated for changes involving other bones because only the lower limb bones and foot bones had survived. However, congenital syphilis is the preferred diagnosis because the thickening and bowing primarily involve the anterior borders of the tibiae, consistent with the known predilection for the disease to affect cooler areas of the bone, close to the skin.

Unsexed adult [4009] had circular depressed lesions, indicative of gumma, on their manubrium, left femur and left tibia (Fig. 4.15). Gumma are characteristic of tertiary syphilis, and may be localised or diffuse, occurring on the face, trunk and legs. They may also form in organs, particularly the liver, but also the brain where they can cause neurologic problems. They have the appearance of small, rubbery, inflamed masses that range in size from 1mm to 1cm in diameter. When they rupture, they leave shallow ulcers that heal slowly. Although gumma can occur in tuberculosis, their distribution in the present case is not consistent with this interpretation.

One individual had inflammatory changes that are probably the result of an overlying chronic skin ulcer and may have been a complication of systemic infection, possibly treponemal disease (Ortner 2003, 213). A raised area of bone, measuring 62mm in the longitudinal axis and 32mm in the transverse axis, was present on the anterior mid-shaft of the left tibia of young adult male [2317] (Fig. 4.16). Healed and active bone inflammation in the form of hair on end and layered bone was present on and around the lesion. Periostitis was also present on both fibulae. A differential diagnosis for the changes is neoplastic disease, but the radiological appearance of the bone showed no evidence for an intra-medullary lesion and therefore a chronic leg ulcer is the preferred diagnosis.

Counting only the definite cases, the overall crude prevalence of syphilis in the Park Street assemblage is 0.6% (2/331). This is much lower than 17th-century skeletons from St Thomas' Hospital (25 skeletons; 25%), where 24 adults and one sub-adult were affected (Bekvalac 2007). However, the high prevalence at St Thomas' would seem to be an exception, with low crude prevalence rates, similar to Park Street, observed at other local sites, such as Cross Bones (0.7%; 1/148) and New Bunhill Fields (one probable case, 0.2%; 1/514) and the wider region, such as St Pancras (0.6%; 4/715) and St Marylebone (0.3%; 1/301). The crude prevalence of syphilis for the period, based on osteological evidence is 0.8% (17/2198) (Roberts and Cox 2003; 341).

Park Street had no confirmed cases of tuberculosis (TB), but an older child [4031] and adult male [4050] should be mentioned here because they had periostitis on the visceral surfaces of their ribs. Rib periostitis has been described in the context of skeletal evidence for tuberculosis, although on its own it is not pathognomic of the disease (Roberts 1999). On the former the periostitis was active and involved the 6th to 10th left ribs, and on the latter the periostitis had healed and involved the right 4th–5th ribs. Since neither case had any associated skeletal lesions, their diagnosis is unconfirmed.

According to Roberts and Cox's (2003, 339) survey of the osteological evidence, the crude prevalence of

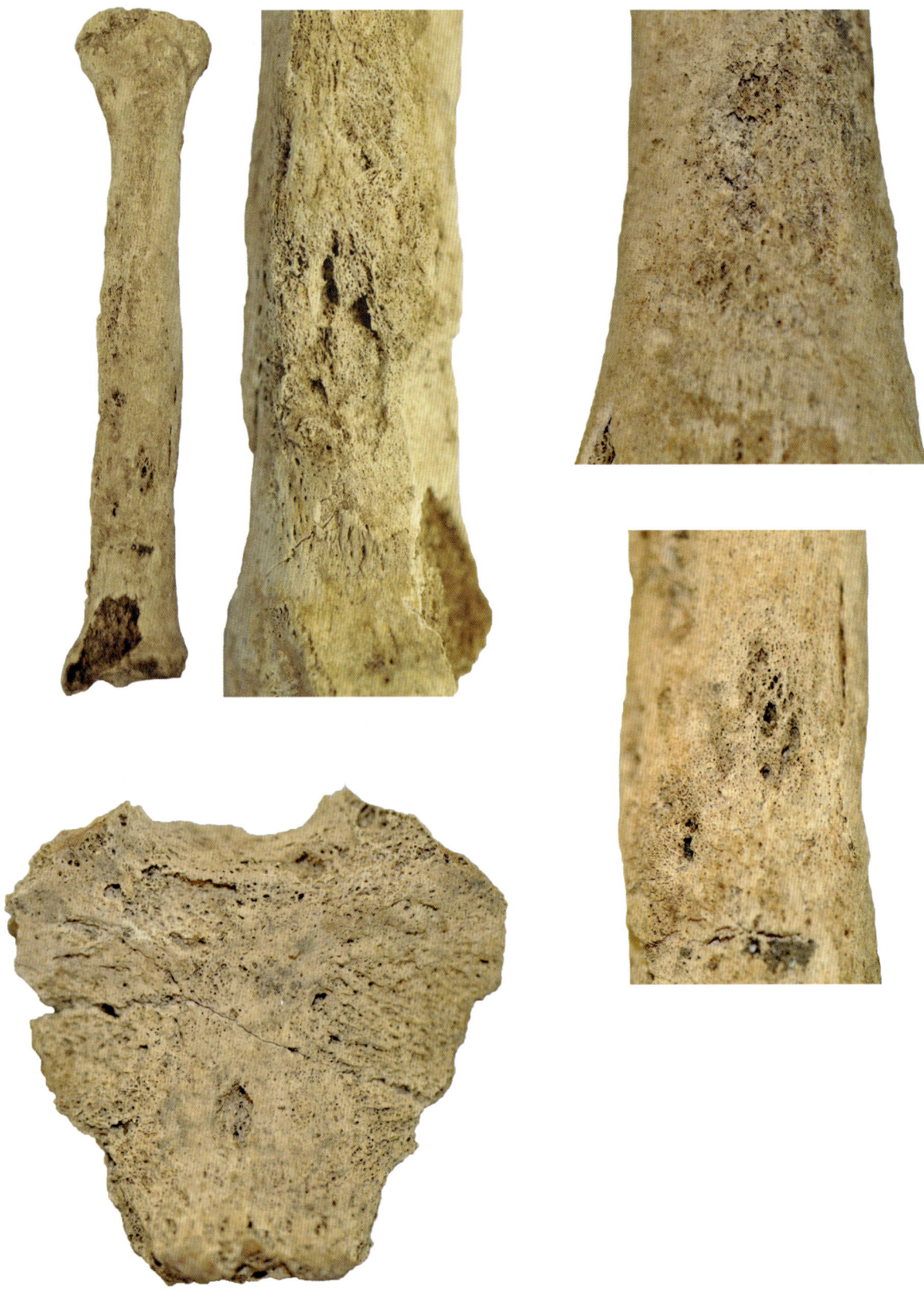

Fig. 4.15 Bony changes on the tibia, femur and manubrium of SK [4009], indicative of syphilis

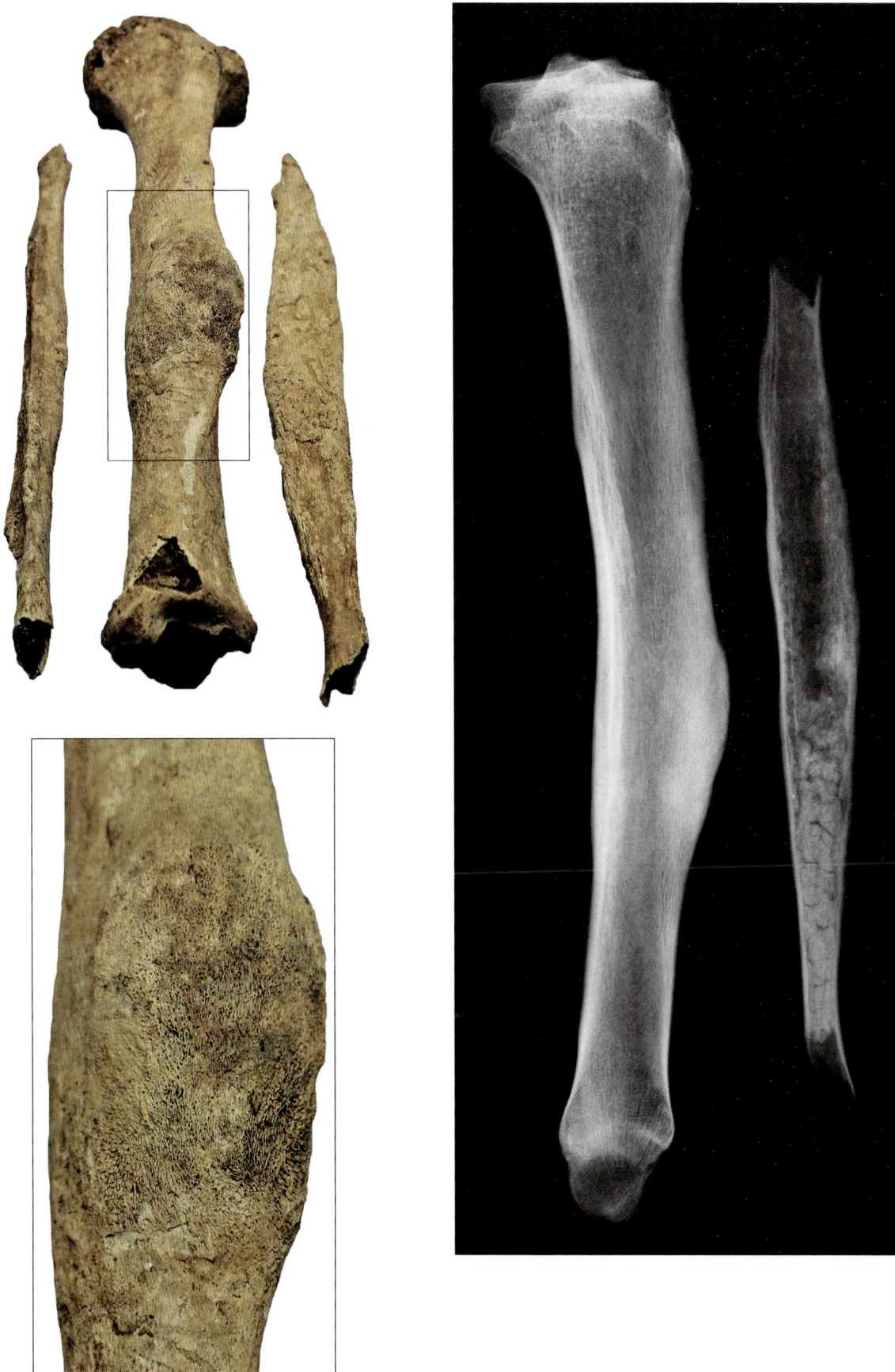

Fig. 4.16 Evidence of possible ulceration as a complication of systemic infection. Left tibia, SK [2317]

tuberculosis during the post-medieval period was 0.5% (8/1690). There were no cases of tuberculosis at Cross Bones, but it was diagnosed at New Bunhill Fields (1%; 5/514 skeletons) and further afield at St Pancras (0.6%; 4/715 skeletons), St Marylebone (1.3%; 4/301) and Chelsea Old Church (1.0%; 2/198).

The examples of specific infection considered here are discussed further in terms of their significance in Chapter 6.

Metabolic disorders
These are triggered by either an excess or a deficiency in the body's dietary requirements and hormones and result in specific changes to the skeleton, such as in the form of increased or decreased bone turn over. Included in this category are scurvy (vitamin C deficiency), rickets (vitamin D deficiency) and cribra orbitalia.

Scurvy
Scurvy is caused by an insufficient intake of vitamin C (ascorbic acid). The disease is generally under-reported in the palaeopathological literature, largely because scorbutic lesions are difficult to identify in the human skeleton (Brickley and Ives 2008; Geber and Murphy 2012). In dry bone, diagnosis relies on the recognition of a certain pattern of skeletal involvement, which can be difficult if skeletons are incomplete. This pattern refers to non-specific bone inflammation – the skeletal manifestation of the haemorrhaging that occurs in the skin, gums joint spaces and subperiosteal regions – which can appear anywhere on the skeleton, but has a predilection for the orbits, temporal bone, sphenoid bone and the jaw.

A young child [775B], (1–2.5 years) had deposits of active and healed new bone on their left orbit, left sphenoid (greater wing), and on the endocranial surface of their occipital bone. The new bone on the sphenoid was inside a *c* 12 mm by *c* 4 mm lytic defect/depression in the cortical bone. Active and healed new bone was also seen on the sphenoid (greater wings), frontal, parietal and temporal bones of adult [885], a possible female. In both cases, the involvement of multiple bones of the skull is consistent with a diagnosis of scurvy (Ortner and Ericksen 1997). In particular, the hypertrophic bone and/or porosity on the sphenoids is considered to be pathognomonic of the disease (Brickley and Ives 2008; Ortner *et al.* 1999; 2001).

There were no other cases from Park Street that presented convincing manifestations of the disease. Skeletons with non-specific bone inflammation, besides those discussed in this section, either showed a pattern of skeletal involvement that linked them to a different disease (for example, syphilis or dental disease), or had patterns that were too general to say what had caused them. Further, a number of skeletons with non-specific bone inflammation were missing skulls, an essential part of the skeleton for diagnosing scurvy.

Rickets
Rickets is a condition in which there is defective mineralisation of growing bone, usually as a result of insufficient amounts of vitamin D. While vitamin D deficiency can result from a poor diet, the lack of exposure to ultraviolet rays has a greater influence on the development of the disease. Ultraviolet rays account for 90% of the body's intake of vitamin D (Stuart-Macadam 1989, 206–7), and hence it is more prevalent among individuals from urban and industrialised settings than those from rural settings. In addition to vitamin D deficiency, chronic intestinal disorders, insufficient amounts of calcium and phosphorous in the diet and chronic renal tubular failure are among other causes associated with rickets (Zimmerman and Kelley 1982).

Vitamin D deficiency may affect adults, in whom the condition is known as osteomalacia. This condition is difficult to diagnose skeletally and relies on detection radiologically.

Frayed metaphyses of long bones, bossing on the frontal and parietal bones of the skull, bowing deformities of the long bones, genu valgum ('knock-knee'), coxa vara (femoral neck deformity), subperiosteal new bone in certain locations on the ribs, femur and tibia, and cupping deformities on the costal ends of ribs are among the lesions observed in juveniles (Lewis 2007). Skeletal manifestations in adults include kyphosis, scoliosis, bowing of long bones, fractures and deformed pelves (Ortner 2003).

Bowing deformities, suggestive of healed rickets, were observed in seven skeletons; three adult females, two adult males and two adults of unknown sex. Active rickets was seen in a further six juveniles. In all, the deformities were identified macroscopically and were confirmed by radiological examination (Table 4.23).

Compared with other assemblages the CPRs for the entire sample (3.9%), adults (2.86%) and juveniles

Table 4.23: Skeletons with probable / possible rickets

SK No	Age category	Probable age range	M/F/?
641	Young adult	18–25 yrs	?
735	Older adult	50–60 yrs	M
839	Prime adult	25–29 yrs	M
891	Young adult	20–24 yrs	F
2107	Mature adult	36–40 yrs	F
2374	Prime adult	23–33 yrs	F
4032	Adult unspec	>18 yrs	?
737	Young child	5 yrs	?
771	Older child	6–12 yrs	?
864	Older child	10.5–11.5 yrs	?
2097	Older child	9.5–10.5 yrs	?
2215	Young child	1.5–3 yrs	?
2338	Infant	1–12 mths	?

(7.0%) were at the lower end of the range. For example, the total assemblage prevalence was higher than St Pancras (2.8%), the same as New Bunhill Fields (3.9%), but lower than St Martin's-in-the-Bull Ring (*c* 7%) and St Marylebone (10.3%).

Osteoporosis
In this disease there is a decrease in bone density and an increase in bone fragility, leading to an increased risk of fracture. Osteoporosis is most common among post-menopausal women, although it can also affect males or individuals suffering from hormonal imbalance, such as hyperparathyroidism and other chronic disease, or as a result of medication. In archaeological material the condition is diagnosed based on the age and sex of the individual combined with the presence of one or more pathognomic fracture types in addition to evidence of reduced bone density.

The present assemblage included two individuals who presented changes that should be mentioned here. Prime adult male [789] had a femoral neck fracture with secondary osteoarthritis affecting the hip joint (Fig. 4.17). Femoral neck fractures are typical in osteoporosis, being prominent among elderly female hospital patients (Brickley *et al.* 2006, 135). However, the sex (male) of the present skeleton, and the lack of reduced bone density, visible radiographically, suggest that osteoporosis is an unlikely diagnosis. This was therefore probably a primary fracture resulting from accidental injury.

The thoracic vertebrae of unsexed adult [4040] had

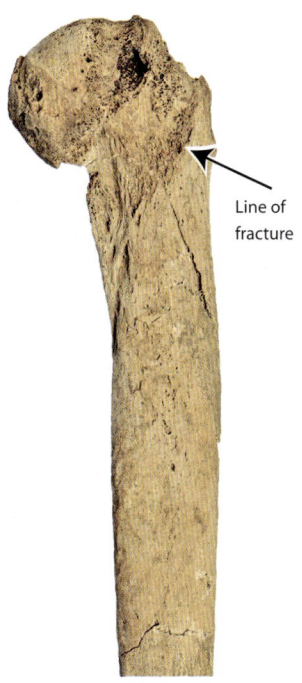

Fig. 4.17 Fracture of the left femoral neck and secondary arthritis of the hip joint, SK [789]

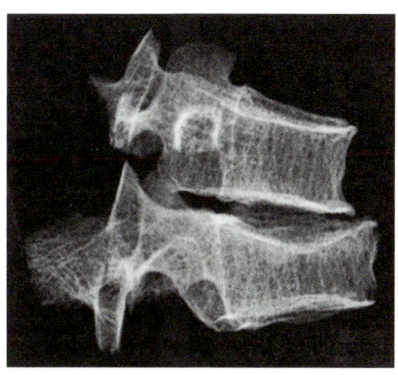

Fig. 4.18 Unsexed adult, SK [4040]. Concave fracture involving the thoracic spine ('cod fish vertebrae')

concave fractures ('cod fish vertebrae') which are typical in osteoporotic spines (Fig. 4.18). Concave fractures are also seen in individuals with vitamin D deficiency, but given the absence of other bowing deformities in [4040], this diagnosis is unlikely.

Cribra orbitalia and porotic hyperostosis
Cribra orbitalia and porotic hyperostosis refer to small porosities or large interconnected trabeculae on the roof of the orbits (cribra orbitalia), and the frontal, parietal and occipital bones of the cranial vault (porotic hyperostosis) (Stuart-Macadam 1991). These changes have traditionally been attributed to iron deficiency anaemia in which marrow expansion causes diploic hyperplasia (thickening) and resorption of the outer table, which exposes the underlying trabeculae (porosity) (Mays 2012). Iron deficiency anaemia may arise as a result of a number of conditions, for example lack of iron in the diet, parasitic infestation in the gut, malaria and lead poisoning (eg Stuart Macadam 1991). More recently, Walker *et* al. (2009) have suggested that iron deficiency may not cause bone marrow hyperplasia and that the lesion may instead relate to a deficiency in vitamin B12 and/or folic acid (megaloblastic anaemia). Regardless of aetiology, cribra orbitalia is often employed as one of a suite of indicators (enamel hypoplasia and periostitis among them) of non-specific health stress, to evaluate the overall burden of disease in archaeological populations (eg Steckel *et al.* 2009). In the present sample, cribra orbitalia was identified on one or both of the orbital bones of 20/245 adults (8.16%), and 13/86 juveniles (15.11%), or 51 adult (38%; 51/133) and 23 juvenile (55%; 23/42) orbits. Only one of two orbits on an individual exhibited lesions in some cases (Table 4.24). The numbers of affected males and females were 7 (7%; 7/100) and 12 (17%; 12/70) respectively. Lesions were classified with reference to the types described by Stuart-Macadam (1991, 109). The most common types were capillary like impressions (type 1), scattered fine

Table 4.24: Cribra orbitalia, true prevalence

Orbit	Male	%	Female	%	Unsexed adult	%	Juvenile	%
Right	11/37	29.7	11/25	44	1/4	25	12/21	57.1
Left	15/38	39.3	11/26	42.3	2/3	66	11/21	52.4
Total	26/75	34.7	22/51	43.1	3/7	42.9	23/42	54.8

Table 4.25: Inter-site comparison of crude prevalence rates for cribra orbitalia

Site	Adult CPR% (n/N)	Adult corrected CPR% (per no. individuals with at least 1 observable socket) (n/N)	Adult TPR% (per socket) (n/N)	Juvenile CPR% (n/N)	Juvenile corrected CPR% (per no. individuals with at least 1 observable socket) (n/N)	Juvenile TPR% (per socket) (n/N)
Park Street, Southwark	8.16 (20/245)	27.4 (20/73)	38.35 (51/133)	15.11 (13/86)	48.15 (13/27)	54.8 (23/42)
New Bunhill Fields, Southwark	-	-	-	-	-	-
Redearth Primitive Methodist Chapel, Darwen	41.07 (23/56)	51.11 (23/45)	50.00 (41/82)	26.74 (23/86)	73.47 (36/49)	73.03 (65/89)
St Hilda's, South Shields	5.98 (7/117)	7.29 (7/96)	No data	6.90 (6/87)	24.00 (6/25)	35.71 (10/28)
St Martin's-in-the-Bull Ring, Birmingham	4.83 (17/352)	5.80 (17/293)	No data	13.73 (21/153)	20.79 (21/101)	No data
St Pancras, London	5.26 (28/532)	No data	9.2 (45/489)	7.65 (14/183)	No data	24.56 (28/114)
St Marylebone, London	23.32 (52/223)	No data	29.77 (78/262)	24.36 (19/78)	No data	28.57 (26/91)
Bow Baptist Chapel, London	2.20 (4/182)	No data	No data	7.69 (13/169)	No data	No data

foramina (type 2) and large and small isolated foramina (type 3). There were no examples of porotic hyperostosis.

Comparison with reported cribra orbitalia rates given for other post-medieval assemblages shows that the Park Street skeletons sit in the middle to upper end of the range (Table 4.25). In their analysis of seven post-medieval British assemblages, Roberts and Cox (2003, 307) report that the CPR for cribra orbitalia ranged from between 0.28% and 24.87%. The Newcastle Infirmary assemblage (24.87%; 47/189) had the highest CPR, followed by Christ Church, Spitalfields (14.57%; 141/968), and Kingston upon Thames (0.28%; 1/360), followed by Cross Bones burial ground (4.05; 6/148) had the lowest CPR (Roberts and Cox 2003, 307). The total CPR (adults and juveniles combined) for cribra orbitalia at Park Street is 9.96% (33/331), which is in the middle of this range.

Joint disease

Osteoarthritis
Osteoarthritis (OA) is the most common pathological condition in both archaeological and modern populations (Rogers and Waldron 1995). It is therefore not surprising to find that it involved the most skeletons of all other disease categories described in this report. Forty-four adult skeletons (18%; 44/245), comprising 16 males, 15 females and 13 of undetermined sex, presented changes that are diagnostic of this condition (Table 4.26). The changes included eburnation (polished bone) or a combination of pitting, bony contour change and/or osteophytosis (new bone growth around the margin of a joint or, less commonly, on a joint surface) (Rogers and Waldron 1995).

The disease affected a greater proportion of the female sample (15/70 females; 21.4%), than the male sample (16/100 males; 16%). Over half of the individuals with the disease were in the older adult age category (Table 4.26), a finding that is consistent with the fact that OA is associated with increasing age (Rogers and Waldron 1995).

Only one young adult [633] had OA which involved the left shoulder. The sex of the skeleton could not be determined. The next youngest individuals with OA were two prime adult males who had the disease in the left hip [789] and the right elbow [897] respectively. In [789], OA was secondary to a fracture involving the femoral neck (Fig. 4.17). In [897] the OA was not secondary to a fracture, but the involvement of the elbow joint is thought to have a stronger activity component in its aetiology than other joints in the skeleton. The same individual also had other conditions that have a strong activity component in their aetiology, including osteochondritis dissecans involving the distal left femur and a healed compression fracture in the thoracic spine.

A total of 33 (13.47%; 212/245) adults had OA affecting one or more extra-spinal joints (Table 4.27; Fig. 4.19). This is approximately half the CPR of 26.34% (255/968) calculated for Christ Church, Spitalfields (Waldron 1993). The most frequently affected joints were in the first toe (metatarsophalangeal joint: TPR 6.61%), followed by the shoulder girdle (sterno-clavicular joint: TPR 4.86%)

Table 4.26: Age and sex distribution of skeletons with OA

Age category	Male CPR (%)	Female CPR (%)	Total CPR* (%)
Young adult	0/23 (0)	0/18 (0)	1/48 (2.08)
Prime adult	4/28 (17.39)	1/17 (5.88)	5/45 (11.11)
Mature adult	4/14 (28.57)	5/12 (41.67)	9/28 (32.14)
Older Adult	4/6 (66.67)	4/6 (66.67)	8/13 (61.54)
Adult unspec.	4/29 (13.79)	5/17 (29.41)	21/111 (18.92)
Total	16/100 (16.0)	15/70 (21.43)	44/245 (18.0)

* Includes unsexed

Table 4.27: Frequency of joints affected with OA

Joint	Total*		Males		Females	
TMJ	1/135	0.74	0/74	0	1/55	1.82
Cervical vertebrae	16/530	3.02	0/74	0	1/55	1.82
Thoracic vertebrae	38/978	3.89	8/303	2.64	4/202	1.98
Lumbar vertebrae	9/427	2.11	21/550	3.82	17/340	5.00
Sacral vertebrae	2/63	3.17	2/243	0.82	6/150	4.00
Sterno-clavicular	7/144	4.86	0/38	0.00	2/23	8.70
Gleno-humeral	7/196	3.57	2/86	3.66	3/53	5.66
Acromio-clavicular	3/137	2.19	3/82	3.66	0/49	0
Elbow	5/182	2.75	2/108	1.85	0/60	0
Wrist	1/163	0.61	1/96	1.04	0/53	0
Hand	0/190	0	0/100	0	0/64	0
Hip	9/220	4.09	5/119	4.20	3/81	3.70
Knee	4/186	2.15	1/81	1.23	2/57	3.51
Ankle	3/164	1.83	0/49	0	0/44	0
Foot	1/163	0.61	0/44	0	0/45	0
MT1-PP1	8/121	6.61	1/33	3.03	2/30	6.67

* Includes adult males, adult females and unsexed adults; Hand=any carpal or metacarpal joints; Hand=any carpal, metacarpal joints or phalangeal joints; Foot=any tarsal or metatarsal joints (except first metatarso-phalangeal joints (MT1-PP1) – counted separately); Thoracic vertebrae= apophyseal joints and costo-vertebral joints

and then the hip (TPR 4.09%). There was a general trend for joints in the pectoral girdle (sterno-calvicular and gleno-humeral) to be frequently affected by the disease. There was low frequency of involvement of joints in the wrists, hands, elbows, knees (eg Fig. 4.20) and ankles. The hip (TPR 4.20%) followed by the sterno-clavicular and acromio-clavicular (both TPR 3.66%) joints were the most frequently affected among males and the metatarso-phalangeal joint of the first toe (TPR 6.67%), followed by the sterno-clavicular joint (TPR 5.66%) were the most frequently affected among females.

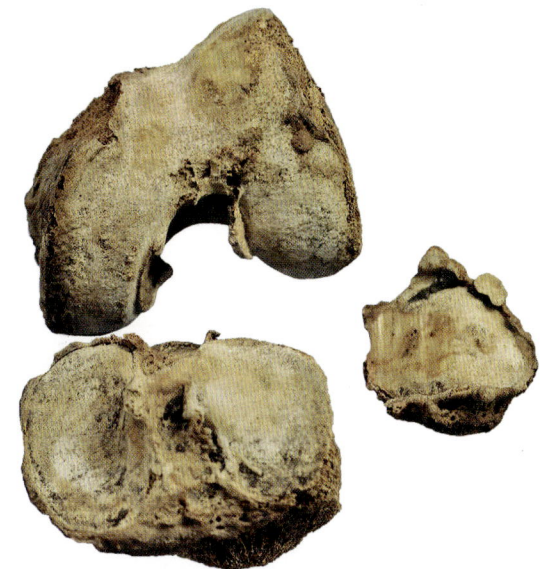

Fig. 4.19 Prevalence of extra-spinal OA by element

Fig. 4.20 Osteoarthritis, left knee joint of SK [627]

A study of the prevalence of OA in different joints among adult skeletons from Christ Church, Spitalfields (Waldron 1991) found that, like Park Street, the involvement of large joints was relatively uncommon overall. However, unlike Park Street joints of the hands were among the most frequently affected sites (Waldron 1991).

Fifteen of the Park Street adults (six males, five females and four unsexed) had OA affecting multiple joints in their skeletons (Table 4.28). A common pattern was spine and shoulder. Different patterns of multiple site involvement may be associated with certain groups. For example, OA affecting the knee and the hand is common among obese individuals and/or individuals with hypertension (Dieppe 1994). Further, OA involving multiple peripheral joints is typical among older individuals, whereas single site involvement of peripheral joints is more common among young males (Cushnaghan and Dieppe 1991).

In two individuals with multiple joint OA, the changes were secondary to trauma in at least one of the affected joints. These were older adult male [856], who had shoulder OA secondary to a fractured clavicle, and unsexed adult [2222] who had trauma and secondary OA in the ankle joints.

In addition to [856] and [2222], there were four further individuals (without generalised OA) in whom OA was secondary to trauma, or possible trauma. These were prime adult male [789], unsexed adult [880], mature adult male [3039] and mature adult female [4036]. In these individuals the OA was observed in the hip joints as a result of a femoral neck fracture [789] and possible trauma [4036], and in the shoulder joints as the result of a possible glenohumeral fracture [3039] and subluxation of the glenohumeral joint [880]. The latter was associated with a pseudo-arthrosis (see below).

Comparison with several other assemblages suggests that Park Street had low rates of extra-spinal and spinal OA (Tables 4.29 and 4.30).

Table 4.28: Skeletons with generalised OA

Skeleton number	Age category	Sex	Joints affected
817	Older adult	M	L sterno-clav, L wrist
856	Older adult	M	L sterno-clav, L gleno-hum, L hip
897	Prime adult	M	Spine, R elbow
956	Older adult	M	Spine, L hip
2119	Older adult	M	Spine, R acrom-clav
2201	Mature adult	M	Spine, L acrom-clav, R acrom-clav, R gleno-hum, R hip, L knee
851	Older adult	F	Spine, L gleno-hum
914	Older adult	F	Spine, R sterno-clav, L sterno-clav
2184	Older adult	F	Spine, R hip
2191	Older adult	F	Spine, R sterno-clav, L sterno-clav, R knee, L knee
2294	Adult	F	Spine, L MT1-PP1
609	Adult	?	L MT1-PP1, R MT1-PP1
627	Adult	?	L knee, L ankle
2222	Adult	?	L ankle, L foot
4009	Adult	?	R sterno-clav, L sterno-clav, R elbow, L elbow

Key: L=left; R=right; sterno-clav= sterno-clavicular joint; gleno-hum=gleno-humeral joint; acrom-clav=acromio-clavicular joint; MT1=first metatarsal; PP1=first proximal phalanx; MT1-PP1- first metatarso-phalangeal joint

Table 4.29: Inter-site comparison of extra-spinal OA

Site	Male CPR% (n/N)	Female CPR% (n/N)	Total adult (n/N)	Total adult TPR% (joints affected/ total number of joints)
Park Street, Southwark, London	12.00 (12/100)	12.86 (9/70)	13.47 (33/245)	2.44 (49/2001)
Redearth Primitive Methodist Chapel, Darwen	35.71 (5/14)	19.35 (6/31)	19.64 (11/56)	3.75 (29/774)
St Hilda's, South Shields	No data	No data	29.06 (34/117)	4.96 (79/1592)
West Butts Street Baptist Burial Ground, Poole	80.77 (21/26)	77.27 (34/44)	76.39 (55/72)	No data
Littlemore Baptist Chapel, Oxford	No data	No data	46.67 (7/15)	8.53 (25/293)
St Marylebone, London	23.58 (25/106)	23.26 (20/86)	21.97 (49/223)	No data
St George's, Bloomsbury (named)	52.63 (20/38)	20.69 (6/29)	38.81 (26/67)	No data
Bow Baptist Chapel, London	10.13 (8/79)	10.34 (9/87)	9.89 (18/182)	No data
Newcastle Infirmary	No data	No data	13.61 (26/191)	2.02 (100/4946)
Chelsea Old Church	26.92 (21/78)	27.03 (20/74)	27.27 (45/165)	No data

Table 4.30: Inter-site comparison of spinal OA

Site	Male TPR% (n/N)	Male CPR% (n/N)	Female TPR% (n/N)	Female CPR% (n/N)	Total adult TPR% (n/N)	Total adult CPR% (n/N)
Park Street, Southwark, London	2.65 (31/1170)	7.69 (8/104)	3.75 (28/747)	15.01 (11/73)	3.25 (65/1998)	8.16 (20/245)
Redearth Primitive Methodist Chapel, Darwen	9.17 (22/240)	35.71 (5/14)	14.43 (58/402)	28.57 (8/28)*	12.84 (86/670)	32.61 (15/46)
St Hilda's, South Shields	8.21 (69/840)	No data	9.73 (68/699)	No data	No data	27.27 30/110
St Martin's-in-the-Bull Ring, Birmingham	No data	No data	No data	No data	7.60 (516/6789)	19.59 58/296
Littlemore Baptist Chapel, Oxford	No data	No data	No data	No data	No data	15.38 (2/13)
St Marylebone, London	4.66 (93/1996)	No data	8.13 (150/1844)	No data	6.54 (272/4162)	No data
Bow Baptist Chapel, London	No data	11.39 (9/79)	No data	18.39 (16/87)	No data	14.29 (26/182)

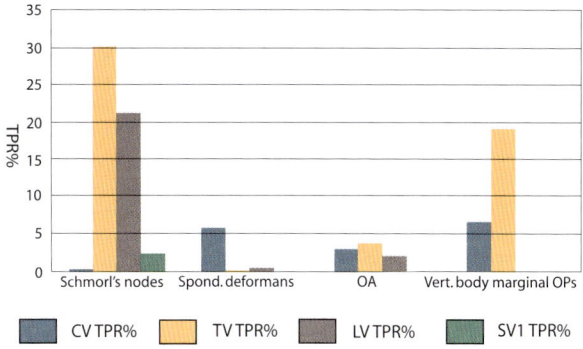

Fig. 4.21 Prevalence of spinal joint disease

Spondylosis deformans and Schmorl's nodes

Spondylosis deformans and Schmorl's nodes are two conditions that involve the spine and are extremely common in both modern and archaeological populations (Fig. 4.21). Schmorl's nodes are caused by intervertebral disc herniation into the vertebral body. They appear on dry bone as depressions, either on the superior or inferior surface of the body. Although associated with degenerative disease, Schmorl's nodes have been linked to activity and trauma, especially in adolescence, or metabolic disorders (Jurmain 1999). Eighty-two adults from Park Street, comprising 50 males, 26 females and six of unknown sex, showed evidence for this condition. They ranged in age from young adult to older adult, but most were from the younger adult age groups (Table 4.31). Schmorl's nodes were most common in the thoracic spine (30.25% of all thoracic vertebrae: Table 4.32), the most common location for this condition (Aufderheide and Rodriguez-Martin 1998).

Spondylosis deformans is identified on dry bone as increased porosity on the surfaces of the vertebral bodies. The condition is mainly caused by degeneration of the intervertebral disc. There were 12 adults with this condition, including five males, six females and one of unknown sex. The condition was most common among mature adults and older adults (Table 4.33) and cervical spines were most frequently affected (5.86% of all cervical vertebrae: Table 4.32). These findings are consistent with the known tendency for the disease to

Table 4.31: Crude prevalence of adults with Schmorl's nodes

Age category	Male CPR%	Female CPR%	Total inc. ?sex CPR%
Young adult	60.87	38.89	47.92
Prime adult	64.29	35.29	53.33
Mature adult	57.14	50	50
Older Adult	33.33	50	38.46
Adult unspec.	27.59	23.53	14.41

Table 4.33: Crude prevalence of adults with spondylosis deformans

Age category	Male CPR%	Female CPR%	Total inc. ?sex CPR%
Young adult	4.35	0	2.08
Prime adult	3.57	0	2.22
Mature adult	7.14	25	14.29
Older Adult	0	33.3	15.38
Adult unspec.	6.9	5.88	3.6

Table 4.32: True prevalence of Schmorl's nodes, spondylosis deformans and vertebral body marginal osteophytosis

	CV TPR%	TV TPR%	LV TPR%	SV1 TPR%
Schmorl's nodes	0.36	30.25	21.26	2.47
Spond. deformans	5.86	0.09	0.47	0
OA	3.02	3.89	2.11	3.17
Vert. Body marginal OPs	6.75	19.25	11.21	6.17

be associated with increasing age (Rogers and Waldron 1995). Spondylosis is uncommon in young individuals, among whom it is probably the result of trauma (Resnick and Niwayama 1995).

Hallux valgus

Three skeletons (CPR 1%; 3/331), two unsexed adults [609] and [753] and one mature adult female [2423], had changes consistent with those seen in hallux valgus. Skeletally, this condition is identified by the lateral deviation of the proximal phalanx of the great toe and can lead to the development of bunions and joint disease. The condition has a close association with the habitual use of restrictive footwear, in particular shoes with pointed toes (Mays 2005, 139). In one of the Park Street cases [609] the condition was bilateral. It was not possible to say whether the condition was bi- or unilateral in [753] and [2423].

A CPR of 3.3% of hallux valgus is reported for the upper-class St Marylebone assemblage (Miles *et al.* 2008). This is over 2% higher than the Park Street assemblage and may reflect the limited access to fashionable shoes afforded to those less well off.

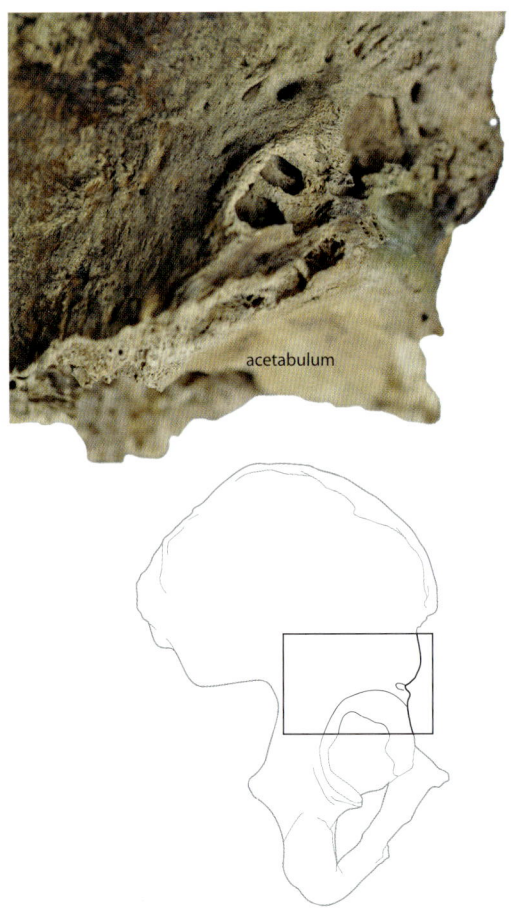

Fig. 4.22 SK [2160] Adult female with lytic lesions around the acetabulum of the right hip ('Egger's cysts')

Other joint disease

Degenerative changes were observed on the tubercles of the humeri of [887], [897] and [3039], and are consistent with rotator cuff disease. In [3039] the condition may have been secondary to a fracture involving the shoulder on the same side.

Adult female [2160] had lytic lesions around the acetabulum of the right hip (Fig. 4.22), associated with periostitis (the latter has been included in the relevant section above). The pelvis was incomplete and no pathology was observed on the femur of the same side. The changes are consistent with acetabular cysts, seen in degenerative arthritis (Eggers *et al.* 1963). Clinically, acetabular cysts may occur independently of other changes seen in joint disease and in individuals who are younger than the age group, typically associated with osteoarthritis (ibid.).

Possible pyogenic arthropathy was observed in the right knee of young adult [641] and the left hip of [856], an older adult. In [641], capillary like bone inflammation was observed on the articular surface of the right patella and was accompanied by erosive changes on the patella surface of the right femur. These changes were not consistent with typical osteoarthritis, and therefore pyogenic arthopathy is the preferred diagnosis. In [856] the acetabulum had reactive new bone that accompanied OA in this joint. The OA was present as eburnation, osteophytosis, porosity and joint cysts.

A first metatarsal distal phalanx of the left foot belonging to unsexed adult [703] had punched out erosions and changes consistent with a 'Martel hook', all typical of gout (Rogers and Waldron 1995). Other erosive arthritis was observed in unsexed adult [631] on the first metatarso-phalangeal joint (Fig. 4.23), but a more precise diagnosis is not possible because the changes were obscured by post-mortem damage. The head of the first metatarsal appeared to have a *c* 4mm by 2mm roughly central smooth margined lytic lesion with a slightly protruding nodule of bone, possibly osteophyte, just lateral to it. There were also punched out areas of bone loss on the superior and lateral regions of the head, also thought to be pathological erosions which have subsequently been damaged post-mortem. The proximal joint surface of the articulating first foot phalanx had porosity and eburnation on its infero-lateral surface, consistent with osteoarthritis in the joint. While it is clear that OA had affected this joint, the lytic lesions point to the presence of erosive disease as well. The skeleton was very incomplete and comprised lower limb and foot bones only. No changes were observed on any other foot bones, including the left first metatarsal. Differential diagnoses include gout, erosive OA or seronegative spondyloarthropathy (for example, Reiter's syndrome).

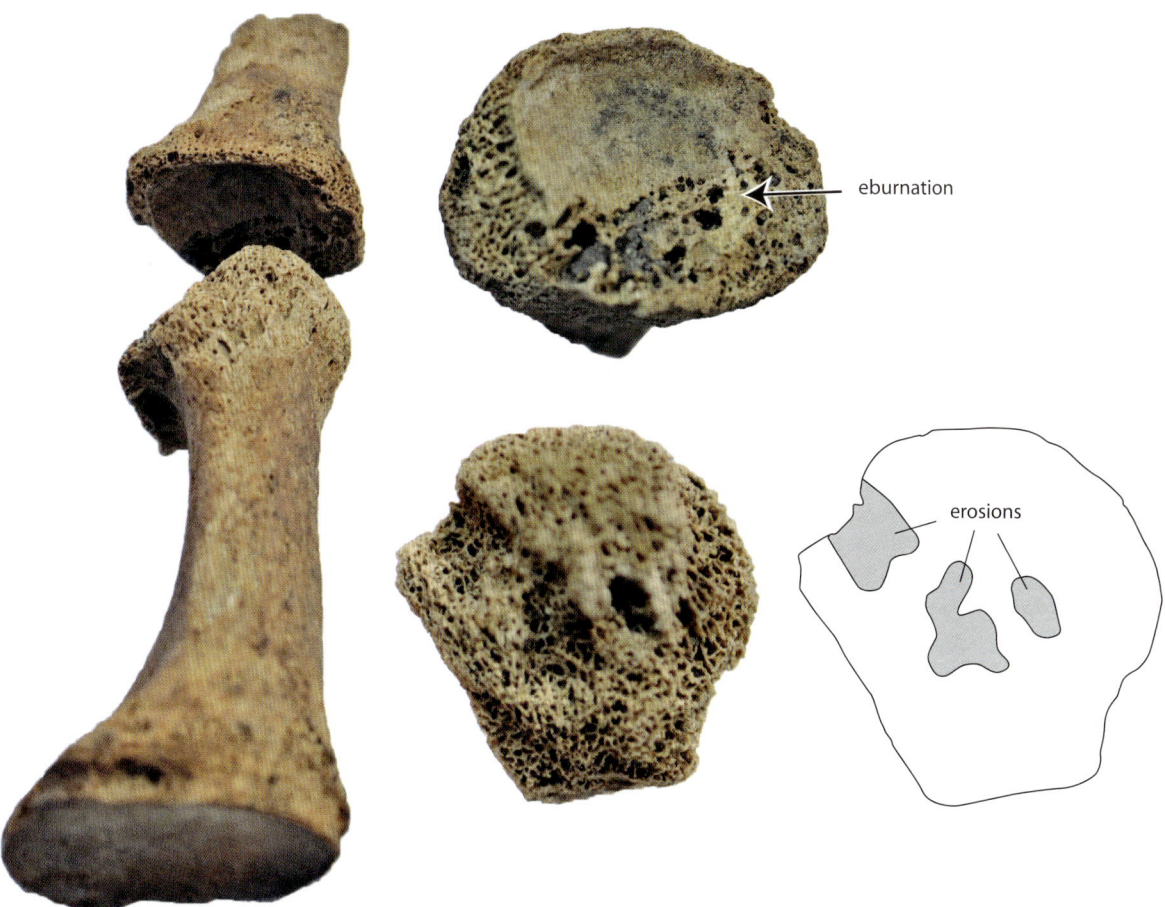

Fig. 4.23 SK [631] Unsexed adult. Osteoarthritis and erosive changes involving the first metatarsophalangeal joint (post-mortem damage is also present on the head of the first metatarsal)

Finally, older adult male [956] and adult male [2217], had lesions that have been classified as possible sero-negative spondylarthropathies. In the former, the changes included bamboo type ankylosis of the cervical (second to fifth) and lumbar (second to fifth) vertebrae and ankylosis of the sacro-iliac joints (Fig. 4.24). Ankylosis between the twelfth right rib and thoracic vertebra were also in progress at the time of death. These changes are seen in ankylosing spondylitis, but in the present case the discontinuity of ankylosis in the vertebral column and the lack of involvement of joints in the hands (the feet had not survived), make this diagnosis less certain. In [2217] the changes involved the right third, left fifth and left fourth metacarpo-phalangeal joints and included unifocal erosions on the margins of the heads of the metacarpals. The erosions were located externally to joint articular surfaces and had rounded margins. These changes may be seen in Reiter's syndrome, but given the limited number of hand and foot bones that had survived for this individual diagnosis remains inconclusive.

Fig. 4.24 Bamboo type ankylosis, second to fifth cervical vertebrae, SK [956]

Table 4.34: Inter-site comparison of fracture crude prevalence rates

Site	Male CPR% (n/N)	Female CPR% (n/N)	Total adult CPR% (n/N)	Juvenile CPR% (n/N)	Total assemblage CPR% (n/N)
Park Street, Southwark	9.00 (9/100)	4.29 (3/70)	7.35 (18/245)	0.00 (0/86)	5.44 (18/331)
New Bunhill Fields, Southwark	29.41 (25/85)	2.78 (2/72)	17.2 (27/157)	0.84 (3/357)	5.84 (30/514)
Redearth Primitive Methodist Chapel, Darwen	57.14 (8/14)	9.68 (3/31)	19.60 (11/56)	0.00 (0/86)	7.75 (11/142)
St Hilda's, South Shields	No data	No data	23.08 (27/117)	1.15 (1/87)	13.73 (28/204)
St Martin's-in-the-Bull Ring, Birmingham	41.67 (75/180)	17.69 (23/130)	30.40 (107/352)	0.65 (1/153)	21.39 (108/505)
St Pancras, London	19.0 (44/231)	8.9 (20/224)	14.08 (69/490)	1.09 2/183	9.93 71/715
St Marylebone, London	27.36 (29/106)	19.77 (17/86)	22.42 (50/223)	1.28 (1/78)	16.94 (51/301)
Whitefriars Anabaptist cemetery, Norwich	30.77 (4/13)	20.00 (4/20)	20.50 (8/39)	4.17 (1/24)	14.29 (9/63)
St George's, Bloomsbury (named)	34.21 (13/38)	10.34 (3/29)	23.53 (16/67)	20.00 (1/5)	23.61 (17/72)
Littlemore Baptist Chapel, Oxford	40.00 (2/5)	0.00 (0/10)	13.33 (2/15)	0.00 (0/15)	6.67 (2/30)
Bow Baptist Chapel, London	13.92 (11/79)	4.60 (4/87)	9.89 (18/182)	0.00 (0/169)	5.13 (18/351)
Chelsea Old Church	20.51 (16/78)	8.11 (6/74)	14.55 (24/165)	0.00 (0/33)	12.12 (24/198)

Trauma

Trauma refers to any injury or wound to the body that may affect the bone and/or soft tissues (Roberts 1991, 226). Dislocations, ligament trauma in the form of new bone formation and fractures are some of the types of change in this category. The most common of these are fractures and these represent the main type of trauma identified in the present sample.

Fractures

A fracture is defined as a complete or partial break in the continuity of bone (Roberts 1991, 226). Fractures may result from underlying pathology, repeated stress or acute injury (Roberts and Manchester 1995). Fractures were identified in the present sample macroscopically based on the presence of discontinuity in bone alignment and/or the presence of a fracture callus. Where macroscopic evidence was ambiguous, radiography was employed.

A total of 36 fractures, all healed, were identified and involved 18 individuals, all adults, including nine males (9%; 9/100), three females (4.29%; 3/70), and six individuals of undetermined sex. These numbers do not include 14 elements (six thoracic and two lumbar vertebrae, one humerus, one radius, one metatarsal and three ribs) that had possible well-healed fractures, that could not be confirmed by macroscopic or radiographic analyses. These involved five males, one skeleton of undetermined sex and mature adult male [2201] (counted among the aforementioned 18 individuals) who had a definite right metatarsal fracture and possible left metatarsal fracture. These possible cases have been excluded from the present analysis.

All of the fractures, either accidental or due to violence, affected adults (7.35%; 18/245). This rate is very low compared with other post-medieval assemblages (Table 4.34). For example, at New Bunhill Fields, St Marylebone, St Pancras, St Martin's-in-the-Bull Ring and St Hilda's the crude adult prevalence rates were 17.2%, 22.4%, 19.0%, 30.4% and 23.1% respectively.

An absence or low prevalence of fractures among juvenile skeletons is a common finding in archaeological populations. Like Park Street, no fractures were observed among the juvenile skeletons from Cross Bones (Brickley *et al.* 1999). This is probably because of the high turnover rate of immature bone, in which fractures heal faster and fully remodel (Glencross and Stuart-Macadam 2000).

A number of fractures were associated with secondary changes that refer to complications arising from the injuries. Prime adult male [789] had a left femoral neck fracture with secondary infection in the form of osteitis of the proximal shaft. In addition, marked shortening and overlap of fracture margins were seen in the left tibia and fibula of male adult [2217] (Fig. 4.25). Unfortunately, poor preservation precluded measurement of these bones and of the right tibia and fibula to quantify the extent of the shortening. The left distal radius of the same individual also showed slight malalignment of another fracture here. Finally, four individuals [789], [856], [2222] and [3039] which had OA secondary to fractures have been mentioned above.

The complications described here provide information about the quality of the individual's lives following their injuries, and their overall health status (Roberts 1988), in addition to the nature and severity of the injury itself. The deformities seen in the bones of [2217] suggest that reduction may not have been practised, or that attempts were unsuccessful. Secondary infection may arise as a result of poor hygiene (not keeping wounds clean) and inadequate treatment, including poor nutrition. Premature OA may occur in joints

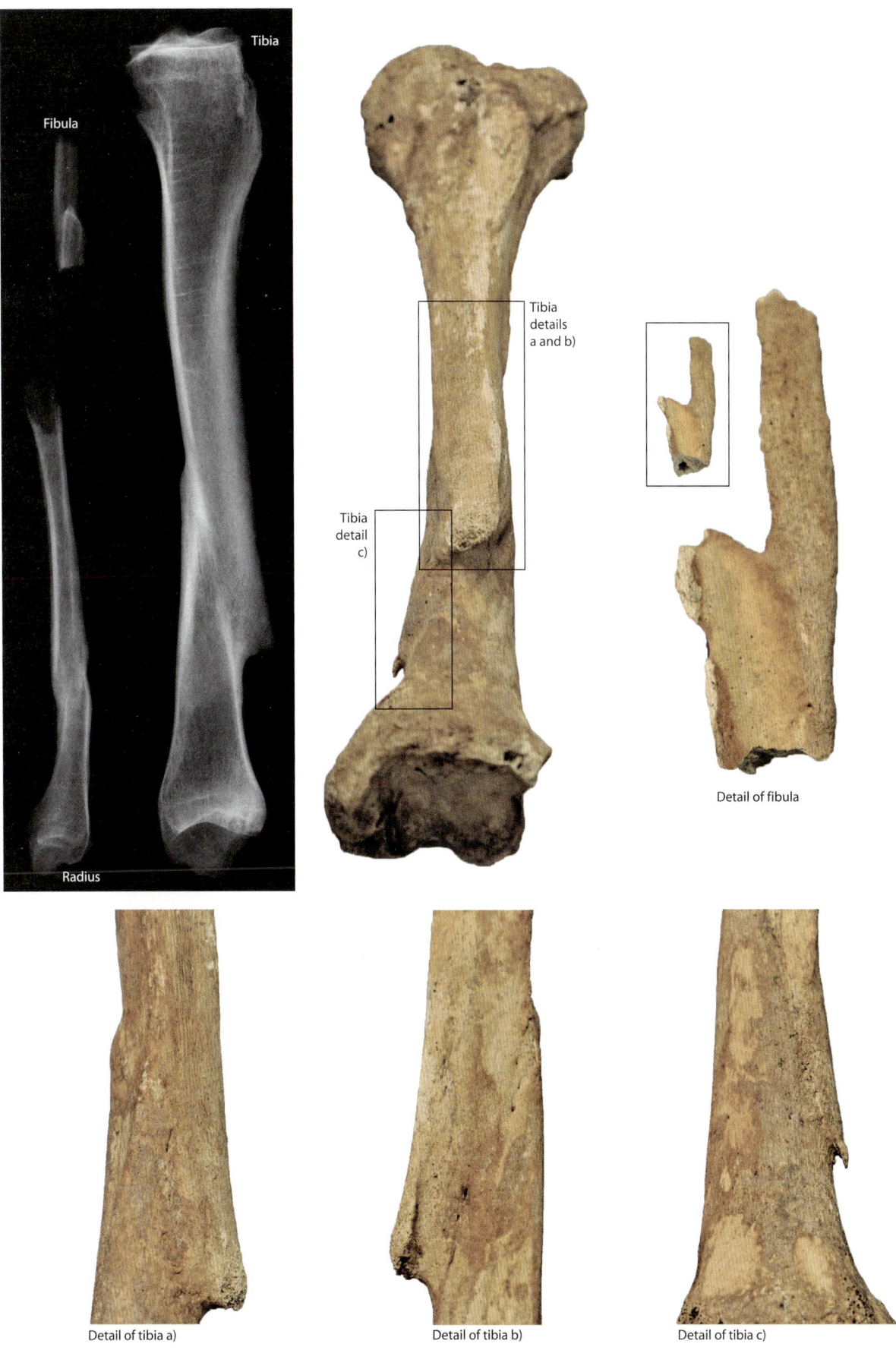

Fig. 4.25 SK [2217] Male adult. Healed fractures involving the left radius (radiograph only), left tibia and left fibula. There is marked overlap of the fracture margins and shortening of the bones

related or unrelated to a fractured bone. It can occur as a result of compensating for the impaired function of the fractured bone, particularly when time for healing and treatment have been inadequate.

The most frequently fractured elements were the skull vault (2.44%), followed by the sesamoid bone in the foot (1.52%), thoracic vertebrae (1.37%), and the facial bones in the skull (1.37%) (Table 4.35; Fig. 4.26). Fractures affecting the skull vault involved two individuals, one prime adult male (skeleton [841]) and one adult female (skeleton [921]). Both had well healed depressed fractures to the frontal bone, which appeared as smooth, sub- or semi-circular indented bone covering an area of up to 18mm. One further skeleton [2107] had a fracture involving the facial skeleton, more specifically the nasal bone. This individual was a mature adult, possibly female, classified for the purposes of this report as a definite female. The nasal fracture was very well healed.

The frontal bone and facial skeleton are common locations for fractures arising as the result of interpersonal violence (Judd 2002; Walker 1997). These injuries usually present as depressed fractures made by a blunt instrument or crushing injuries to the bones of the cheek or nose from a blow with a fist (Judd 2002, 49). Other injury patterns seen in cases of interpersonal violence include fractures to the forearms, sustained when parrying a blow, and metacarpal fractures, sustained when delivering a blow with a fist (Brickley and Smith 2006; Galloway 1999; Jurmain 1999). Transverse rib fractures and multiple rib fractures are others (Judd 2002). Among the Park Street skeletons, an adult male [3013A] had a transverse fracture to the right fifth metacarpal, but the location of the fracture (the distal shaft) is not typical in injuries arising from violence (Galloway 1999). Two skeletons, young adult [2226] (sex unknown) and mature adult male [2158] had rib fractures and show patterns consistent with interpersonal violence. In [2226], the fracture was transverse and involved the anterior shaft of one left rib. In [2158] the mid- to proximal portions of four rib shafts were fractured, two of which may have been green-stick fractures. It was not clear what the pattern of these fractures was.

Fractures involving bones of the hands and feet are rare in archaeological populations, and this probably reflects the low recovery rate of these bones during excavation (Roberts and Manchester 1995). The sesamoid fracture seen in the present sample involved a prime adult possible female, classified as a definite female for the purposes of this report. Fractures involving this bone are typical in individuals who have fallen from a height or have had heavy weights dropped onto their forefoot (Galloway 1999, 222).

Vertebral fractures were primarily diagnosed based on the identification of fracture lines. Three skeletons had these lesions; prime adult male [897]; unsexed adult [4009] and unsexed adult [4040] (Fig. 4.18). In [897] and [4009] one vertebra each was affected, a thoracic and a lumbar respectively. In [4040] fracture lines were present on two lower thoracic vertebrae. In addition, this skeleton had three lower thoracic vertebrae that displayed loss of vertebral body height, typical of the concave deformity seen in osteoporotic vertebral fractures. These have therefore been counted as fractures even though no fracture lines were visible.

Two further individuals [2158] and [2403] had probable vertebral fractures (nine thoracic in total) because their vertebrae displayed a marked loss of body height in association with osteophytosis. On its own, loss of vertebral body height is not diagnostic of a fracture, because this may also be seen in spines with metabolic disease and developmental conditions. Further, mild loss of body height may even be a normal accompaniment to ageing (Watt pers. comm.). In the present cases, the loss of height is very marked, and in [2158] the changes were also associated with rib fractures, increasing the probability that these are also fractures.

Multiple fractures were seen in five individuals, three males and two of undetermined sex (Table 4.36). Those sustained to the tarsal bones had involved the posterior tubercle of the right and left talus bones

Table 4.35: Fracture true prevalence rates by element

Elements fractured	TPR%	No. obs (total L+R)	No. affected
Skull vault	2.44	82	2
Skull facial	1.37	73	1
Clavicle	0.49	204	1
Rib	0.31	1598	5
TV (bodies)	1.37	1091	15
LV (bodies)	0.23	428	1
MC	0.14	734	1
Femur	0.48	210	1
Tarsal	0.75	801	6
MT	0.33	603	2
Foot sesamoid	1.52	66	1

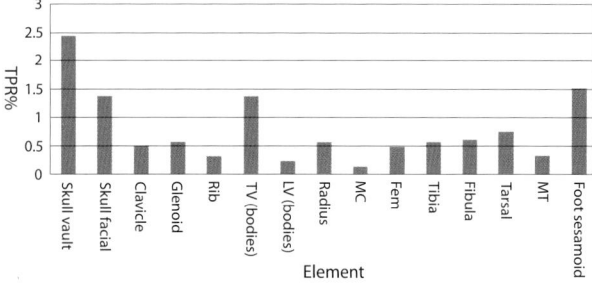

Fig. 4.26 Prevalence of fractures by element (lefts and rights combined)

Table 4.36: Skeletons with multiple fractures

Skeleton number	Age	Sex	Fractured elements
2158	Mature adult	M	x4 R ribs; x5 TV
2217	Adult	M	L distal radius; L tibia, L fibula
2394	Adult	?	x1 L tarsal; x1 R tarsal
2403	Mature adult	M	x4 TV; x2 L tarsals, x1 L MT
4040	Adult	?	x5 TV

TV = thoracic vertebrae; L = left; R = right; MT = metatarsal

belonging to [2394]. Injuries in this location may arise as a result of forced plantar flexion or when the foot is pronated and dorsiflexed (Galloway 1999, 210). Other tarsal bone fractures involved the left medial and intermediate cuneiform bones of [2403] and were associated with a fourth left metatarsal fracture. They may relate to an injury sustained as a result of a fall from a height, or a blow to the foot (Galloway 1999).

It is not possible to say whether the multiple fractures on each skeleton represent one or several traumatic events (vertebrae excluded – see above). A single event is more likely where articulating elements are involved, for example, the left tibia and fibula of [2217] and the thoracic vertebrae in [2403] and [4040]), or where several skeletal regions are involved, for example, the foot bones in [2403].

The cases of multiple fracture do not reflect a pattern that is consistent with a type of individual identified by Judd (2002a; 2002b) as 'injury recidivists'. This term refers to young males with multiple injuries at different stages of healing, reflecting trauma sustained over a period of time as a result of several different incidents, accidental and/or violent. The age of only two of the Park Street individuals with multiple injuries could be estimated and both were mature adults. Further, the lesions in all of the Park Street skeletons had healed.

Sub-periosteal ossified haematoma
This refers to the ossification of undissolved haematoma, usually in areas of bone where blunt force trauma has been sustained. Ossified haematomas occur when excessive stress is placed on the periosteum at the site of an injury, preventing successful resorption of the haematoma that forms as a part of the initial healing process. They are frequently observed on archaeological bone, where they appear as smooth bony masses (Ortner 2003, 88). They may be visible on bone after approximately two months of healing (Lovell 1997, 145).

Ossified haematomas were identified on the right femurs of adult males [839] and [2201]. No fractures were identified on either of the femora, but other traumatic lesions were observed elsewhere on the

Fig. 4.27 Dislocation involving the left gleno-humeral joint, SK [880]

skeletons. Skeleton [839] had a possible crush fracture involving the first lumbar vertebra, and [2201] had fractures involving the metatarsals and neural arch of the sixth lumbar vertebra (spondylolisis).

Prime adult male [2410] had a possible haematoma on the left ulna shaft. The lesion was present as a smooth raised area of bone with a focal area of increased porosity. There was no evidence of a fracture. A differential diagnosis for this lesion is neoplastic disease.

Dislocations
Three individuals displayed evidence of dislocations, involving the left gleno-humeral joint [880] (Fig. 4.27), the right talo-calcaneal joint [2222] (Fig. 4.28), and the fourth tarso-metatarsal joint [2403]. In all of these, the dislocations were subluxations, meaning that they were incomplete or partial. The talo-calcaneal dislocation was secondary to a crush fracture in the talus bone and tarso-metatarsal dislocation was associated with fractures involving the fourth metatarsal and the medial and lateral cuneiforms.

Soft tissue trauma
Evidence of trauma to the muscles was observed on young adult male [2382], who had an exostosis on the distal right humerus at the insertion site of the brachioradialis muscle. In addition, unsexed adult [849] had a bony protrusion at the site of the medial flexor attachment of the right fifth proximal hand phalanx. This may be an old healed fracture, but no evidence for a break could be seen, and therefore muscle trauma is the preferred diagnosis.

Fig. 4.28 Dislocation involving the left talo-calcaneal joint, secondary to fracture of the talus, SK [2222]

Spondylolisis
Spondylolisis is a stress fracture in which the neural arch separates from the vertebral body, most commonly in the fifth lumbar vertebra (Mays 2006). It may be caused by an underlying congenital weakness in this part of the spine (Aufderheide and Rodríguez-Martín 1998).

In the present sample the condition was seen in three individuals, one adult male [837] and two mature adult males [2201] and [2403], giving a crude male prevalence rate of 3% (3/100). This rate is higher than that reported for males from Christ Church, Spitalfields (2.2%; Molleson and Cox 1993), but lower than the rate reported for males from St Pancras (3.5%; Powers 2011, 148).

In two of the individuals [2201] and [2403] the fractures were accompanied by probable spondylolisthesis, which refers to slippage of the vertebral body in an anterior direction away from the detached neural arch. This was indicated on the present skeletons by osteophytosis and anterior defects on the surfaces of the first sacral bodies.

Os acromiale
Os acromiale refers to the non-fusion of the acromial process of the scapula, which usually occurs in late adolescence. Once considered to be a non-metric trait that is genetic in origin, the condition has been linked to activity-induced trauma occurring at a young age (Stirland 1998), which is why it is considered here.

Three individuals from Park Street had the condition, two adult males [635] and [793] and one older adult female [851]. All of these skeletons were incomplete and thus it was not possible to observe whether the condition was unilateral or bilateral. The presence of the condition in these individuals implies strenuous use of the upper arm from a young age (Knüsel 2000a).

Miscellaneous trauma
A sub-oval porous lytic defect was present in the right acetabulum of mature adult female [4036]. The margin of the acetabulum was remodelled and had osteophytosis. The right femur had not survived and so it was not possible to say whether any pathological changes were present on the other side of this hip joint. The changes possibly refer to micro-avulsions in this joint.

Abnormal fusion of the composite epiphysis of the distal right humerus was identified in adolescent [681]. This was possibly a result of trauma occurring in childhood causing disrupted development of this joint.

Circulatory disorders
This refers to conditions arising as a result of a loss or reduction in blood supply to bone which can lead to necrosis (bone death) of the affected region and subsequent dysfunction. Trauma, inheritance and developmental disorders are among the aetiological factors associated with circulatory disorders (Aufderheide and Rodriguez-Martin 1998).

The only condition in this category that was observed in the Park Street assemblage is osteochondritis dissecans. Osteochondritis dissecans refers to focal necrosis on the convex joint surface of diarthrodial joints, and results in the partial or complete detachment of a segment of the subchondral bone and articular cartilage. The aetiology of this condition is not fully understood but it may be caused by low grade chronic trauma or micro-trauma (Aufderheide and Rodriguez-Martin 1998; Federico et al. 1990).

Twelve individuals, comprising six adult males, one adolescent male, one adult female, and one adult and three adolescents of undetermined sex, had osteochondritis dissecans in one or more joints (Table 4.37). This gives a CPR of 7.0% (7/100) for males, 1.43% for females (1/70) and 3.63% (12/331) for the entire assemblage. The knee (for example, Fig. 4.29) and elbow joints were the most commonly affected, but the ankle and

Table 4.37: Skeletons with osteochondritis dissecans

Skeleton number	Age	Sex	Affected joint
727	Adult	M	R knee
757	Adult	M	L shoulder
811	Juv (adolescent)	M	R knee
897	Adult	M	L knee
934	Adult	M	L knee
2314	Adult	M	L + R knees
2410	Adult	M	R elbow
663	Adult	F	R elbow
813	Juv (adolescent)	?	R elbow
843	Juv (adolescent)	?	L + R ankles
2352	Juv (adolescent)	?	R elbow
2394	Adult	?	L + R ankles

L = left; R = right

shoulder were also involved. All of the elbow examples involved joints on the right side of the skeleton, while those seen in the knee involved both right and left sides.

In modern populations, the knee and elbow are among the most common sites to be affected by osteochondritis dissecans (Aufderheide and Rodriguez-Martin 1998). The condition is more common among males and individuals aged between 10 and 25 years old (Aufderheide and Rodriguez-Martin 1998). In the elbow, it is more predominant on the right side of the body, possibly as a result of right-sided dominance in strenuous activities involving the arms (Aufderheide and Rodriguez 1998). In the present examples, the lesions would not have greatly impacted on the daily lives of the individuals, who may have experienced a clicking in the affected joint and some pain with movement.

Compared with five other post-medieval populations, Park Street has the highest CPR rates for males, females and total assemblages (Table 4.38). This result is most notable among the males whose CPR was 7% compared with between 0% and 5.26% for other sites.

Neoplastic disease
A neoplasm is an abnormal mass of tissue resulting from cell proliferation and new growth exceeding that of the normal surrounding tissues (Aufderheide and Rodriguez-Martin 1998). Neoplasms may be benign (not harmful), pre-malignant or malignant (harmful to health). Without treatment, pre-malignant tumours may become malignant.

Two individuals had neoplastic disease including young adult male [699] and adult male [887]. Both had ivory button osteomas, which are benign and are common among archaeological and modern populations. They may be described as smooth dense expansions of cortical bone that are usually small and tend to occupy the

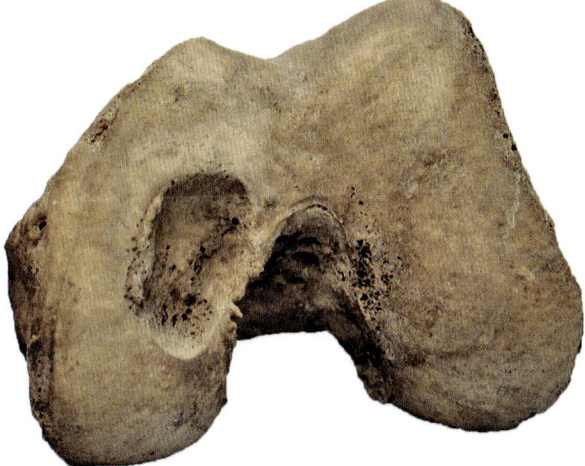

Fig. 4.29 Bilateral osteochondritis dissecans involving the knee joint, SK [2314]

Table 4.38: Inter-site comparison of CPR for osteochondritis dissecans

Site	Male CPR% (n/N)	Female CPR% (n/N)	Total adult CPR% (n/N)	Total assemblage CPR% (n/N)
Park Street, London	7.00 (7/100) inc. 1 male adol	1.43 (1/70)	3.27 (8/245)	3.63 (12/331)
Redearth Primitive Methodist Chapel, Darwen	0.00 (0/14)	16.13 (5/31)	8.93 (5/56)	3.52 (5/142)
St Martin's-in-the-Bull Ring, Birmingham	4.44 (8/180)	0.77 (1/130)	2.70 (10/371)	1.98 (10/505)
St Marylebone, London	No data	No data	3.14 (7/223)	2.33 (7/301)
St George's, Bloomsbury (named)	5.26 (2/38)	0.00 (0/29)	2.99 (2/67)	2.78 (2/72)
Bow Baptist Chapel, London	2.50 (2/80)	1.16 (1/86)	1.65 (3/182)	0.85 (3/351)

outer table of the skull or the sinuses. Their cause is unknown, but some have suggested that they are a response to trauma (Aufderheide and Rodríguez-Martín 1998). In the present cases, four osteomas were present on the left parietal (two) and frontal bones (two) of [699] and one was present on the right parietal bone [887].

No other confirmed cases of neoplastic disease were observed in the assemblage, although this is a differential diagnosis for the ulna lesion described above for [2410]. In addition, mature adult female [2421] had a raised area of cortical bone on the anterior of their distal femoral shaft. Differential diagnoses include a subperiosteal haematoma or an osteoid osteoma. Osteoid osteomas are small benign tumours of uncalcified bone matrix due to the over proliferation of osteoblasts (Aufderheide and Rodriguez-Martin 1998). The lack of bony reaction around the lesion, its location and the age of the individual suggest that an osteoid osteoma is the likely diagnosis.

Congenital and developmental conditions
This refers to abnormalities in growth or development. They may not become evident until the period of growth or young adulthood, or they may be present at

Table 4.39: Details of skeletons with congenital and developmental conditions

Skeleton number	Age	Sex	Description
Congenital fusion of vertebrae			
629	Young adult	F	CV6–7 – fused via bony bridging of posterior body margins
773	Older child	/	LV3–4 – fused via bony bridging of arches, + abnormal vert body morphology
Bifid ribs			
651	Prime adult	??F	Bifid R rib
Supernumerary ribs			
797	Older child	/	Bilateral cervical ribs, or malformed first ribs? (see vertebral border shifting) L upper rib is fused to the second rib
2201	Mature adult	M	Facet on LV1 for a lumbar rib (but rib not actually present) (x6 LV also)
2408	Adolescent	M	Additional rib facets (bilateral) on additional (13th) TV
Vertebral border shifting			
694	Prime adult	?M	Lumbarisation of SV1 (x6 Lvs, x4 Svs)
797	Older child	/	x6 CV, x13 TV (?cervical ribs also)
837	Young adult	M	Lumbarisation of SV1 (x6 Lvs, x4 Svs)
2079	Young adult	M	Lumbarisation of SV1
2408	Adolescent	M	x6 CV, x13 TV (supernumerary rib facets also)
Additional vertebral segment			
701	Prime adult	?M	x6 SV
731	Prime adult	?M	x6 LV
2201	Mature adult	M	x6 LV
Abnormal vertebral morphology			
773	Older child	/	Abnormal morphology of LV3-4 bodies (these vert are also fused via bony bridging of arches)
841	Prime adult	M	LV4+5 – inf body surfaces exhibit smooth, symmetrical depressions (not SNs) – prob developmental
2226	Young adult	?	Abnormal TV12 + LV1 arch morphology
2378A	Older child	/	Bifurcated LV5 arch
Spina bifida occulta (SBO)			
2406	Mature adult	F	Complete hiatus (SV1-5)
Symphalangism			
2193	Prime adult	M	R 5th intermed + dist foot phals fused
2403	Mature adult	M	Bilateral – single case in each foot
2415	Mature adult	M	Bilateral – single case in each foot
2419	Prime adult	?M	Bilateral – single case in each foot
Absent MC3 styloid (not trauma)			
2314	Adult	?M	R MC3 affected (L=NR)
2350	Young adult	?M	R MC3 affected (L=NR)

CV = cervical vertebrae; TV = thoracic vertebrae; LV = lumbar vertebrae; SV = sacral vertebrae; R = right; L = left; SNs = Schmorls nodes; MC3 = 3rd metacarpal; phals = phalanges; ad = adult; juv = juvenile; NR = not recordable

the foetal stage or at birth. The most common abnormalities are relatively minor and involve the spinal column (Barnes 1994).

In the present assemblage 24 individuals (CPR 7.21%; 24/333) had congenital or developmental conditions (Table 4.39). All of these were relatively minor and the majority involved the axial skeleton. By far the most common condition was symphalangism in the foot (TPR 4.55%). This primarily inherited condition involves ankylosis of the interphalangeal joints in the hand or foot due to the failure of the developing bone to fully separate during foetal growth. Apart from some stiffness, the condition does not greatly affect overall function.

Miscellaneous pathological conditions

Hyperostosis frontalis interna (HFI) was present on the endocrania of four adults (TPR 4.88% 4/82; CPR 1.63% 4/245) including a prime adult male [841], an older adult female [914] and two adult females [2151] and [2207]. HFI is identified on dry bone as thickening and nodule formation on the endocranial surface of the frontal bone. This condition has associations with virilism and obesity, and it is common among post-menopausal women. Its cause is unknown but it has been known to occur in pregnancy and accompany changes associated with acromegaly, thereby implicating some sort of pituitary gland disorder in its aetiology (Aufderheide and Rodríguez-Martín 1998).

Number of observed elements	TPR%
Total no. sks with obs vert (ad + juv) 210	TPR of congen fusion of vert (block vert) 0.95%
Total no. juv sks with obs vert 67	TPR of congen fusion of vert (block vert) 2.99%
Total no. obs ribs 1598	Rate of bifid ribs 0.06%
Total no. sks with obs ribs (ad + juv) 203	TPR of supernumerary ribs 1.48%
Total no. sks with obs vert (ad + juv) 210	TPR of vert border shifting 2.38%
Total no. sks with obs vert (ad + juv) 210	TPR of additional vert segment 1.43%
Total no. sks with obs vert (ad + juv) 210	TPR of abnormal vert morphology 1.90%
Total no. ad sks with obs sacrum 87	TPR of SBO 1.15%
Total no. sks with obs foot phals (ad + juv) 88	TPR of symphalangism 4.55%
Total no. ad sks with obs foot phals 73	TPR of symphalangism 5.48%
Total no. MC3s (ad) 158	TPR of absent MC3 styloid 1.27%

One prime adult female [2234] had distinctive bowing of the proximal and intermediate hand phalanges, which, in life, had probably caused the fingers to be visibly curved. The skeleton also had three abnormally bowed right ribs (all other observable ribs appeared to be normal).

Bowing deformities are seen in osteomalacia, but this is perhaps unlikely in the present case, because the skeleton did not display any other abnormalities, such as bowed weight bearing bones, associated with the disease. It is possible that the rib and hand deformities are unrelated and the former are the result of wearing a corset. The hand deformities may refer to contracture, or abnormal shortening of the muscle tissue which becomes highly resistant to stretching. Such contracture may result from tissue fibrosis or disorders of the muscle fibres. Fibrosis can occur secondary to trauma or erosive joint disease (Watt pers. comm.), but there were no lesions on any of the hand or wrist joints (which generally had a 'youthful' appearance), and neither was there any abnormality that indicated trauma. Another possibility is Dupuytren's disease, in which contracture results from shortening, thickening and fibrosis of the palmar or plantar fascia. Dupuytren's disease tends to affect males more than females and occurs among individuals aged between 40 and 60 years (Flatt 2001). The cause is unknown, but inheritance is thought to be a key factor; it is usually seen in individuals with a Nordic ancestry (Flatt 2001). Trauma and occupational stresses (eg occupations that involve the power grip) have also been cited as possible causes and associations with alcoholism, diabetes and pulmonary tuberculosis have been noted (Flatt 2001)

The same individual exhibited rib deformities involving the 8th, 9th and possibly 7th right ribs, the sternal parts of which, from the angle region, projected inferiorly and appeared to be slightly straightened. From the angle region the rib shafts 'dropped' suddenly, rather than following the normal gradual curvature. The left ribs were too fragmentary to say whether they were also deformed. These changes are consistent with the plastic deformation associated with wearing a corset in life (Stone 2012). Other changes include anterior displacement of the articular facets on the thoracic vertebrae (Groves et al. 2003), but were not observed on the present case.

ISOTOPE ANALYSIS by Rowena Henderson

The enamel from the teeth of 42 adults was taken for dietary isotope analysis at the Research Laboratory for Archaeology and the History of Art, University of Oxford. $\delta^{15}N$ and $\delta^{13}C$ stable isotope analysis was used to consider the infant and childhood diet of those buried at Park Street. The aim was to identify which individuals were breastfed and whether some were not.

Background

$\delta^{15}N$ and $\delta^{13}C$ stable isotope analysis is used to understand diet in past populations. When a person consumes food it is broken down and incorporated into the tissues of the person. Nitrogen is obtained from the protein component of the diet and the nitrogen isotopes reflect the position of the organism within the food chain (Deniro and Epstein 1981). At each step up the food chain the tissues become enriched by around 3–6‰ (Minagawa and Wada 1984). This means it is possible to predict how much meat and fish a person was consuming. Because of the large number of trophic levels in an aquatic food web, the $\delta^{15}N$ values of organisms consuming fish can be the most highly elevated (Schoeninger et al. 1983). The same occurs when an infant breastfeeds. When a child consumes breast milk it is feeding from a trophic level above its mother or carer, resulting in a 3‰ elevation (Fogel et al. 1989).

Carbon is obtained from the whole diet, with a bias towards proteins (Fernandes et al. 2012; Jim et al. 2006). The carbon can show whether a person had a diet based on plants which photosynthesize using the C4 pathway (such as maize, sorghum and millet) or the C3 pathway, which is standard in temperate climates such as England (Van der Merwe and Vogel 1978). Like the $\delta^{15}N$, the carbon isotopes also become elevated by 1‰ up the food chain (DeNiro and Epstein 1978). This has been shown to occur when infants consume breast milk (Katzenberg et al. 1993; Prowse et al. 2008; Nitsch et al. 2011). The carbon isotopes are further used to consider whether a diet had a marine or freshwater input. When a marine diet is consumed, the $\delta^{13}C$ becomes elevated, but is highly variable in fresh water systems, often being depleted relative to C3 terrestrial systems but sometimes as elevated as marine ecosystems (Chisholm et al. 1982).

Isotope analysis research questions

During the post-medieval period, historical sources suggest many infants were 'dry-fed', meaning they were given foodstuffs such as pap (breads soaked in water with spices) rather than breast milk (Fildes 1986). This has wider implications, as without the immunologically protective colostrum and breast milk dry-fed infants did not always survive into adulthood (Lönnerdal 2000). This was further compounded by the use of contaminated dry foods and food/liquid containers. These combined influences have the potential to influence infant mortality and population dynamics (Anderson *et al.* 1986).

Identifying variability in childhood diets within a population has other implications, including how homogenous a society was. Breastfeeding is both biologically and cultural influenced, meaning patterns differ between populations depending on factors such as religion, class, fashion, subsistence strategy and a mother's need to return to work (Ineichen *et al.* 1997; Hannan *et al.* 2005; Howie *et al.* 1990). Southwark was an area which experienced a high level of immigration and was essentially a working-class area. How variable infant feeding patterns were and how these compare with other sites is therefore important in our understanding of the area. Two other sites have been analysed using stable isotopes, a middle-class population from Spitalfields (Nitsch *et al.* 2011) and a Catholic working-class group from Lukin Street, Tower Hamlets (Beaumont *et al.* 2012).

The questions can be summarised as follows:

- How long were infants breastfed for?
- Were there any adults who survived and were not breastfed?
- How homogenous were infant feeding practices in the population, and what can this tell us about class?

The results presented here have been reported in full in Henderson *et al.* (2014), where additional analysis is made.

Sample selection and method

Forty-two first molars and 10 third molars were selected for $\delta^{15}N$ and $\delta^{13}C$ stable isotope analysis. Teeth without carious lesions, damage and attrition were preferentially chosen. These teeth were cleaned using aluminium oxide air abrasive, and dental calculus was reserved for future analysis. The enamel was removed using a hand held drill, after which each tooth was cut in half using a Buehler Isomet with diamond-tipped blade. The selected half teeth were demineralized in 0.5 M HCl and the resultant tooth was cut into 10 strips horizontally from the crown to the tooth. These represent different age brackets during a person's early life and were aged according to a developmental chart (Massler *et al.* 1941) (Fig. 4.30). The intra-tooth sampling method of adult teeth described allows the childhood diet of adults who survived infancy to be studied.

The strips were rinsed in distilled H_2O three times and heated at 70°C in pH3 H_2O for two days following a modified Longin method (Longin 1971). The third molars were treated the same way, but only

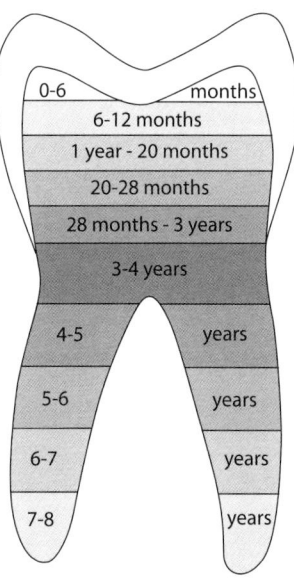

Fig. 4.30 An illustration of segments of the tooth taken and the age brackets assigned to them. Adapted from Henderson *et al.* (2014)

the root tips were processed, representing the late teenage/early adult diet. After filtration and freeze-drying, the collagen from these strips was weighed into tin capsules. They were measured in duplicate, using a continuous flow mass spectrometer (Sercon 20-22) at the University of Oxford. The standard, Alanine, was used to check the quality of the data and the results were calibrated using a two-point calibration curve, based on multiple aliquots of international standards IAEACH6 and USGS40. Analytical reproducibility is 0.1‰ and 0.2‰ for $\delta^{13}C$ and $\delta^{15}N$ respectively.

Results

The average collagen yield was 12.9%, indicating good preservation. All samples had C:N ratios within the acceptable range of 2.9-3.6 (DeNiro 1985) with the exception of [2417] and [799]. These were subsequently omitted. The $\delta^{15}N$ peaked at 0–6 months of age, averaging 13.6±1.9‰, ranging between 8.2–17.3‰. This suggests that breast milk was being consumed by most individuals, although not all. The $\delta^{15}N$ then declines, averaging 11.4±1.3‰ at 3–4 years old, indicating that other non-breast milk foods were being consumed. There is a general upward trend in $\delta^{15}N$ throughout later childhood and by adulthood, $\delta^{15}N$ from the third molar averages 13.3±0.5‰, ranging between 12.4–14.1‰. $\delta^{13}C$ in comparison was consistent over time. At 0–6 months of age the average was -18.7±1‰ ranging between -16.8 to -21.2‰. In the third molars the average was -18.6±0.5‰, demonstrating the consistency (Fig. 4.31)

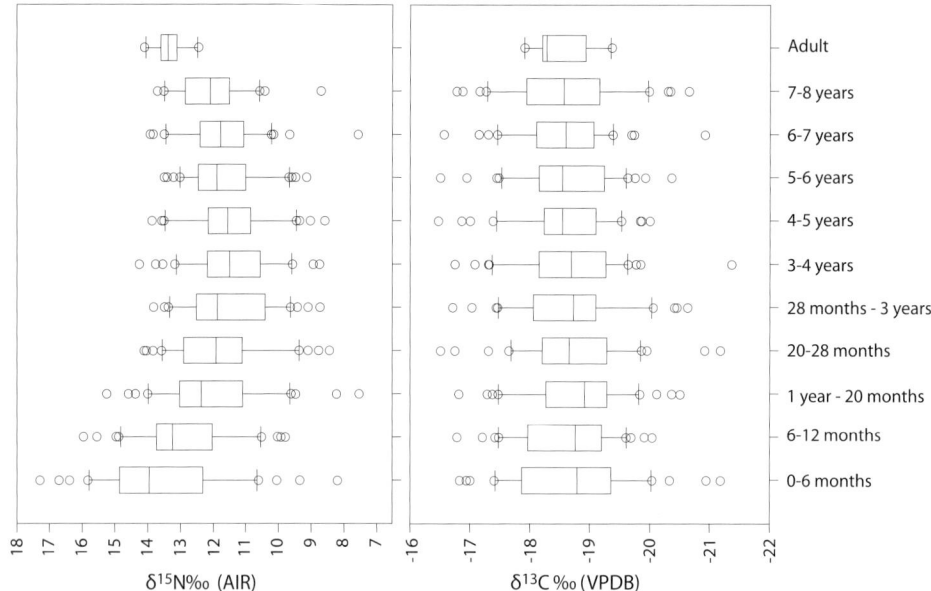

Fig. 4.31 Box and whisker plots of the first and third molars showing the δ15N and δ13C results from each age bracket. Taken from Henderson *et al.* (2014).

A General Linear Model was used to test for the effects of age and sex. The results from all 40 individuals showed age has a significant effect on the $\delta^{15}N$ (p=0, F= 10.163) but did not have a significant effect on $\delta^{13}C$ (p=0.961, F= 0.342). From the limited number of sexed individuals, it was shown that there was a small difference in $\delta^{13}C$ between males and females (p=0, F= 17.327). Males averaged -18.5±0.8‰ and females averaged -18.9±0.9‰. A small difference was also found with the $\delta^{15}N$ (p=0.019, F= 5.581). Females averaged 12.1±1.2‰ and males averaged 11.8±1.3‰.

Conclusions

With reference to the above stated aims, the overall findings of this study indicate that:

- Most infants were generally weaned at around 6 months old.

- Some adults (nine in total) had not been breastfed, but had survived into adulthood.

- Infant feeding practices were variable, and this was reflected in different contributions of breast milk, variable mother/carer diets and, possibly isotope differences between males and females.

- Findings are similar to other studies of London sites and therefore suggests that infant feeding practices were not influenced by class.

These observations are discussed further below.

SCIENTIFIC ANALYSES OF THE HUMAN SKELETAL REMAINS: SUMMARY AND CONCLUSIONS *by Louise Loe*

A good proportion of the assemblage was very incomplete, but generally well preserved, presenting the opportunity for a range of data to be collected with regard to demography, physical attributes, health and disease and dietary isotopes. The findings have identified a total of 331 individuals, and less than a third (86) of these were juveniles (individuals less than 18 years of age). Ages at death peaked among adults between 18 and 35 years, and numbers of individuals dying below five years and over 45 years were low. Males outnumbered females by 31 (104 minus 73) and were also more frequent among individuals from a group burial of 36 skeletons from the mass grave excavated in Pile Cap D.

The population showed evidence for deprived growth resulting in under-achieved final height. In addition, some individuals had experienced vitamin C and D deficiency, and there was evidence for childhood health stress in the form of cribra orbitalia, enamel hypoplasia and non-specific bone inflammation, although these were less prevalent than in other comparable assemblages. Examples of specific infection were also limited in number. Besides infection and non-specific stress indicators, other pathological conditions observed included joint diseases, such as osteoarthritis and gout, conditions of the spine, congenital and developmental conditions, and neoplastic disease. These showed patterns of skeletal involvement and prevalence rates that are unremarkable for a post-medieval British assemblage.

There was also evidence for trauma, primarily in the form of healed fractures, but this, too, was not very prevalent. Carbon and nitrogen isotope ratios indicate patterns in weaning and childhood diet that are in keeping with other London assemblages.

The following discussion considers the results with reference to several themes. These include mortality patterns, behavioural changes, childhood health and cultural/fashionable practices. Lastly, the overall health status of the population is considered with reference to other post-medieval populations from London and beyond.

Mortality patterns

Does the mass grave in Pile Cap D represent a catastrophic assemblage?

Thirty-six individuals recovered from a single grave [969] in Pile Cap D comprised males, females and children. Group burials such as this may take place as a result of a catastrophic event, or when a cemetery runs out of space, either because its catchment area increases and/or the population suddenly expands, for example due to an influx of migrants. Disturbance followed by reburial is another factor and is particularly relevant to Park Street where it is known that burials were moved during the construction of the railway in the 1860s, although details concerning this activity are limited.

One possible explanation for the mass burial is that it was the result of an epidemic, such as plague, typhus, ague, smallpox (among others, see Roberts and Cox 2003, 328–344 and 'mass fatality', Chapter 6), prevalent at the time. This can be further explored using the demographic data, considering that the mortality profile of a group dying suddenly – a catastrophic assemblage – will be different to that of a group with a normal pattern of mortality – an attritional assemblage (Paine 2000). However, investigation using archaeologically derived skeletal assemblages is hampered by the fact that constructed age profiles have the tendency to be biased by the methods employed to estimate age. To this end, the application of Bayesian statistics has been proposed (Gowland and Chamberlain 2005).

Nevertheless, the signature of an epidemic in mortality profiles, constructed from archaeological skeletons, remains unclear, as different epidemic diseases can affect different age groups. This is illustrated in work on the mortality profile of a Black Death assemblage from East Smithfield (1348–50), London. Here, an almost entire absence of neonates and young infants, a male to female ratio of 1.98:1 and a high proportion of juveniles (40.5%) were identified (Grainger et al. 2008). However, further manipulation of age at death data presents a mixed picture. Margerison and Knusel (2002), employing a life table approach, concluded that the Black Death was an indiscriminate killer, but more recent analysis, employing a new method of age estimation, which addresses the biases of more traditional methods ('transition analysis'), suggests that this plague killed selectively, targeting the elderly and those in poor health (DeWitte 2016).

East Smithfield is the only known plague assemblage published to date, but there are other mass graves from London where epidemics are suspected. For example, and local to Park Street, 17th century mass graves were found in a burial ground believed to be associated with St Thomas' hospital (Bekvalac 2007; Dawson 2002; Jones 1990). The graves may be those of paupers or of victims of an epidemic (ibid.; and see further discussion in Chapter 6). Osteological analysis of 193 out of 227 excavated skeletons identified 160 adults (58 males, 29 females and 73 unsexed) and 33 juveniles (Bekvalac 2007). Male deaths were highest in the mature adult (36–45 years) age category, female deaths, in the young adult (18–25 years) age category and juvenile deaths, in the adolescent (12–17 years) age category, and the male to female ratio was 2:1 (Bekvalac 2007). Unusually high rates of syphilis (CPR 13% – see above) and periostitis (CPR 35.2%) were observed, but no conclusions were drawn about whether the osteological findings pointed to pauper burials or victims of an epidemic (ibid.)

Another relevant assemblage is from St Mary Spital, where individuals were found in several mass graves dating between c 1120 and 1539 (Connell et al. 2012). These were observed to have a higher number of deaths among 16–17 year olds compared with attritional burials from the same cemetery. Overall, the mass grave age at death distribution tended to amplify the attritional mortality profile and, combined with osteological indicators of physiological stress, was attributed to famine coupled with epidemics. A mortality profile which amplifies an attritional distribution is classic of famine, which targets the very young and very old (Margerison and Knusel 2002; Dyson and Ó Grada 2002).

The Park Street mass grave age at death distribution showed a higher number of deaths among older children and prime adult males, and a higher ratio of males to females (4.7:1 compared to 1.1:1) compared with the rest of the burial ground. Considering that current osteological methods tend to under-age the old, the peaks in age at death are consistent with the mortality profiles of individuals dying from famine and smallpox, the latter of which affects young migrant workers often migrating from rural to urban environments. Further, the higher number of males is in keeping with the historical literature on famine, which reflects a female mortality advantage (Macintyre 2002) and the fact that most migrant workers were young males (Weinreb *et al.* 2008).

In conclusion, the mass grave in Pile Cap D has a mortality profile which is consistent with a catastrophic event. The characteristics of the profile would point to famine and/or an epidemic such as smallpox as contributory factors.

Other demographic trends

The higher proportion of males to females at Park Street has been seen among contemporary assemblages from London and elsewhere (eg St Bride's Lower Churchyard). Numerous factors, such as population mobility, zoning within a burial ground, differences in the religious and social treatment of males and females and a higher male birth rate, may explain this. However, the fact that the sex of 68 adults could not be estimated owing to missing elements is of primary consideration here.

It is likely that infant burials were lacking at Park Street because they had been truncated as a result of later burial activity and subsequent disturbance from the works associated with the 19th-century railway. Generally speaking, infant burials encountered in the archaeological record are more vulnerable to disturbance and loss than other burials, because they were often shallow, some having being inserted into the top of adult graves (Chamberlain 2000; Lewis 2007).

Overall, the assemblage had a high number of 18–35 year olds, even discounting the high proportion of prime adults in the mass grave. This trend is in contrast to other London assemblages discussed in this report and is more in keeping with the mortality profile of individuals dying as a result of a catastrophic event, such as massacre or epidemics – as described above. Massacre, or other violent episode can be ruled out here, because no peri-mortem trauma was identified on the skeletons. There were several epidemics during the lifetime of the burial ground, and map regression highlights a number of areas in the vicinity of the present site potentially marked out for the burial of plague or other epidemic victims (Chapter 2, Table 2.2). Unfortunately, the inability to assign the skeletons to finer date ranges precludes further consideration to explore an association between known epidemics and the date of those assigned to the 18–35 year range.

Another factor that may have contributed to the peak in deaths between 18–35 years is migration, particularly among males, considering that they outnumbered females in this age category. In addition, at least one individual in the assemblage was noted for possessing mixed ancestral cranio-facial traits. The lack of preserved cranio-facial regions in the rest of the assemblage has precluded a more detailed consideration of ancestry, but this observation could indicate a relatively heterogeneous population. This is supported by the estimated male statures, which showed a fairly mixed distribution. The range of estimated male statures (1.57–1.83m) was greater than the female range (1.4–1.65m) (Table 4.10) and greater than those estimated for contemporary males from more closed groups, such as the Baptists from Littlemore, Oxford (1.68–1.69m) and the Methodists from Redearth, Darwen, Lincolnshire (1.62–1.77m).

During the 16th century, London's population experienced unprecedented growth. This was more pronounced in the 17th century, and by the beginning of the 18th century London contained 10% of the nation's population with more than twenty times the number of inhabitants than the largest English town (Weinreb *et al.* 2008, 655–6). Increasing numbers of unskilled labourers, the poor and the destitute flooded into the city from the provinces as well as other migrants from different countries reflecting various factors, such as religious intolerance (eg Huguenots in Spitalfields and Southwark, Molleson and Cox 1993).

Even during the second quarter of the 18th century, when gin drinking had reached epidemic proportions among the poor and the burial rate exceeded the baptism rate, overall numbers were sustained by immigration on a massive scale. As Weinreb *et al.* (2008, 656) state: 'The effect of surplus births in the Home Counties, the Midlands and farther afield was that thousands of people poured into London, often to die within a short time'. The growth of London's population resumed in the late 18th century, and by the first half of the 19th century it had expanded to more than double its size as previously rural, discrete settlements were absorbed and migrants populated the city. The 1841 census return indicates that 40% of Londoners had been born elsewhere (Weinreb *et al.* 2008). According to Weinreb *et al.* (2008, 656), an average of around 300,000 individuals came into the capital each decade between 1841 and 1871. Migrants were coming from all over the Britain and Europe, with numbers breaking down into about a third from neighbouring counties, half from the Home Counties in general, and the remainder largely comprising those from other parts of England and Wales, but also Scotland, Ireland and the continent.

Immigrants have been identified in the archaeological record from several sites around the city, including French émigrés at St Pancras (Emery and Wooldridge 2011), a 'Lascar' at Sheen's burial ground (Henderson *et al.* 2013) and individuals of Huguenot descent at Christ Church, Spitalfields (Molleson and Cox 1993). In addition, the Catholic Mission of St Mary and St

Michael probably served a primarily Irish descent migrant population (Powers 2015), and migrants from London's hinterlands and the far reaches of northern and western Britain have been identified isotopically among the skeletal assemblage from East Smithfield Black Death cemetery (Kendall *et al.* 2013).

Reasons for the high rate of migration to London between the 17th and 19th centuries are varied. London depended on a regular intake of economic migrants in order to sustain its manpower, and this requirement would have increased at times of war and during epidemics such as plague (Kendall *et al.* 2013). Famine is another factor, in particular the Great Irish Famine of 1845–52, which resulted in population movement to urban centres, including London. Direct evidence to support this has recently been identified through analysis of stable dietary isotopes in a sample of skeletons from Lukin Street cemetery, Tower Hamlets, London (Beaumont *et al.* 2013).

In conclusion, it would seem to be reasonable to suggest that the higher number of 18–35 year olds at Park Street was the result of high numbers of individuals of that age group migrating into the population from elsewhere in Britain and Europe. This is supported by the mixed distribution of statures observed among the skeletons (consistent with a heterogeneous population), historical evidence and other archaeological examples where immigrants have been confirmed through isotope analysis. Immigrants were perhaps more susceptible to earlier deaths than the local population because of exposure to new diseases, possibly epidemics, that they lacked immunity against.

Behavioural changes

Osteoarthritis, trauma and enthesial changes were all observed in the assemblage. These are some of the primary forms of data employed by anthropologists to explore skeletal responses to its mechanical environment (Pearson and Buikstra 2006, 210, 220). These analyses are based on the principle that bone has the ability to respond proportionally to functional pressure by increasing or decreasing its mass (Wolff's Law, 1892). However, there are a number of shortfalls associated with this approach, the main one being that none of the datasets have a direct correlation with activity, because of a number of underlying factors, such as age, diet, body mass and climate (see eg Jurmain 1999; Michopoulou *et al.* 2015; Pearson and Buikstra 2006; Stock 2006). In addition, and most important, is that despite considerable interest in the skeleton in relation to activity, research is yet to identify signatures for specific activities (Pearson and Buikstra 2006).

Post-medieval skeletal assemblages are considered to be key in behavioural studies of the past, because of the availability of documentary source material, especially when this can be employed at an individual level to explore occupation. For example, Campanacho and Santos (2013) examined enthesial changes in manual and non-manual workers from early modern and modern identified collections from Lisbon and Coimbra (Portugal) and in Spain and concluded that occupation does not predispose individuals to develop these changes at an earlier age. Other work has examined the relationship between osteoarthritis and occupation, most notably Waldron and Cox (1989) on patterns of hand OA in a named sample of weavers from Christ Church, Spitalfields, but have found no association. There has also been a large volume of work on activity and trauma, including that on skeletons of retired sailors from Greenwich Royal Naval hospital which has identified fracture patterns associated with activities performed aboard ship (Boston *et al.* 2008).

The prevalence and distribution of osteoarthritis (OA) in the Park Street assemblage were consistent with most other archaeological populations in that it was the most common pathology observed and was most prevalent among older adults. It is very unlikely that occupation and activity will have played a unique role in the manifestation of OA in this population, because of the many factors, including age, sex, ancestry and genetic predisposition, as well as activity or occupation, which play a part in the manifestation and course of the disease. Age is a major factor and may be controlled for by considering those less than 45 years of age with the disease. In the present study only three individuals with OA were less than 45 years, including one with changes secondary to trauma, another with primary shoulder OA and another with primary elbow OA. OA affecting upper limbs, such as the shoulder, is thought to be more closely associated with hereditary factors than the weight-bearing joints of the lower limb (Resnick and Niwayama 1995). Perhaps more interesting, however, is the fact that OA affecting the elbow might be more closely associated with activity because of the bio-mechanical properties of this joint (Jurmain 1999).

Like OA, enthesial reactions showed a strong correlation with increasing age. This trend has variously been interpreted as the accumulation of micro-trauma through life (Robb 1998) and, where the epiphyses are involved, increased age-related tendon stiffness (Jurmain *et al.* 2012). In the Park Street assemblage changes involved the upper limbs more frequently than the lower limbs. Beyond the stage of crawling, the bones and joints of the upper limbs are used almost exclusively in voluntary activities (i.e. the manipulation of objects and tools) and are therefore more likely to reveal information about activity (Knüsel 2000b). Thus, the presence of reactions in this group from Park Street could indicate that they were experiencing repetitive and, probably, heavy mechanical stresses from a young age.

Trauma was observed on several individuals, evidenced by fractures, ossified haematomas, dislocations and soft tissue trauma. These lesions probably account for a fraction of the trauma that was actually present in the population, because many will have involved soft tissues sparing bone entirely.

Fractures were the most common type of skeletal trauma observed, but when rates were compared with other assemblages they were generally low. This may suggest that the Park Street individuals were less predisposed to occupational hazards and interpersonal violence than their contemporaries. One or two of these were suspected to have been pathological fractures, such as a fractured femoral neck, probably secondary to osteoporosis, considering the age and sex of the individual and the fracture location (Brickley and Ives 2008). In others, mechanical pressure on the lower back leading to fracture of the neural arch (spondylolisis) may be indicated, although interpretation is obscured because this type of fracture in particular may be the result of an interaction between genes and activity (Pilloud and Canzonier 2014). A small number (possibly five) of fractures may have been due to interpersonal violence, while the majority are likely to be accident related. Interestingly, two of the possible interpersonal violence examples were a female and a possible female.

Childhood health

Pathology – scurvy and rickets

A relatively limited range of pathological conditions was observed among the juvenile skeletons compared with the adult assemblage. This is not altogether surprising considering the lesser number of years during which they were exposed to a risk of disease or trauma. In addition, most diagnostic skeletal lesions are longstanding ones which relate to chronic conditions and, as such, are usually only detected in adult skeletons.

Only one juvenile (1.16% of all juveniles, or 0.30% of the total assemblage) had lesions that were readily recognisable as scurvy. It is difficult to say how this compares with other assemblages and what this might mean in terms of the health status of the children from Park Street. Among some comparable assemblages (eg St Pancras and New Bunhill Fields) the disease has not been identified, while a small number of cases, or possible cases, are reported for others. For example, at St Marylebone and St Martin's-in-the-Bull Ring four cases (6.5% of all 77 juveniles or 1.7% of the total assemblage: Miles et al. 2008; Powers 2009) and six cases (Brickley and Ives 2012) are reported respectively. This mixed picture is likely due to the fact that developments in the understanding and recognition of skeletal lesions arising from scurvy are fairly recent (Brickley and Ives 2008; Mays 2013; Ortner and Erikson 1997). In addition, not all cases can be confirmed solely by macroscopic analysis, but require the application of other analytical techniques, such as radiography (Brickley and Ives 2008). Further, some lesions are not diagnostic of the disease alone, and this was certainly the case for Park Street where at least one additional case may be present but cannot be confirmed because other changes were lacking and/or bones were missing.

Besides shortages of fresh fruit and vegetables, scurvy in archaeological populations may relate to cultural practices influencing dietary habits and/or cooking methods (Mays 2013). It has been suggested that a shortage of potatoes, resulting from blight, may have contributed to the cases observed among low status individuals from St Martin's-in-the-Bull Ring, Birmingham, during the 18th and 19th centuries (Brickley and Ives 2006). During the 17th to 19th centuries potatoes were a main source of vitamin C among the urban poor (Mays 2013). Further, the London Bills of Mortality data shows a marked correlation with the introduction of potatoes and the decline in the number of individuals reported as having scurvy at the time of their deaths (Roberts and Cox 2003).

Rickets is another deficiency disease, the prevalence of which has been shown, both historically and osteologically, to have increased in Britain during the 18th and 19th centuries (Mays 2003; 2013), possibly reflecting climatic shift and increased urbanisation (Roberts and Cox 2003). It was identified in 3.9% of the Park Street skeletons. As with scurvy, the development of criteria for diagnosing this disease is relatively recent and therefore rickets is sporadically reported in the comparative literature. The most detailed study undertaken to date is on the assemblage from St Martin's-in-the-Bull Ring where a prevalence of around 7% (11/148) was identified (Brickley et al. 2006; Brickley and Ives 2006). In addition, at St Marylebone rates were found to be especially high: 26.9% among juveniles and 4.6% among adults (Miles et al. 2008; Powers 2009). Less industrialised sites show lower prevalence rates. For example, Roberts and Cox (2003, 310) present data for six London assemblages which have an overall crude prevalence rate of 3.63% (89/2452) and range from 0.56% (Kingston upon Thames) to 6.76% (Cross Bones). These rates are probably an artefact of the socio-economic status of the assemblages, however (ibid.). Overall, it would seem that although vitamin D deficiency was present in the Park Street population, it was not excessive.

Several factors have been attributed to vitamin D deficiency in post-medieval assemblages. For example, Cox (1996) suggested that fashionable infant feeding practices had contributed to the cases observed among skeletons from Christ Church crypt, Spitalfields. A lack of exposure to sunlight as a result of climate change, working indoors, sickly children being kept indoors, and a lack of unadulterated cow's milk (eg from cattle kept in stalls and cellars) in towns and cities are other possibilities (Roberts and Cox 2003, 309–10; Brickley and Ives 2006; Mays 2013). The condition may also be secondary to disease, such as those involving the kidneys or liver and other rare conditions (Ortner 2003, 393).

It is impossible to say which factors may have contributed to the cases observed in the Park Street population and, indeed, whether they were the result of acute, isolated, episodes, or chronic, recurrent disease which, according to historical sources, peaked in the low sun winter months in the industrial centres of post-medieval Britain (Mays *et al.* 2009, 413). Isotope analysis suggests that a total of nine Park Street juveniles may not have been breastfed (see below), but no macroscopic lesions of rickets were detected on them, as might perhaps be expected. The fact that most skeletons with the disease were above the age of five years (only three with rickets were between the ages of birth and five years) would seem to point to other causes besides infant feeding practices. In addition, the disease did not seem to show a sex bias, perhaps ruling out sex-specific cultural practices and activities that could have been predisposing factors. For example, a high prevalence of rickets was observed among females from St Marylebone and this may have been related to dietary fashions (Miles *et al.* 2008, 153). The Park Street skeletons date to a period of climatic deterioration, including the 1739–41 'Great Frost', so it is possible that this had been an important factor in the disease in this population.

As rickets does not itself cause death, Mays (2013) has suggested that infantile cases represent sickly children who were kept indoors away from sunlight. However, there is limited evidence for this in the juvenile skeletons with rickets from Park Street. The presence of several cases of healed or resolved rickets in adults – as seen at Park Street – may suggest it was a common ailment among children whose health was otherwise not particularly compromised (Mays 2013).

Growth and final achieved height

Besides scurvy and rickets, other indicators of childhood health captured during the analysis of the Park Street skeletons are non-specific and, as such, give a more nuanced picture. One of these is growth, generally regarded as a useful barometer of health in archaeological populations (Lewis 2007). Growth may be explored by comparing measurements of long bone lengths with dental age to determine whether children were short for their age and therefore under-nourished (Lewis 2007). Only six juveniles had the required intact long bone (in this case the femur) and dentition preserved for this assessment to be undertaken. The results showed that dental age was generally older than bone length age. Although this comparison is rather crude (for example, comparison with contemporary juveniles is required and the small sample precludes statistical analysis), it seems to suggest that environmental factors were having a detrimental impact on the growth of juveniles from Park Street.

A study by Mays *et al.* (2008) found that endochondral growth (as expressed by long bone length) was a poor indicator of health stress among low status children from St Martin's-in-the-Bull Ring, Birmingham. However, Lewis (2002) reported up to a 3cm deficit in height among middle-class children from Christ Church, Spitalfields compared with medieval populations. Further, Pinhasi *et al.* (2006) concluded that data captured from Anglo-Saxon, late medieval and post-medieval assemblages implicated socio-economic status, rather than industrialisation, urbanisation or rickets as the principal factor in growth differences among post-medieval populations, and that this was only significant in infancy, a time of maximum growth velocity.

The impact of health stress on growth may be further explored by considering the data obtained for final achieved height from the adult skeletons. While final achieved height is primarily determined by genetics, environmental factors play a significant role in influencing an individual's ability to realise their full height potential (Larsen 1997; Steckel 1995). In addition, nutrition, provided by the mother via the placenta to foetuses and by mother/carer breast milk to infants and young children, has a significant impact on adult stature; thus heights are a reflection of maternal nutritional status as well (Gowland 2015, 533). The Park Street individuals were ranked among the lowest of all comparative post-medieval assemblages considered in this report, which might suggest childhood exposure to physiological health stress, especially inadequate nutrition and poor maternal/carer health.

Isotope analysis and nutritional status
(by Rowena Henderson)

A more detailed insight into the nutritional status of the population was achieved by incremental dietary isotope analysis of adult teeth. A relatively new technique, this approach affords the unique opportunity to perform retrospective analyses of dietary life histories in childhood, as well as examine maternal (or carer) nutritional status.

The findings of the analysis indicate that, in general, weaning practices were variable in the Park Street population, although most were breastfed up to 6 months old (Henderson *et al.* 2014). This finding is similar to those reported for other sites, including the middle-class Spitalfields population and the Catholic Lukin Street cemetery, suggesting class did not influence practices (Nitsch *et al.* 2011; Beaumont *et al.* 2012). A total of nine individuals [659], [661], [885], [962], [2127], [2362], [2423], [4044] and [4052] were not breastfed but were able to survive into adulthood. They included three males, three females and three unsexed skeletons with ages at death which ranged from adolescent to mature adult, although the group was predominantly below the age of 25 years. Using this technique, it is not clear what proportion of the dry-fed infants would have died.

The variable $\delta^{15}N$ elevation in infancy not only suggests different contributions of breast milk, but also suggests that the mothers/carers had variable diets. Londoners during this era could have had access to a wide variety of foods. Looking at the population as a whole, the $\delta^{15}N$ is generally high compared to other populations, but is comparable to other post-medieval London sites thus far analysed. This might be caused by the manuring of crops, which elevates the $\delta^{15}N$ throughout a food chain, or might be caused by the frequent and widespread consumption of fish (Bogaard *et al.* 2007).

A feature of many of the life history projections is a 'dip' in the $\delta^{15}N$ during childhood. This has been observed across a variety of populations and probably represents a physiological rather than dietary change (Henderson *et al.* 2014). It is proposed that due to high growth rates during this period the children's bodies are not able to preferentially select the ^{15}N isotope (Schurr 1997). The isotopic difference between males and females was unexpected, but may indicate males and females were fed different foods throughout the first eight years of life. Alternatively, there could be a physiological cause. Further research will help to clarify this.

Skeletal health of breastfed children versus non-breastfed children

All but one of the non-breastfed skeletons had stress indicators, that is, either cribra orbitalia, non-specific bone inflammation (including periostitis and endocranial lesions) and/or enamel hypoplasia (Tables 4.40 and 4.41). Analysis of final achieved height was precluded by the lack of measurable long bones. The stature of only one of the skeletons could be estimated, but had to employ the maximum length of the humerus, which is the least reliable bone, and therefore the result is not very useful.

By comparison, osteological analysis of the breastfed skeletons showed that there were more-or-less even numbers of males and females (12 males, 14 females and seven unsexed skeletons) and no apparent bias in ages at death. Ages at death included adolescents (nine unsexed skeletons); young adults (five females and five males); prime adults (one male and one female); mature adults (three females and one male); an older adult (one male) and unspecified adults (three females, one male). Eight (24%; 8/33) of the skeletons had no stress indicators. Stature could be estimated for 11 of the skeletons and ranged from 152.9cm to 182.87cm, but if those estimates that employed the least accurate bone (the humerus) are excluded, the range is 152.9cm–176.13cm.

Table 4.40: Non-breastfed individuals

Skeleton number	Age at death	Sex	Adult stature (m)	Stress indicators / other metabolic disease
659	Adult unspecified	Male	No data	Cribra orbitalia; enamel hypoplasia (1.5–3.5 yrs / 4.5–5.5 yrs)
661	Young adult	Male	No data	Enamel hypoplasia (7.5–10.5 mths / 10.5–18 mths / 1.5–2.5 yrs / 2.5–3.5 yrs)
885	Adult unspecified	Female	No data	Cribra orbitalia; endocranial lesions; probable scurvy; enamel hypoplasia (0.5–2 yrs)
962	Adolescent	unsexed	Not relevant	Inflammation (associated with dental disease); maxillary sinusitis; enamel hypoplasia (2–5 yrs / 4–5.5 yrs)
2127	Mature adult	unsexed	No data	Cribra orbitalia; periostitis visceral surfaces of ribs; enamel hypoplasia (2.5–3.5 yrs)
2362	Young adult	Female	No data	Cribra orbitalia
2423	Mature adult	Female	No data	Cribra orbitalia
4044	Adolescent	unsexed	Not relevant	None
4052	Young adult	Male	1.65 (humerus)	Ecto-cranial inflammation

Approximate age at which enamel hypoplasia appeared in parentheses

Table 4.41: Breastfed individuals

Skeleton number	Age at death	Sex	Adult stature (m)	Stress indicators/ other metabolic disease
603	Adolescent	Female	/	Cribra orbitalia; endo-cranial lesions; enamel hypoplasia (2.5–3.5 yrs / 3.5–4.5 yrs)
607	Mature adult	Female	/	Enamel hypoplasia (5.5–6.5 yrs)
629	Young adult	Female	/	None
677	Young adult	Female	/	Enamel hypoplasia (3.5–5.5 yrs)
681	Adolescent	unsexed	/	Cribra orbitalia
709	Young adult	Male	1.64 (humerus)	Enamel hypoplasia (7 mths–3.5 yrs)
767	Adolescent	Male	/	None
785	Prime adult	Male	1.67 (humerus)	Cribra orbitalia
799	Adult unspec	Female	1.64 (humerus)	None
801	Adolescent	unsexed	/	Cribra orbitalia; enamel hypoplasia (1.5–2.5 yrs / 4.5 yrs)
809	Young adult	Male	1.83 (humerus)	Cribra orbitalia
813	Adolescent	unsexed	/	None
823	Young adult	Female	1.53 (femur)	Cribra orbitalia; maxillary sinusitis; Inflammation – ectocranium; enamel hypoplasia (2–3 yrs/7–8 yrs)
843	Adolescent	unsexed	/	None
889	Prime adult	Female	1.57 (femur)	Endocranial lesions; periostitis; enamel hypoplasia (2.5–3.5 yrs)
895	Older child	unsexed	/	Enamel hypoplasia (1–5 yrs)
921	Adult unspec	Female		Cribra orbitalia
949	Older child	?	/	Cribra orbitalia
956	Older adult	M		None
2079	Young adult	M	1.74 (femur)	Cribra orbitalia
2097	Older child	?	/	Cribra orbitalia; enamel hypoplasia (4–6 mths / 1–4 yrs) rickets
2151	Adult unspec	F		Cribra orbitalia; maxillary sinusitis; enamel hypoplasia (10–12 mths)
2199	Mature adult	F	1.61 (humerus)	Cribra orbitalia
2350	Young adult	M		Cribra orbitalia; periostitis; enamel hypoplasia (4.5–5.5 yrs)
2406	Mature adult	F	1.64 (humerus)	Cribra orbitalia
2408	Adolescent	M	/	Maxillary sinusitis
2417	Young adult	F		None
3011	Young adult	M		Max sinusitis
3065	Adolescent	F	/	None
4005	Young adult	F		Enamel hypoplasia (4.5–5.5yrs)
4050	Adult unspec	M	1.69 (humerus)	Periostitis
4084	Adolescent	M	/	Periostitis
2272A	Mature adult	M	1.76 (femur)	Periostitis

Approximate age at which enamel hypoplasia appeared in parentheses

Cultural and fashionable practices

Osteological evidence provides some information on cultural and fashionable practices adopted in the past. Among those which have received most attention in studies of post-medieval populations are pipe smoking, footwear and the wearing of corsets. Infant feeding is another practice and has already been considered under 'childhood health'.

Corsetry

Corsets are rigid garments which are worn to hold the body in a desired shape. They were ubiquitous during the Victorian period, worn by all classes and especially by women who reportedly wore them from around the age of nine years (Cole 2010; Stone 2012). Although also used to treat medical conditions (eg spinal deformities) they were primarily worn among females and males alike to achieve a small waistline (Steele 2001; Cole 2010). They could have serious health implications, the tight lacing used to contract the corset resulting in displacement of internal organs, placing pressure on the lungs or bowels and bladder (depending on the direction of displacement) and causing shortness of breath, obstructed bowels, incontinence, uterus prolapse and immobility (Stone 2012). Over the long-term, corsets could result in deformities in the ribs, vertebrae and pelvis leading to complications in pregnancy and childbirth among women (Stone 2012), even though they were worn throughout pregnancy (Miles *et al.* 2008). Another long-term consequence was muscular atrophy (wastage) as a result of disuse, which could result in the wearer being unable to stand upright without support, digestive problems and, in extreme cases, herniation (ibid.).

Only one skeleton from Park Street was identified with deformities consistent with corset wearing. This probably under-estimates the actual number of Park Street individuals who had deformities from wearing corsets because, in keeping with most skeletal assemblages, the rib cage did not survive well in the burial environment; most ribs were highly fragmentary and this will have obscured any evidence.

During the 18th and 19th centuries corsets were worn for fashion as well as to treat medical conditions such as spinal deformities. The example from Park Street did not have any skeletal pathology that would imply a medical motivation, although this cannot be entirely ruled out. For example, corsets were worn to treat soft tissue conditions, such as hernias, which do not leave traces on the skeleton.

At Wolverhampton, rib deformities in a 20–35 year old male have been linked to wearing a corset to treat Pott's disease of the spine, caused by tuberculosis (Moore and Buckberry 2016). Other examples of corset wearing have been observed at St Marylebone (Miles *et al.* 2008), St Mary and St Michael, Tower Hamlets (Henderson *et al.* 2013) and the Bow Baptist Church, Tower Hamlets (Henderson *et al.* 2013), presumably all for fashion. These include males and females, although they are more common among the latter.

Pipe smoking

Two individuals (one male and one ??female) in the sample had pipe stem facets on their teeth, consistent with having smoked a pipe in life. This is undoubtedly an under-estimation of pipe smokers in the assemblage, considering that pipe facets take a number of years to form on the teeth.

Notches are one of the markers of smoking in archaeological populations, dental staining on the lingual (tongue facing) surfaces of teeth being another. Detailed analysis of both these indicators in a post-medieval (1843–1854) Irish migrant population from St Mary and St Michael, Whitechapel, has identified a high prevalence of pipe smoking (Walker 2010). In this study, apparent smokers showed a lower life expectancy and more evidence for lung disease than apparent non-smokers and, in keeping with historical sources, indicators of smoking were higher among males than females (ibid.).

Overall health and well-being: Park Street in context

The foregoing discussion has primarily focussed on skeletal changes as discrete entities in relation to cultural practices, childhood and behavioural patterns. However, what do the datasets tell us about the overall health and well-being of the population? This section considers the evidence with reference to other comparable assemblages from London and elsewhere in Britain.

Throughout this report osteological findings have been compared with a number of assemblages from high- and low-status contexts, from London and elsewhere in England. The Park Street individuals had comparatively low levels of dental disease (except for caries), non-specific inflammation, maxillary sinusitis, trauma and enamel hypoplasia. They also showed less evidence for specific infection and deficiencies (scurvy and rickets), although the latter are probably more a reflection of methodology, than a real trend (see above). These observations are inconsistent with the high burden of disease and high mortality known among the working classes of London from historical sources (eg Boulton 1987; Roberts and Cox 2003; Watts 2015). However, this depends on how the data are interpreted because low levels of non-specific inflammation may refer to individuals who had weak constitutions and, when inflicted by disease, did not survive long enough for changes to manifest on their bones (DeWitte and Stojanowski 2015; Wood *et al.* 1992). This is certainly the picture suggested by the limited evidence for specific infection, such as syphilis and tuberculosis, diseases which only manifest skeletally in their advanced stages and after a long period of time. In fact, estimated stature supports this argument, because it ranked Park Street among the lowest of all assemblages. In addition, cribra orbitalia was comparatively high.

The enamel hypoplasia may indicate recovery rather than indicating health stress (Ribot and Roberts 1996; see relevant section above). Further, it may reflect short periods of illness that did not have a lasting impact on health or predispose to early mortality, as has been observed among other high/middling and low socio-economic status London assemblages (Watts 2015, 577). Thus, low assemblage rates of enamel hypoplasia could be consistent with populations who experienced chronic health stress. Sex and socio-economic status are also important factors to consider here. According to Watts (2015, 578), London assemblages reflect a trend whereby chronic stress leading to greater susceptibility to infections and increased risk of adult mortality is apparent among low-status males and high/middling-status females, but not among high/middling-status males and low-status females. This is interesting considering the higher number of males from the Park Street assemblage.

Another factor that may account for the apparent low levels of pathology in the assemblage is the mortality profile, or more specifically, the high number of individuals dying between 18 and 35 years and low number of older adults. It is likely that they simply did not survive long enough to develop those conditions, for example, ante-mortem tooth loss, which have a positive association with increasing age.

Conclusions

Scientific analyses of the skeletons have considered the demographic, palaeopathological and isotopic composition of the burial population. Essentially, the burials comprised two types of death assemblage, including a group of 36 individuals who appear to have died and been buried as the result of a one-off event ('catastrophic assemblage'), and 295 individuals who presumably died as a result of natural wastage and been buried over the course of several hundred years ('attritional assemblage'). The demographic composition of the catastrophic assemblage points to famine and/or epidemic (eg smallpox) rather than war or some other cause. The attritional assemblage may also include significant numbers of individuals who died sudden, unnatural deaths (considering the high number of individuals dying between 18 and 35 years), in particular immigrants, aged between 18–35 years, exposed to hitherto un-encountered pathogens after migration.

Several datasets have been considered in respect of interpreting behavioural patterns within the population, but these present a very limited picture. Perhaps the most useful observation is that the data has identified a group of individuals who had pronounced muscle markings on their upper limbs, suggestive of mechanical loading from a young age. In addition, bone deformities, from wearing corsets, and notched teeth, from smoking pipes, provide some insight into their daily habits and cultural practices. Evidence for trauma was lacking, but it is hard to believe that the individuals had had limited exposure to violence and especially accidents, considering the occupational hazards and the living conditions of the time (see Chapter 6). Rather, the incompleteness of the assemblage may have had a greater influence on this result.

Evidence for scurvy and rickets was observed, possibly as a result of famine and climate change respectively. However, interpretation is limited because the diseases have probably been under diagnosed in this group due to difficulties associated with identification in archaeological bone. Indeed, considering growth and stature, it does seem that childhood and maternal health were compromised, in particular as a result of inadequate nutrition. Further insight is provided by isotopy which suggests that diets had been varied, and that boys and girls may have been given different diets in their first eight years of life. These observations could be reflective of the mixed composition of the population and/or differential access to foods; it may also point to physiological differences between males and females. Most children appear to have been weaned at about six months of age, while some individuals had not been breastfed as children, but had survived into adulthood with no discernible differences in their skeletal health status compared with those who had been breastfed.

Overall, these observations would seem to be consistent with 18th- and 19th-century assemblages from elsewhere in London and beyond. That is, the osteology, palaeopathology and isotopy are consistent with low- to middling-status 18th- and 19th-century individuals who experienced longstanding health stress resulting from inadequate living conditions, over-crowding, poor sanitation and health care during their lives that were, for many, unnaturally short. In particular, immigration, increased disease burden, and pressure on food supplies seem to be the most notable factors that have defined this group in terms of the osteological evidence.

Chapter 5

Coffins and coffin furnishings

by Mark Gibson

This chapter describes and discusses the coffin fittings found during the excavations, exploring aspects such as their status connotations and symbolism. It also presents the known biographical details of the only individual identifiable from the inscribed breastplates: William Pope, who died in 1816.

The remains of 223 wooden coffins, representing 67.4% of all burials, were identified during the excavation, either from traces of decayed wood or stains in the shape of the decayed coffin and/or coffin fittings, most often iron fixing nails associated with a skeleton. Some of the stains incorporated small fragments or flecks of highly decayed wood, but no recoverable pieces survived.

A total of 139 coffin fittings from 97 coffin contexts was recovered, and another two definite and 39 possible coffin fittings were present in four non-coffin contexts. Nails and coffin studs were not always precisely quantified during excavation, often recorded as 'occasional' or 'not known', so these have been excluded from the quantification. The coffin fittings are fully catalogued in the archive.

Background to post-medieval coffins

Many 16th-century coffins were plain, of a rectangular or trapezoidal shape, often with a gable lid (Litten 1991). They were usually the preserve of the nobility and gentry, but by the 17th century their use had increased within the general population, and by the 18th century their use was prevalent (ibid.). Over time the gabled lid developed a more flattened shape.

By the late 17th century the single-break coffin (tapered at the shoulders) had become more popular than the trapezoidal or wedge shape (Litten 1991). Financial investment in coffins and funerals increased from 18th and into the 19th centuries, resulting in increasing elaboration, and decorated coffins became common. The wrought iron grips and sheet iron grip plates typical of simple furniture on the earlier coffins were replaced by purpose-made and often highly decorative cast grips and die-stamped grip plates, mass-manufactured and affordable to a wide market (ibid.). Breastplates displaying the details of the deceased became more commonplace, as did other coffin decorations, such as escutcheons, lid motifs and stud work.

By the end of the use of the Cure's College burial ground, investment in coffins and funerals had reached its peak. It was perceived as one of the most important ways of reflecting a person's respectability and position in society (Richmond 1999). Whilst the wealthy could afford highly elaborate affairs with processions of black-draped hearses, black-plumed horses, mutes and chief mourners, the poor performed more simple ceremonies. However, even amongst the less affluent, providing a decent burial was important, and many families placed themselves into financial hardship to do so (Friar 2003; May 2003).

Methodology

The coffin fittings were examined by context and state of preservation, material and type of coffin fitting were recorded, along with decorative details, inscriptions or maker's marks. Where preservation allowed, motifs on the fittings were described and, where possible, matched to types recorded in the catalogue of Christ Church, Spitalfields (Reeve and Adams 1993), and styles recorded from other excavated post-medieval sites.

Results

Coffin construction and carpentry
Where preservation was sufficiently good to observe coffin details, there was no evidence for double-skinned wooden coffins or metal shells, and it appears that all of the coffins were constructed with a single skin of wooden planking. Due to the poor condition of the wood, no details of coffin construction, such as jointing, were identified, even where larger fragments of wood survived.

Coffin shape

It was possible to determine the shape of only 66 coffins (29.6%) due to truncation and the advanced states of decay. All of these were of the single-break style or shouldered style still commonly in use today. Where the superior half of the coffin was truncated it was frequently noted that the coffin stain tapered towards the foot. As this was the case with both trapezoidal and single-break coffins it was impossible to determine which shape the coffin would have been.

Fixing nails

Iron fixing nails were recorded in only 30.0% of coffins (67/223). A total of 85 nails were retained from 24 coffins, and the presence of nails was recorded in the case of the other 43 coffins. The maximum number of nails found per coffin was 11, of which most were in a fair condition. These figures are probably a significant under-representation of the original number, which would have been reduced due to truncation and corrosion.

Where recordable, the shanks are angular, and square or rectangular in cross-section (Fig. 5.1). This is characteristic of early cut nails or machine-cut nails, which predate the smooth-shanked wire nails ubiquitous from the later 19th century to the present day (Taylor 1999).

The only other type of coffin fixing recorded is a single hinge from context [890], suggesting the coffin had a hinged lid. As it is unlikely that the lid had a single hinge, the other hinges must have been lost to truncation or not recovered, or the single hinge may have been an intrusive object from elsewhere.

Coffin fittings

Only 41 coffins (18.4%; 41/223) were fitted with either a breastplate, grips, grip plates, a lid motif and/or upholstery studs. Other fittings found elsewhere in cemetery excavations of this date, such as coffin lace and escutcheons, were entirely absent. Most of the fittings were heavily corroded and, in the case of breastplates and grip plates, generally highly fragmented. All of the fittings were made of iron, sometimes painted black.

Grips and grip plates (Table 5.1)

Coffins of the 18th and 19th centuries were usually fitted with between four and eight grips backed by a plate. Grip plates could be plain or cast in a decorative design (Litten 1991), the decoration either engraved, punched or embossed. Grips were not used to carry the coffin, but to steady it whilst it was carried to the church or graveside. This was the most common coffin fitting in the assemblage, found in 13.0% of burials. A total of 48 grips was recovered from 27 coffins, and the presence of unrecovered grips of unspecified number was recorded in another two cases. A single grip was by far the most common occurrence (59.3%). Only one coffin had a near full suite of grips, a total of seven unadorned Christ Church Spitalfields (CCS) type 1 (Reeve and Adams 1993) associated with context [2351]. Where their location could be recorded it was observed that they were present on the head and foot of the coffin as well as the sides. This suggests that the absence of grips on many coffins was due to truncation, destruction by corrosion or failure of observation.

Over half of the grips (52.1%, 25/48) could not be identified to type due to their poor condition. Of the remainder, 23 from seven coffins are CCS type 2a, a type found at Spitalfields on coffins dated 1763–1837

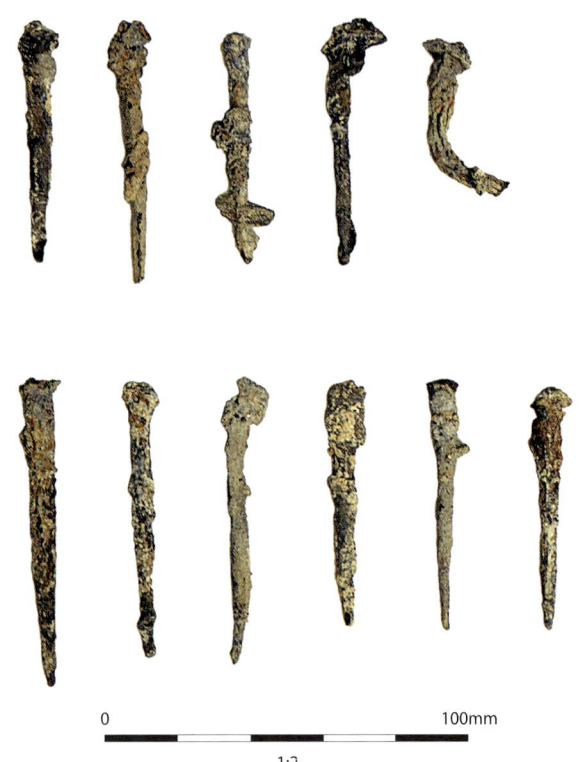

Fig. 5.1 Coffin fixing nails from coffin [2202]

Table 5.1 Coffin grips

Grip type	No. of grips	No. of coffins	Length mm (when complete)
CCS 1	7	1	115
CCS 2a	9	7	145 (Adult) 64 (juvenile)
PQC 7152	1	1	-
Angular	6	2	-
Unidentifed	25	16 (+2 with no. grips not recorded)	-
Total	48	27+2	-

(Reeve and Adams 1993). Seven grips from one coffin are CCS type 1, dating to 1747–1847 (ibid.). A single grip found on coffin [710] is identical to one found at St Paul's Church, Hammersmith (PQC7152; OA forthcoming) (Fig. 5.2). This decorated example has two winged cherub heads located centrally on a curved grip surrounded by flowers and foliage. It stylistically resembles CCS type 4, found on coffins dating from 1743–1847 (Reeve and Adams 1993). Another six grips from two coffins were too corroded to decipher the detail, but their overall shape is a simple straight bar with a right angle return attachment to the coffin (Fig. 5.3).

Grip plates composed of thin metal are highly prone to destruction. Fragments frequently adhere to the back of grips but often go unobserved, and when they are, details of any decoration are often impossible to determine. Fragments of grip plates were universally found on the back of grips from St Paul's Church, Hammersmith (OA forthcoming), and this was frequently the case at Park Street. Seventeen coffins had grip plates (7.6%), although in the case of two coffins they were not retained. A total of 27 grip plates were recovered from the remaining coffins, six being the maximum number associated with any single coffin. They were all either in poor condition or damaged beyond the possibility of identification to type.

Breastplates

Outer breastplates were one of up to four types of *depositum* plate attached to coffins, in addition to an inner breastplate, a headplate and a footplate. Outer breastplates were located on the coffin lid, usually over the neck, chest and abdomen of the deceased. Their function was both decorative and informative. The cheaper iron ones would have been painted black with details of the deceased's name, title, date and age of death painted in white or yellow on the central panel.

At Park Street, outer breastplates were observed in 16 cases (7.2%). All were made of a thin sheet of embossed iron, which had corroded and generally fragmented upon lifting. They were similar to examples excavated from earth-cut graves at St Hilda's Church, South Shields (Raynor *et al.* 2011), St Martin's-in-the-Bull Ring, Birmingham (Hancox 2006), Bonn Square, Oxford (Boston 2010), and St Paul's Church, Hammersmith (OA forthcoming), amongst others.

Most of the Park Street examples were too fragmented and corroded for identification, paint, or for even a general impression of shape to be recorded. Occasional fragments of black paint were observed and have been noted in the archive. In addition, decorative motifs such as floral designs, foliage, radiating crowns, urns, angels, borders of concentric shapes, and even a skull were recognisable in some

Fig. 5.2 Grip from coffin [710] (top) and PQC 7152 (middle and bottom) for comparison

Fig. 5.3 Grips from coffin [2128]

96 Living and Dying in Southwark 1587–1831

○ Fragments recovered from coffin 890
○ Fragments recovered from coffin 915

Fig. 5.4   Breastplate type CCS6 with fragments recovered from coffins [890] (blue) and [915] (red)

cases. The breastplate from coffin [602] was rectangular in shape, but no detail survived. Although both highly fragmented, the breastplates from [890] and [915] (Fig. 5.4) could be classified. Both had angels blowing trumpets towards an urn, as well as columns, and [890] also had a pedestal with a centrally located skull motif, which corresponds to CCS type 6 dating from 1783–1852. Complete examples are rectangular with a border of geometric designs and a second border of floral designs, and within this a datum plate. The datum plate is flanked by a column either side which stands upon a pedestal, one of which is decorated with a skull, the other with crossed bones. In front of each column is an angel on the pedestal holding a branch above it. Surmounting the columns and the datum plate is an architrave upon which sits an urn with spouting flames, and radiating beams of light behind it. Either side of the urn is an angel holding a branch and blowing a trumpet towards the urn. Beneath the urn and architrave are three winged cherub heads.

A breastplate resembling a CCS type 49 was observed on coffin [4030] (Fig. 5.5). It consisted of scrolling foliage borders around a roughly shield-shaped datum plate, but unlike CCS type 49 there were additional open floral designs at the four corners and another centrally located at the top.

A breastplate from coffin [604] (Fig. 5.6) could not be classified by type, but common decorative motifs were present. A sunburst on top of a wreath of stylised foliage surmounted the datum plate, and a bordered oval with a winged cherub head beneath were at the base of the datum plate.

Writing survived on seven of the 16 breastplates (43.8%). The details by context are presented below:

[602]   M….
           'Eliz[abeth]…
           Die[d]…. De[c]..

[604]   Miss
           ……Mille[r?]..
           Die[d] 9th F[eb]
           ..78..
           …9 yea[rs]

[2281]   ….llia…Pop…
           ….[5]3 Y[ears]

[4002]   …er….
           [D]ied
           …ye..2..D
           36
           [A]ge[d] … Wee[ks]

Fig. 5.5 Breastplate from coffin [4030]

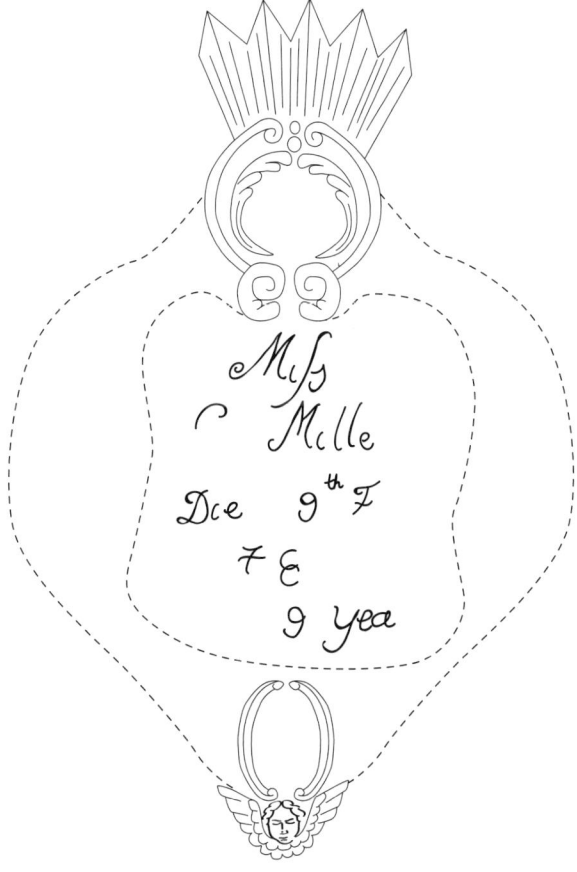

Fig. 5.6 Breastplate from coffin [604]. Dashed lines are extrapolated edges

[4028]   Fr...

[4030]   Wa ...
          ...ber 6...
          Ag[ed]...Months

[4082]   M[r/rs?]
          I......Du...

Lid motifs

A single lid motif was recovered from the excavations. It was located above the skull on coffin [638] but no recordable motifs survived, and it did not survive lifting.

Upholstery studs

Given the common use of studs on coffins during the 18th and 19th centuries (Janaway 1993), the association of upholstery studs with Park Street coffins was surprisingly rare. Studs usually formed continuous lines around the margins of coffins, and were used to form decorative panels on the lids and sides on which other fittings were also placed. The low numbers observed at Park Street may reflect the fact that most of the coffins were actually plain and unupholstered, but truncation may also have been a factor, and the studs would have been easy to overlook during fieldwork due to their small size. Their presence was recorded in only eight cases (8.1%), and they were recovered from only four contexts. A total of 17 iron studs were associated with four coffins, a maximum of eight on a single coffin. The recorded size is 13–15mm diameter, and where corrosion had not destroyed the detail in the case of three coffins, they were enamelled in black (Fig. 5.7). Preservation was not sufficient in any cases to allow identification of decorative patterns, but some notes on their position were recorded.

Three coffins had continuous lines of studs around the outline of the lid, six had a continuous line of studs, and on one coffin studs formed triangles of three studs a side.

Fixtures and fittings from non-coffin contexts

Four non-coffin contexts produced possible examples of coffin furniture. Fill [2061] of pit [2072] contained a deposit of disarticulated human bone and two coffin grips (Fig. 5.8) of PQC 7152 type (see above). Given that they were redeposited in the charnel pit with disarticulated human bone, and decorated with foliage and winged cherub heads, they clearly would have originally ornamented a coffin.

Fill [2006] of construction cut [2004] contained three iron nails and a coffin grip attached to a grip plate. Both grip and grip plate were in a poor condition and too corroded to identify to a type. Dump layer [3000] contained a single unidentifiable grip along with five upholstery studs, and soil layer [3001] contained 24 iron nails, a grip of CCS type 2a, and three ferrous objects with a heavy conglomeration of stones. In the absence of distinctive decoration, it was unclear whether these belonged to a number of disturbed coffins, or were redeposited survivals from domestic wooden furniture, which commonly featured grips and grip plates.

Discussion

The preservation of the coffins and coffin fittings was poor overall. Most of the recorded coffins were very

Fig. 5.7 Studs embedded in mineralised coffin wood, coffin [915]

Fig. 5.8 Grips from pit fill [2072] (of type PQC 7152, shown in Fig. 5.2)

plain, the surviving fittings often restricted to nails. Taking into account the levels of disturbance, the poor condition of the wood, and corrosion of iron fittings and fixtures in most burials, it is likely that the recorded number of coffins is under-represented. However, the number of coffin fittings may be low for the same reasons as fixing nails. Coffins of the 16th to 19th centuries were constructed with butt-joints held together with nails (Litten 1991, 90), and so the record of nails from only 67 of the 223 coffins must be a significant under-representation. Determination of the shape of most coffins was hampered by poor preservation and truncation, but only single-break coffins were identified. This was the preferred shape of the 18th and 19th centuries (Litten 1991).

Status
A fully decorated 18th- and 19th-century coffin was constructed of up to three layers of wood (or occasionally wood-metal-wood in the case of wealthier individuals), and between four and six decorative grips with grip plates. A breastplate with details of the individual, along with lid motifs and escutcheons, all decorated with funerary symbols, would be present on the lid. The coffin would have typically been upholstered in fabric, most often baize or velvet, held in place with upholstery studs. Upholstery studs, in common with other coffin fittings, were once purely functional, but became highly decorative during this period, forming elaborate patterns on the sides and lid of the coffin (Litten 1991).

The coffins from Park Street were not of this elaborate middle- to upper-class style, as seen at St George's, Bloomsbury, for example (Boston *et al.* 2009). They were of a simpler, lower-class tradition of more functional coffins, and decoration was the exception. Whilst corrosion and truncation would have reduced the number of surviving fittings, this cannot fully account for the plain and unadorned condition of most of the Park Street coffins.

Inscriptions
Of the seven breastplates with legible inscriptions, none was complete. Although the legible inscriptions consisted mostly of fragments of words, all but [4028] was able to yield some biographical details. The high central location of the 'M' observed on [4082], which the excavator thought likely to be Mr or Mrs, is of limited use except to confirm that skeleton [4081] was an adult. On the breastplate from coffin [602] the partial name 'Eliz' probably continued as Elizabeth, which confirms that skeleton [601], an incomplete middle or mature adult of >36 years, but of indeterminate sex, was female.

Adolescent or young adult (17–18 years) skeleton [603], recorded as possible female (??F), was confirmed as a young adult female of 19 years by the biographical details on a breastplate from coffin [604]. She was unmarried and had a surname beginning with Mille, possibly Miller. The date of her death appears to have been on either the 9th, 19th or 29th of February, although the year could not be confirmed. Given that the cemetery was used between 1587 and mid 1800s, the possible years are 1678, 1778 and any year in the 1780s. As biographical details tended to be outlined in studs rather than on a datum plate prior to the 18th century in all but the richest burials (Litten 1991), it is likely that this individual died either in 1778 or the 1780s.

The breastplate from [2281] had both a partial first and surname, which is likely to have been William Pope. Whilst no date of death survived on the datum plate, a partial age with a '3' at the end did. It was recorded as most likely to be 53 years, although the '5' was too incomplete to confirm this. Records of a William Pope who died in April 1816 in Southwark (see text box) are likely to have been referring to this individual. Skeleton [2280] was of a mature adult male of between 44 and 55 years, corresponding well to the age 53 recorded.

The biographic details from the datum plate of [4002] show a partial name 'er', but it is not clear whether this forms part of a first name or surname. The '36' is most likely to be part of the year of death. The estimated age of individual [4001] of 38 weeks in utero to 1.5 months (neonate) fits with the partial age at death on the datum plate. Whilst no number was observed for the age, the fact that it referred to the age in weeks rather than months or years confirms that the individual was very young.

Skeleton [4029] was estimated to be between 1 and 12 months of age (infant) at death, which correlates to the use of 'months' on the datum plate from [4030], although the use of 'months' rather than 'month' shows that the infant was probably between 2 and 11 months. The first name began 'Wa' but no other letters survive. However, it is clear from the 'ber 6' that the individual must have died in the latter part of the year, between September and December and on the 6th day of that month.

Symbolism
Breastplates, as well as grips, grip plates and other coffin fittings were often deeply imbued with Christian, classical and secular symbolism. The ancient Greek symbol of mourning, the urn, was a very popular motif until the 1850s, and cherubim were popular on coffins of infants and children (Boston *et al.* 2009). All of the motifs had at least one meaning, some obvious, such as

> ### William Pope 1763–1816
> *by Kirsty Smith*
>
> Burial records were searched for William Pope (www.findmypast.co.uk) and the following record represents the most likely match. The probability of the match is increased by the age of death at 53 years which is consistent with the coffin plate and the sex and age of the skeleton. The burial registers do not offer details of the relevant burial ground, only the address of the individual.
>
> | | |
> |---|---|
> | First name(s) | William |
> | Last name | Pope |
> | Age at death | 53 |
> | Birth year | 1763 |
> | Burial year | 1816 |
> | Burial date | 02 Feb 1816 |
> | Address | Church Yard |
> | Parish | Southwark, St Saviour |
> | City | London |
> | County | Surrey |
> | Source | City of London Burials 1754-1855 |
>
> William Pope's will and probate record provide more details. His probate record states that he was a labourer and had 5% Navy annuities. Navy annuities were shares that were sold between 1810 and 1821 as a way of funding the British Navy. They were paid back at 5% interest and so became a popular form of investment for ordinary people (www.immediateannuities.com/annuitymuseum/annuitycertificatesofthebankofengland/). The probate record is ambiguous as there are two sums of money recorded: £156.11 and £143.11.3. Nonetheless, it is notable that Pope had over £100 to invest in this 5% scheme which suggests that he was not a pauper, but a relatively wealthy labourer.
>
> Pope was buried on 2 February 1816, his will (National Archives prob 11/1579) was read on 26 April 1816, and his probate record is dated 30 April 1816. The probate record refers to his will. In this record he names James Potter as his sole executor, and his son Richard Pope the beneficiary. There is no mention of a wife in either record. The only family member mentioned is Richard, and the fact that he was not made an executor could suggest that he was a minor at the time that the will was made. James Potter is mentioned in the will as living in Park Street.
>
> *I approvist James Potter sole exactor. And as to the sum of one hundred pounds Navy five per cent Bank annuities belonging to me at the bank of England and all other the residue of my Estate and Effects whatsoever and whomsoever I give the same .. the said James Potter his executors and administrators in trust to be applied and disposed of for the benefit of Richard Pope my natural Son at such time on times and in such manner as he the said James Potter his executors or Administrators shall think proper.*
>
> *£100 Navy 5 per cent to be transferred to James Potter the devise in trust and the sole executor & left at his disposal*
>
> Pope's will and probate record both show that he lived in Soap Yard, Park Street. However, this is at odds with his burial record, which cites Church Yard, a street just south of St Saviour's Church. This discrepancy could be explained if he lived for most of his life in one address and moved to the other at the end of his life. Soap Yard was located next to Cure's College and also had almshouses. This close association can be seen on Howe's plan of the College dated 1844 (Fig. 2.10). Pope was perhaps moved into the almshouse shortly before he died, with the burial register recording his old address.

skulls and cross bones representing death, other less so and variable, such as a flaming torch which symbolises both life and death, depending on whether it is upright or inverted (May 2003).

Although in low numbers, decorative coffin fittings were present in the Park Street assemblage. Most designs were observed on breastplate fragments, but decorative symbols were recorded on a number of coffin grips. The designs included flowers, foliage, radiating crowns, urns, angels, borders of concentric shapes and even a skull. Whilst the majority of foliage and floral designs were stylised, and so unidentifiable as particular species, the one surmounting the datum plate of [4030] (Fig. 5.5) is likely to have been a daisy. Daisies represented childhood innocence, youth, and Jesus the infant, highly appropriate as skeleton [4029] was an infant. Poppies were present on the decorative grips found on coffin [710] and in pit fill [2072] (Figs 5.2 and 5.8). They symbolised peace, sleep and consolation (Boston *et al.* 2009, 163) whilst the accompanying winged cherub heads represented the departed soul (May 2003).

A winged cherub head was present on the base of the breastplate from [604] (Fig. 5.6), and would have also been present on the breastplates from [890] and [915] (Fig. 5.4) had they been complete. All three breastplates included a sunburst surmounting the datum plate, symbolising renewed life after death (May 2003). The breastplates from [890] and [915] were further imbued with symbolism – the urn and the flames representing mourning and eternal life respectively, and death represented by the skull and crossed bones (ibid.).

The angels standing on the pedestals are obvious symbols of heaven, whilst the palm fronds that they carry symbolise spiritual victory over evil and Jesus' victory over death (Boston *et al.* 2009, 163). God's glory over death and the Day of Judgement are represented by the pair of angels blowing the trumpets (May 2003).

Chapter 6

Discussion: social history, funerary practice and skeletal studies

by Louise Loe and Kirsty Smith

Summary of the main findings

Although earlier burial activity is known at the site, map regression suggests that the assemblage relates to the burial ground of Cure's College, established in 1587, within the parish of St Saviour. The burial ground was in use until the 1850s, possibly as late as 1862 (see Chapter 3 and below), but the present assemblage probably dates to up to 1831, before the burial ground was re-ordered and reduced in size.

The extent of Cure's burial ground pre-1831 was approximately 1300m², suggesting that the Park Street excavations, which covered 448m², accounted for approximately 34% of this area. This sample is larger than elsewhere from London, for example New Bunhill Fields, Southwark and North-East London Cemetery at Cambridge Heath, Bethnal Green, where c 10% of these burial grounds have been excavated (Miles and Connell 2012, xi; Powers 2015, 49).

The burials were broadly aligned east–west and were plain earth cut graves which contained single or multiple interments. Some graves were evenly spaced, but the majority were heavily intercutting. In fact, considering the number of excavated burials and the area excavated, it has been estimated that the density of burial activity at Cure's ranged from a minimum of 12 to a maximum of 43 bodies every metre square. This would suggest that between 16,000 and 56,000 burials were made at Cure's, considering that the extent of the burial ground at the time of the Park Street burials was c 1300m². This number far exceeds estimates of 7950 bodies made by surveyors during the 1860s, prior to the development of the burial ground by the railway, but their survey relates to the burial ground post-1831 after it had been re-ordered and made significantly smaller (760m²).

Finds associated with the burials were extremely few, consisting of a few dress items and coffin remains, and this has precluded attempts to assign precise phasing. At least 39 burials pre-date 1799 and seven date to 1816 or later, but most of the assemblage could not be assigned to either of these phases. One burial, possibly early in the sequence was a mass grave which contained a total of 36 individuals.

The burials involved a total of 331 individuals of all ages, the youngest having died at around the time of birth, and the oldest was at least 45 years. There were 104 males and 73 females, giving a male to female ratio of 1.42:1. The physical attributes of the assemblage and skeletal pathology were considered in the context of a number of broadly contemporary burial grounds from elsewhere in London and the country. Estimated statures ranked them among the lowest, and there was one individual with mixed cranio-facial traits, although this need not mean they were non-local or, in fact, non-Caucasoid. There was some evidence for infection and nutritional deficiency, as well as generalised health stress and stunted growth. Evidence for trauma included healed fractures, dislocations and lesions associated with torn ligaments. Incremental isotope analysis, performed on a sample of the adults, explored dietary life histories in childhood and maternal (or carer) nutritional status. A relatively new method, this work has afforded a much more detailed consideration of dietary practices in post-medieval London than other similar studies. In particular, because the method analyses adult teeth for markers established in childhood, it has provided the opportunity to consider childhood health in an assemblage otherwise limited by low numbers of child skeletons.

Archaeological context

Park Street is one of a growing number of London burial grounds to have been archaeologically excavated and analysed since the late 1980s. Most of these relate to sites that lie to the north of the Thames, and which have tended to focus on the 18th- and 19th-century middle to upper classes, and on burial assemblages from church crypts and vaults (eg Christ Church, Spitalfields; St George's, Bloomsbury; St Bride's). Consequently, publications on sizeable working class burial grounds from Greater London, covering the 16th and 17th centuries, have been less common, although this picture is changing (eg Miles and Connell 2012; Ives *et al.* forthcoming).

According to a recent audit of sizeable, key historical burial grounds excavated in Greater London, five such sites in addition to Cure's are from the borough of Southwark (Powers 2015; see Table 6.1). These refer to a variety of time frames (most dating to the mid-19th century) and types, including Christian (churchyards and pauper burial grounds), hospital, and private non-conformist burial grounds. They also cover a spectrum of different sectors of society, from wealthy vault burials at St Mary's Newington to pauper burials at Cross Bones. These have undergone varying levels of excavation and analysis (Table 6.1).

At New Bunhill Fields, in addition to almost 800 skeletons, a wealth of funerary remains was recovered, including very well preserved coffins, coffin furniture (including types not previously found), floral tributes, personal items (including plates), textiles and burial clothing (Miles and Connell 2012). The analysed skeletal assemblage comprised 157 adults and an especially large number of sub-adults (357), the latter reflective of the excavation strategy, which sampled approximately 10% of the burial ground and primarily impacted on the uppermost burials (Powers 2015). Part of the burial ground believed to be associated with St Thomas' Hospital excavated in 1990 exposed mass graves which contained 227 skeletons, of which 193 were fully analysed (Bekvalac, 2007; Jones 1990; see Chapter 4 and below).

The only archaeological investigation of crypts in the borough have been at St Mary's, Newington where 316 churchyard burials were also excavated. This latter group is currently undergoing full osteological analysis (Langthorne 2014). Burials excavated at St George the Martyr are believed to be associated with the pre-1734 church.

Cross Bones burial ground, originally established as a single women's (prostitutes') cemetery, served the poor from St Saviour's parish. The excavated assemblage probably spans 10–30 years of the mid-19th century and is believed to include *c* 18% of individuals from the workhouse. It is especially relevant here because of its situation within the same parish as Cure's College.

Finally, although not large, the assemblage excavated at St Saviour's Church, now Southwark Cathedral, is relevant because it is from the same parish as Cure's and Cross Bones. Here, comprehensive archaeological investigation of the burials, in particular the human osteology, was precluded by the nature of the fieldwork, which comprised keyhole excavation in small focussed areas where flood lights were being installed, along with other small works (Divers *et al.* 2009, 88). Seventy-seven burials were recorded in the southern graveyard, of which 58 were present as skeletal remains, seven as coffins, and 12 as brick-built tombs (ibid.). These were associated with a quantity of coffin furniture, comprising grips, breastplates, coffin nails and upholstery studs from the churchyard soils. To the north of the church, three shaft graves containing 24 stacked coffined burials, believed to date to between 1832 and 1853, were investigated. Skeletal remains from the Southern churchyard were too incomplete for osteological examination but the skeletons from the stacks were examined (Dodwell 2002).

Appearance, organisation and management

Much evidence of the original layout of Cure's burial ground has been lost as a result of its re-ordering in 1831 and clearance in the 1860s. Three paintings by Thomas Hosmer Shepherd from the British Museum's collection provide some perspective (Figs 6.1–6.3). These date to between 1851 and 1852, post-dating the rebuilding of the college in 1831 and evidently after the reordering of earlier burial ground to which the present burials date (Chapter 2). Although not directly relating to the excavated material, they provide some useful observations and are interesting to compare with the excavation record.

Table 6.1: Summary of sizeable, key historic burial grounds excavated from the Borough of Southwark

Site Name	Reference	Location
New Bunhill Fields	Miles and Connell 2012	New Bunhill Fields, Deverell Street, Southwark
St Thomas' Hospital	Jones 1990	North of St Thomas' Street
Cross Bones burial ground	Brickley *et al.* 1999	Redcross Way, St Saviour's parish
St George the Martyr	Powers 2006	East side Borough High Street
St Mary's	Haslam 2014	Newington, Southwark/Elephant and Castle Leisure Centre

Discussion

Fig. 6.1 Cure's College Almshouses and burial ground facing north-west, 1851 (© British Museum)

Shepherd's 1851 paintings (Figs 6.1 and 6.2) depict north-west and north facing views of the almshouses, and his 1852 painting (Fig. 6.3) depicts south-east facing views, with the burial ground in the foreground in a central area surrounded by railings. In these images, burials are organised in rows marked by a variety of headstones, and several are mounded, suggesting the ground had not yet settled following interments made a relatively short time before the paintings were created. Further, in the 1852 painting other burials may have been relatively new because the mounds are not covered by grass. A sparsity of monuments is shown in the foreground (to the north) of the 1852 painting.

There are at least two hard surface footpaths depicted in the burial ground images, including one running north–south and aligned off centre, and another running perpendicular to this in a westwards direction. A third path is illustrated in the south-east facing painting (Fig. 6.3), but appears to be a less permanent, possibly less formal trackway. Some degree of organisation was observed in the excavated assemblage, with the earliest and latest burials found to be well spaced and in rows (Chapter 3). Otherwise, the majority of burials were heavily intercutting, and no spaces or gaps that might be interpreted as paths were encountered. Presumably, the sheer quantity of burials used all available space, and this is consistent with the

Date of excavated assemblage	Type	Numbers excavated/analysed
c 1821–1853	Private burial ground. Largely Non-conformist	827 coffins and 796 skeletons recorded at excavation 766 skeletons assessed, 514 skeletons fully analysed
17th century	Hospital burial ground	227 skeletons excavated, 193 analysed
Mid-19th century	Pauper's burial ground	148 skeletons fully analysed
Associated with the pre-1734 church	Churchyard	163 skeletons assessed but not fully analysed
Mid-19th century to 1854	Large vault containing 25 crypts and churchyard burials	316 inhumation burials from churchyard assessed. Full analysis underway

Fig. 6.2 Cure's College Almshouses and burial ground facing north, 1851 (© British Museum)

overcrowded situation of burial grounds of this date (see below).

Heavy intercutting and limited dating information have obscured further details of how Cure's burial ground might have been organised and managed. For example, the coffin plates detailing dates of death and the limited intercutting of graves observed at St Mary and St Michael's, Tower Hamlets suggested that the graveyard had been filled from east to west and that there had been reasonable record keeping (Henderson *et al.* 2013, 29). At Bow Baptist Church, Tower Hamlets the practice of reserving zones for certain individuals, in this case infants, was identified (Henderson *et al.* 2013, 41), although this is probably a feature of non-Conformist burials.

The positions of the headstones in the paintings suggest burials were orientated with the head end at the north-west and the foot end to the south-east, typical of Christian burials, and in keeping with the majority of the excavated assemblage (Chapter 3). There was no deviation to this except in the case of one headstone, depicted in one of the 1851 paintings (Fig. 6.2), which appears to observe a different orientation. It is possible that it could be marking a burial on the very edge of the burial ground, made on an alternative alignment to the others because of limited space. Burials occupying alternative alignments on the edge of burial grounds are not uncommon in cemeteries of this date, where there was a need to maximise space. This has been observed elsewhere in the archaeological record, for example at New Bunhill Fields (Miles and Connell 2012) and St Benet Sherehog (Miles and White 2008). A few of the excavated Park Street burials occupied alternative alignments, possibly due to the same activity and/or an earlier burial phase which respected a different layout and the position of buildings.

The paintings show that most of the burials were plain graves with a single headstone and, in a few cases, footstones. Large headstones seem to be marking group burials, while smaller ones may have marked single burials, most likely of children. There is at least one brick shaft grave depicted in the north-west-facing painting (Fig. 6.1), and there were probably more, considering the recumbent slabs shown in the foreground.

Other 19th-century paintings and drawings of Cure's College burial ground reside in the London Metropolitan Archives, among them a watercolour of

Fig. 6.3 Cure's College Almshouses and burial ground facing south-east towards the chapel, 1852 (© British Museum)

1808 by George Smith (see front cover), probably of Cure's, and an undated painting, probably pre-1831, by an unknown artist (Brickley *et al.* 1999, fig. 7). Like Shepherd's paintings, these also show recently dug graves and headstones and footstones. Workers/grave diggers are depicted excavating the ground, possibly to make a new grave or erect a headstone. The burials include earth cut and brick shaft graves, and no paths are depicted. These paintings do not give the impression of a crowded burial ground.

No evidence for headstones, footstones or burial structures was found during the Park Street excavation. During the early part of the burial ground's use, graves may not have had markers, as was typical at this time (Gittings 1999). Over time, however, monuments, inscriptions and gravestones to the dead became increasingly common as commemoration of the individual grew in popularity.

Twenty-one grave cuts contained multiple burials or stacks, a common feature of contemporary London burial grounds which probably represent grave cuts that were left open for burials made over a relatively short space of time, and then dug over once full (Miles and Connell 2012, 22). At the nearby New Bunhill Fields burial ground, good preservation of coffin plates, giving the date of death of the deceased to the day, allowed Miles and Connell (2012, 22–5) to conclude that most multiple stacks were kept open and filled after no more than a week. Similarly, at St Mary Newington churchyard, Southwark, two stacked burials were interpreted to have been made at or around the same time (Haslam 2014, 69). Unfortunately, no such conclusions can be made for Cure's ground due to a lack of dating evidence. For example, very few breastplates survived to provide dates and, typical of any intensively used cemetery, the homogenous soil matrix precluded detailed observation of grave cuts that might suggest whether they had been reopened. Therefore, it remains unclear whether stacked burials were made over relatively short spaces of time, as at Bunhill and St Mary, or whether they were reopened after some time had elapsed.

Whether any of the stacked burials contained members of the same family is unknown because of the absence of name-plates. The skeletons from these graves were investigated for shared non-metrical traits and certain pathologies (see Chapter 4), which have a tendency to run in families. However, no compelling trends were found, and this type of data is not sufficiently robust to identify families alone, which requires analysis of DNA for genetic relationships. A similar investigation undertaken on the Cross

Bones assemblage also did not identify any useful patterns (Brickley *et al.* 1999, 33). On the basis of evidence from excavated assemblages from nearby sites (eg Bunhill Fields), and considering the pressure on burial space (see below), the burial of families within the same grave could perhaps be regarded as uncommon.

A maximum of nine individuals was found within one grave at Park Street, which seems to broadly correspond to burials elsewhere, such as New Bunhill Fields (14 burials; Miles and Connell 2012, 22), St Mary's (seven burials; Haslam 2014, 77), and the north side of St Saviour's Church (24 stacked burials in three graves; Divers *et al.* 2009, 91). This perhaps reflects the maximum depth to which graves could be safely dug manually. At these and other contemporary assemblages (eg Cross Bones), infants, when present, tended to be at the tops of burial stacks, probably as attempts by undertakers to make efficient use of space, possibly for a smaller fee or no fee (Miles and Connell 2012, 26). This trend is not apparent at Park Street, where multiple burials contained very few infants and young children (see Table 3.2, Chapter 3). This is in stark contrast to New Bunhill Fields where the uppermost burials were infants or children (0–5 years) in 66.2% of the graves (Miles and Connell 2012, 26). It is possible that any infant or child burials made in the tops of graves at Park Street were lost to truncation during post-burial activity.

In the first half of the 19th century, when the population of London had more than doubled since the 18th century, burial grounds were severely overcrowded, grave diggers were forced to abandon traditional methods of churchyard management, and had to resort to desperate measures (Cherryson *et al.* 2012). This situation resulted in the passing of the 1852 Burial Act and, in reflecting health concerns, especially about cholera, contributed to the introduction of public health measures, such as those of 1848 (Public Health Act), 1853 (compulsory smallpox vaccination), and 1854 (improvements in hospital hygiene). The possibility that alternative alignments were adopted in order to fit interments at Cure's has already been mentioned as one such management method (see above), but a far more desperate picture is painted in historical sources. For example, vestry minutes record the state of burial grounds in St Saviour's parish as 'repulsive' 'surcharged with dead' and presenting a 'formidable' array (Brickley *et al.* 1999, 11) because of their over-crowded state. Graves were frequently disturbed, resulting in the exposure of corpses and, at Cross Bones, a committee set up to improve the burial ground commented in 1831 on the lack of space as a 'consequence of the irregular manner of burial heretofore' (cited in Brickley *et al.* 1999, 9). Vestry minutes from 10 July 1823 are perhaps of most interest here because direct reference is made to Cure's on the subject of burial ground management, regarding the use of head- foot- or ledger stones, which were to be prohibited in order to economise on space (Brickley *et al.* 1999, 10). It is possible that there had never been head- or foot-stones in association with the excavated assemblage (see above).

Funerary practice at Cure's College

The archaeological record provides some evidence of the contemporary funerary practices. All of the burials were conventional Christian interments. They were supine, extended, and generally unremarkable in terms of how they had been placed in the ground. Evidence of coffins survived in some cases in the form of wood and fittings, but there were no associated textiles or grave goods. Overall, general impressions gained from analysing the funerary record are that it seems to reflect the doctrines and traditions that existed at the time, and of a burial ground that was used primarily by the working classes, of some financial means, but by some poorer individuals as well (see Chapters 3 and 5).

Funerals

Around the time that Cure's was established fundamental changes were taking place in funeral practice, set against a context of considerable change in religion, politics and society, as a result of the Reformation. The concept of purgatory, which had been widespread since the 12th century, was rejected, profoundly altering the relationship between the living and the dead (Cherryson *et al.* 2012). Religious services became shorter and there was less praying for the dead, less sacramental activity and less commemorative ritual (Gittings 1999). Despite this, the belief that the living could have an effect on the dead persisted in traditional customs for many centuries. For example, wakes and keeping vigil over the corpse prior to burial continued well into the 17th century (Cherryson *et al.* 2012).

A number of beliefs and rituals associated with the dead were rooted in folklore and placed great emphasis on the metaphysical attributes of the corpse (Richardson 2000, 15). Fear of revenants and ghosts was common (Cherryson *et al.* 2012) and is reflected in the emphasis placed on a good death (*Ars moriendi*). A good death required being at peace with God and fellow men, to have made speeches prior to death to show readiness for what lay ahead, and to be conscious of death. As a result, dying from sudden or painful illnesses and dying whilst asleep were greatly feared. The significance attached to such deaths and ideas surrounding preparations for death changed over time; by the 18th century, for example, a sudden death was considered a positive outcome for a 'well prepared Christian' (Houlbrooke 1999, 184). That aside, it was the concept of a good death that had a significant impact on funerals. A bad death could be counteracted by a good funeral, and this was epitomised by the heraldic funerals of the wealthy, which were highly elaborate affairs with processions of black-draped hearses, black-plumed horses, mutes and chief mourners (see Houlbrooke 1999 and Litten 1991).

The human corpse was believed to hold sentience and spiritual power, and it was believed that respect for the dead would assure comfort and repose of the souls of the mourners (Richardson 2000). Thus, providing a decent burial was significant, and not disturbing the dead and belief in the sanctity of the grave gained great emphasis (Richardson 2000). By the end of period during which Cure's burial ground was in use, great importance was placed on providing a decent funeral, even among the less wealthy, who put themselves into financial hardship as a result (Friar 2003; May 2003). Funerals became more focussed on the individual and their family and were less often community affairs, as had earlier been the case.

The importance of the sanctity of the grave was keenly felt in towns and cities during the 18th and 19th centuries when over-crowding in burial grounds was common, causing the disturbance of recent burials and unsightly piles of corpses (see above), and opportunities for the 'resurrectionists' (body snatchers) who exhumed corpses to supply anatomists (Richardson 2000). The wealthy buried their dead in double or triple wooden and lead coffins (see below) under the church in vaults and in brick shafts, or in mausolea, and burial thereby became more 'sanitised' (Rugg 1999, 227).

Another theme was grief, or lavish mourning, which continued into the 19th century. The Bills of Mortality of 1665 list 45 people who died of grief, and dying of 'a broken heart' is also a common entry in the 19th century (Roberts and Cox 2003). However, while grief was expected, obsessive mourning was considered indecent by the Church (Houlbrooke 1999).

The burial of the dead was largely the responsibility of the parish, managed by the vestry and churchwardens who determined and collected burial fees and made provision for space (Harding 1993). A typical funeral for less wealthy individuals, like those from Cure's, during the 17th century is described by Gittings (1999, 156). Key elements were the tolling of a bell as the individual lay dying, coffin bearers, who were usually friends and/or family (there were no undertakers as such until slightly later – see below),

and a ceremony performed by a minister. Various elements could be added for a fee, for example, sermons could be preached and different grades of palls could be hired to cover the coffin (ibid.). Sermons became central to funerals from the late 17th and early 18th centuries, but most likely were not delivered at funerals of the poor because a fee was usually required (Houlbrooke 1999).

Thus, funerals covered a spectrum of ritual and display that was dependant on wealth and religious belief (some non-conformists, eg Quakers, rejected, doctrinally at least, opulence and ostentation in funerals), and this is a trend which continued into the 18th and 19th centuries. Cure's seems to have been no exception to this because a variety of choices and different grades of funeral are reflected in the parish fee books (1782–91). Entries relating to Cure's suggest that a minister, register, clerk, sexton, grave-making, bearers and bell-ringing, were common extras that were paid for. Three types of bell could be rung, the size reflected in the cost; the small bell (1 shilling 8d), the lady bell (4 shillings 4d) and the great bell (6 shillings 19d). Apparently, basic funerals were primarily afforded to the pensioners of Cure's College, their fees perhaps having been paid for by the parish. However, the cheapest funerals held at the college appear to have cost six shillings, and were afforded to infants dying below the age of one year.

The most expensive funerals at Cure's, which seem to have been for adults over approximately 30 years, cost over one pound and included a church service, referred to as a desk service. A desk service was almost certainly a funeral service conducted inside a nearby church or chapel. Examples of this practice at Cure's include the funeral of William Cheale, who was buried in January 1783 with a desk service which cost 10 shillings, in addition to the cost of the funeral at £1, 05 shillings and 2 pence (P92-SAV-3093). It is likely that most people in the parish could not afford this, although it was comparably cheaper than St Saviour's Church which, in 1782, charged over £5 for a funeral, including 11 shillings for a desk service (P92-SAV-3093). It is not clear where desk services for Cure's were conducted, but they were possibly held at St Saviour's Church or, more likely, in the chapel, depicted in Gwilt's 1821 survey of the College (Chapter 2, Fig. 2.9), and in two images of the exterior and interior of the college chapel (Fig. 6.4 and 6.5 respectively).

From the late 17th century the formalisation of funerals and elite funerals had become an important trend, particularly under the influence of the College of Arms and the establishment of undertaking firms in the 18th century, prior to which it was necessary to employ different people for each aspect of the coffin construction and funeral itself. The latter, in particular,

Fig. 6.4 Cure's College Almshouses showing the chapel on the left, prior to the rebuild of 1831 (© London Metropolitan Archives)

meant that funerals began to be mass-produced. Investment in coffins and funerals was perceived as one of the most important ways of reflecting a person's respectability and position in society (Richmond 1999). This not only concerned the funeral and the coffin but, especially for the wealthy, the presentation of the deceased, who were clothed in elaborate garments and their coffins lined with mattresses and pillows (eg see Molleson and Cox 1993). Unfortunately, there was no evidence from Park Street for clothing of the deceased, but a few upholstery studs suggest that some coffins were covered with fabric (see Chapter 5; see Reeve and Adams 1993).

Paupers were afforded funerals paid for by the parish, but there was an increasing stigma attached to poor relief, and deliberate measures were put in place to make pauper funerals degrading. For example, cheap, inferior coffins were deliberately ordered for paupers by the poor-law unions, and even palls marked 'pauper' had to be used in some cases (Rugg 1999, 224). However, even more degrading was the passing of the 1832 Anatomy Act, which permitted the dissection of unclaimed paupers from workhouses and hospitals. Dissection was greatly feared at this time because of the belief in resurrection which required the body to be intact on the Day of Judgement (Richardson 2000). Dying on the parish was therefore greatly dreaded.

By the late 18th and early 19th centuries, when the later burials of the Park Street assemblage were taking place at Cure's, attitudes towards death had become increasingly secularised as a result of Enlightenment theory, medical advances, and neoclassical aesthestics (Rugg 1999, 209). Physicians treated the sick in their homes (at least those who could afford it) and their attendance at death-beds became increasingly more important than that of the minister. Another factor was the need to address problems of over-crowding in cemeteries, which took the focus away from church building and churchyard burial, and was to later lead to the development of large extra-mural cemeteries (Cherryson *et al.* 2012).

Coffins and coffin furniture

Many of the Park Street burials lacked any evidence for a coffin. There are several reasons why this might have been the case, including one or more of the following: preservational bias, burial tradition and economic status. Firstly, evidence for coffins may simply not

Fig. 6.5 Interior view of the chapel of Cure's College Almshouses showing benches, the pulpit and a painting hanging on the wall, 1825 (© London Metropolitan Archives)

have survived, and especially if they had been very basic without metal fittings, the wood might simply have completely decayed. This is certainly a possibility in some cases, considering that where coffin remains survived preservation was usually extremely poor, often limited to traces or 'shadows' of wood, and/or a few coffin nails and fittings. However, some coffin remains did survive, suggesting that where groups of burials were found to be consistently with or without associated coffin remains, preservational bias was not always a factor. Another explanation is that some of the burials lacking coffins were of the poorest members of the community, who had not been able to afford them. In some parishes a communal coffin was used to carry the dead to their grave, the body then removed and buried in a shroud directly in the ground (Houlbrooke 1999).

It is also possible that some of the burials without evidence of coffins were among the earliest to be made at Cure's (*c* 16th century), at a time when coffined burial was uncommon. Individuals were instead wrapped in a winding sheet, tied at the head and feet, and placed in the ground. This possibility cannot be ruled out, considering the limited dating evidence for the burials. During the medieval period burial within a coffin was a minority rite but became universal in the 17th century (Litten 1991), possibly earlier in London (Cherryson *et al.* 2012, 46). It is not clear why coffin burials became common at this time, but some possible reasons include the enhanced personal significance of the corpse, the unpleasant sight of victims of the Great Plague of London, the increasing affordability of coffins, and the greater emphasis placed on bodily privacy during the early modern period (see Cherryson *et al.* 2012, 46–7).

Information obtained from the coffin remains and coffin furniture from Park Street seems to reflect late, 18th- to 19th-century burial activity, the fittings in particular being consistent with styles used at this time (see Chapter 5). During this period, coffins were constructed in a variety of shapes, most commonly single break (ie tapered at the shoulders; popular from the late 17th century), out of wood, lead, or both if they comprised double or triple shells. The evidence from Park Street suggests that only single-shell wooden coffins were used, and that they were single break. This is keeping with the hierarchy of burial location during the 18th and 19th centuries, summarised by Miles (2011, 166):

1. Private vault within the parish church (lead coffins)
2. Public vault within the parish church (lead coffins some wooden ones)
3. Private vault in the parish churchyard (lead coffins and some wooden ones)
4. Parish churchyard (wooden coffins and some lead ones)
5. Parish extramural ground (wooden coffins)

The extent to which all burials at Park Street were made in single break wooden coffins could not be determined. However, there are examples in the archaeological record of burials of institutions using standardised containers to the extent that some individuals appear to have been squashed in (Cherryson *et al.* 2012).

There was no evidence from the Park Street burials for the type of wood used for the coffins, but considering the working class status of the individuals buried there, most were probably of elm or even cheaper alternatives, such as soft wood timbers (spruce, larch and pine), collectively referred to as deal. Elm (*Ulmus* sp.) is considered to have been the traditional wood that was used during the 18th and 19th centuries, with walnut and oak used as more expensive alternatives (Litten 1991, 90; Miles 2011, 176). The commonly used single break shape coffins were usually constructed of six pieces of wood, which were nailed or sometimes screwed together (Miles 2011, 176). The internal base of the coffin was sometimes sealed with resin or pitch and covered in sawdust or bran and aromatic herbs (rosemary or balm) to absorb body fluids and reduce the malodourous by-products of decay (ibid.).

Good examples of coffins that survive from other burial grounds in the borough provide a perspective on the limited evidence from Park Street. The remarkably well-preserved coffins used by working class individuals at New Bunhill Fields were made of elm and constructed from the standard six pieces of wood described above. Some of them had six kerf lines from a saw on the insides of the sides, which were created to help bend the wood into place. At Cross Bones, most of the coffins typically associated with paupers were crudely constructed of deal. At the other end of the spectrum were more expensive double or triple shell lead and iron coffins, found in locations reserved for the wealthy in the southern graveyard of St Saviour's Church (Divers *et al.* 2009).

Forty-one of the 223 coffins from Park Street (18.4%) were enhanced with either name plates, grips, grip plates, lid motifs and/or upholstery studs. This number is considerably lower than St Saviour's (42%), and slightly lower than Cross Bones (23.4%). Proportions of decorated coffins from different burial grounds may be relative to the socio-economic status of those buried there, the higher proportion at St Saviour's compared with Cross Bones, reflective of the wealthier classes using the burial ground (Divers *et al.* 2009). However, for Park Street, preservation is a key factor because with few exceptions the furniture was highly fragmentary and heavily corroded, much of it beyond identification. It is therefore very likely that many fittings did not survive.

Decorating the outer surface of coffins to convey the status of the deceased became increasingly important during the 17th century. The practice was not confined to the wealthy, but was also common among the lower working classes. As discussed above, many less affluent families put themselves into financial hardship to provide a decent burial (Friar 2003; May 2003), of which coffin decoration was a key element. Several breastplates, inscribed with biographical information (mostly illegible), found at Park Street reflect the importance at this time attached to identifying the deceased. Name plates seem to have become common during the 17th century, for practical reasons, but also perhaps because of an increasing focus on commemoration, and because it was linked to continuing strong personal identities beyond death, among other reasons (see Cherryson *et al.* 2012, 59–60).

Who was buried at Cure's College burial ground?

The Cure's burial ground was not exclusive to residents of the almshouse, but was used by a good proportion from St Saviour's parish as well as individuals from other London parishes, especially South London. According to fees books dating between 1782 and 1797 for example (Chapter 2), only 10% of those buried were college inmates. Nor were all of those interred there necessarily local to the area; migration to London from the rest of Britain, especially the Home Counties, and continental Europe was especially high between the 17th and 19th centuries (Chapter 4).

European and Irish migrants have been identified in a growing number of 18th- and 19th-century assemblages from London, including St Pancras, Sheen's burial ground, Christ Church Spitalfields, Lukin Street and East Smithfield (see Chapter 4). In the Park Street assemblage, no direct evidence (eg a name on a breastplate) for migrants was found, but osteological analysis highlighted a high number of 18–35 year olds, which could reflect higher numbers of that age group migrating into the population. There were more male than female 18–35 year olds, and it is interesting to note that, according to Boulton (2005, 135), there were much higher numbers of male servants than female servants in Southwark during the late 17th century, compared with London. This was possibly because of the large concentration of taverns, coaching inns and heavy industry in the borough (ibid.).

The 1841 census for St Saviour suggests that approximately two-thirds of residents were from outside the county, the majority from the Home Counties, in particular Surrey and Kent, which had particularly strong trade connections with the Borough Market. A small minority was from Ireland, Scotland or abroad. Names listed in the burial registers relating to Cure's between 1782 and 1797 appear to be typically English, although one – 'Sullivan' – is likely to be Irish. The Great Irish Famine of 1845–52 resulted in large numbers of the population moving to London, and Irish are known to have lived in Southwark in the 19th century when they worked on the London to Greenwich railway. Irish migrants have been identified using analysis of stable isotopes on skeletons from Lukin Street cemetery, Tower Hamlets (Beaumont *et al.* 2013), but no such analysis was undertaken on the Park Street skeletons.

Several names in the Cure's burial registers refer to the individual's trades, for example 'Smith', 'Baker', 'Taylor', and 'Wheelwright'. Analysis of the fee books dating between the 17th and 19th centuries suggests that the most common occupations were labourer, skilled craftsman, and trader, primarily in food and drink. A small number of gentlemen of independent means was also registered.

One named individual, William Pope, was identified in the assemblage from a coffin plate associated with Skeleton [2280]. He died at the age of 53 years and was buried on 2nd February 1816. His cause of death was not identified in any of the records consulted. Pope was a pensioner at Cure's College and had been a labourer, but perhaps unusually one whose financial means were such that he had enough capital to invest in shares in the British Navy. Little else is known about him but he was evidently not a man of impoverished means (Chapter 5).

Pope may be typical of individuals buried at Cure's during the 18th and 19th centuries. The Almshouse burial ground was originally for the poorest members of the parish, including the unemployed, the sick and elderly pensioners, whose burials were paid for by the parish in part or in full. However, during the 18th and 19th centuries, when other burial grounds for the poor opened (eg the Union Workhouse burial ground) and space ran out, Cure's seems to have become a more exclusive burial ground in the parish, because it was charging higher fees (see Chapter 2). While it is important to remember that even the very poor went to great lengths to save for their funeral, the importance of a decent burial being keenly felt, the increase in fees does suggest that those buried at Cure's from around the 18th century were individuals who were in established trades, of some financial means and were therefore not the poorest of the parish.

The burial ground contained individuals of all ages and both sexes. Analysis of a sample of fees books (Chapter 2) identified more females (211/397 individuals) than males (186/397 individuals) and individuals of all age categories, but in particular those over the age of 45 years (147/399 individuals). Over 80 of the burials were those of infants less than one year old. The oldest individual was a Mary Piliatt, a pensioner of the College who died aged 105 years. Broadly speaking, osteological examination of the excavated assemblage identified similar trends – individuals of all ages and both sexes, although there were more males (104) than females (73). Unlike the fee books there were few individuals who were over 45 years (13 skeletons), likely to be an artefact of the militated accuracy of age determination (see below), or less than five years of age (two neonates, six infants, 18 aged one to five years).

These comparisons are hampered by the various biases and weaknesses inherent in the two datasets. For example, the fee book data refers to a relatively small number of burials and, like any historical record of this nature, is subject to transcription errors. Similarly, the osteological data suffers from a number of drawbacks which are worth some detailed consideration here.

First, the assemblage represents only a proportion of the total buried population and of the parish. The collection is not a biological sample of the population of which it was once part, but a social or cultural sample (Waldron 1994, 12). That is, it is not a random sample, but one determined by religious beliefs, place of residence, 'social mores' of individuals, and other such factors (ibid.). It is also a sample determined by preservation and location and extent of excavation. Burials are known to have been removed as a result of the construction of the railway, and infant burials are likely to have been lost due to truncation, the latter perhaps explaining their apparent absence in the dataset compared with the fee book data.

Another drawback is that studies using adult skeletons of documented age have demonstrated that present methods tend to over age the young and underage the old (Cox 2000), and this must also be borne in mind. Many of the skeletons in the present assemblage were incomplete and this meant that age had to be estimated using fewer, and sometimes, less accurate, skeletal indicators than the desired range. This is reflected in the high number of adult skeletons (111) that could not be assigned an age category. If it had been possible to estimate more precise ages for these individuals, the mortality profile for the assemblage may appear quite different.

Health status and cause of death

Osteological, palaeopathological and isotopic analyses concluded that the assemblage comprised individuals who had probably experienced longstanding health stress as a result of a high burden of disease and inadequate nutrition. There was evidence for nutritional deficiency in the form of rickets, scurvy and deprived growth, consistent with this picture. However, perhaps unexpected, was that several conditions, such as infection and trauma, were found to be less prevalent than in other London assemblages, including those of higher status individuals. This might simply highlight the fact that individuals in the Cure's assemblage had succumbed to disease more readily than higher status contemporaries from elsewhere, dying before lesions had started to affect their bones, and the high number of individuals dying between 18 and 35 years could support this interpretation. In addition, it is in keeping with Champion's (1993) analysis of London hearth tax data and the Bills of Mortality, which identified the tendency for poorer households to experience higher numbers of deaths than those that were wealthier.

Information obtained on the causes of death of members of the Cure's burial population from a sample of fees books (see Chapter 2) reminds us that many fatal illnesses and diseases that affected the population would have left no trace on the human skeleton. For example, measles, convulsions and smallpox are recorded as the causes of death for some of the infants. A Sarah Arnold is recorded to have died from mortification (infected tissue) at the age of 16, and a John Dewe, aged 76, from asthma. Roberts and Cox (2003, 291) provide further information on the causes of death listed in the London Bills of Mortality in 1775, and identify convulsions (principally in teething infants), pulmonary tuberculosis, smallpox and other fevers as the most common. Leprosy and St Antony's Fire (ergotism) were also recorded, but as less significant conditions, and there were also non-natural causes such as drowning, suicide and execution (ibid.). These records may not be accurate; they reflect what the person present at death reported, so are the conditions that they knew the deceased experienced at the time of death. However, they do highlight a range of conditions and causes not conveyed by the skeletal record. Measles was one of the most common causes of death among children in the 18th and 19th centuries, in addition to scarlet fever, whooping cough, and diphtheria, and in the general population cholera, typhoid and typhus (Roberts and Cox 2003, 330). However, despite the significant impact on mortality, they cannot be observed macroscopically on the human skeleton.

A further caveat is offered by Ives (2015) in an integrated analysis of skeletal pathology and death registers associated with 19th-century named individuals, excavated at Bethnal Green cemetery. One child, documented as a three year old female, had considerable changes in her skeleton caused by tuberculosis, but her acute cause of death in the registers was measles (Ives 2015, 153). Chronic conditions are rarely fatal, but compromise immunity and resistance to acute diseases resulting in death. Thus, the many nuances of historical and osteological datasets can only be properly appreciated when they are considered together. It also highlights the multi-faceted and heterogeneous nature of health status among individuals from the same population.

Ives' (2015) analysis also identified some fatal accidents, including being run over by an omnibus and falling onto iron spikes, which had left no changes on the skeletons concerned (Ives 2015, 154). Such scenarios could explain the apparent dearth of trauma in the Park Street individuals compared with other London assemblages. Certainly the living and working environment was no safer or freer of hazards than those of other London populations. In fact, considering the scale of commerce and industry in Southwark at the time, individuals were likely to have been exposed to more accidents and violence than most other parts of London. A good proportion – 70% – of the skeletons were less than 50% complete, another factor that has undoubtedly contributed to the low prevalence of trauma recorded.

Living conditions and disease

Cure's College burial ground dates to a period when living conditions provided the perfect breeding ground for infection, with the result that epidemics were a constant risk and accidents and minor infections could readily develop into life-threatening conditions. Urban contexts were characterised by poor sanitation and water supply, high population density and high levels of atmospheric pollution. In addition, high numbers of migrants would have introduced new diseases into the population and they, themselves, would have been exposed to infections they had not previously encountered (Roberts and Cox 2003, 167).

Southwark, and more specifically St Saviour's parish, was no exception. In his account of Southwark William Rendle remarks upon the unsanitary conditions, describing Foul Lane as a place with 'open ditches, dirty wharves, swarming with pigs and houses of office ...' (1878, 201). 'House of Office' was a euphemism for toilet, implying that the ditches in Foul Lane were used to dispose of sewerage as well as of slaughtered and knackered animals. He comments that the area around Foul Lane was not much healthier either. Until the early 17th century, cattle and horses were kept in urban areas and slaughtered in back yards; the vestry minutes for St Saviour's contain numerous complaints about the noise and pollution that this caused. Drinking water was also polluted, and in the late 18th century Concanen and Morgan (1795) mention that Southwark had a plentiful water supply but it was abused by visitors. This presumably suggests they polluted it with industrial waste and/or sewerage. Drainage was also poor; a drawing of the Ship Inn on Borough High Street by John Chessel Buckler dated to 1827 depicts houses fronting onto a cobbled alleyway which has a drain (or sewer) running down the centre of it (Fig. 6.6a). Further details on the unsanitary, unhygienic conditions that prevailed in Southwark are described by Brickley *et al.* (1999, 20–3) in relation to the Cross Bones assemblage.

Considering this historical context, the osteological evidence for infection at Park Street – only six skeletons with possible or probable syphilis, tuberculosis and treponemal disease – is perhaps underwhelming. Further, it does little to support evidence such as the London Bills of Mortality, which attributes 25% of deaths to 'consumption' (Roberts and Cox 2003). In addition, frequent descriptions of syphilis in contemporary novels, journals, medical treatises and plays, including descriptions of mercury treatment, possibly identified in 17th-century syphilitic skeletons from the burial ground associated with St Thomas' hospital, reflect the fact that it was commonplace (Tucker 2007). However, the cases observed at Park Street probably represent only a fraction of the individuals who suffered infectious diseases such as tuberculosis and syphilis because some of the observed skeletal lesions were too general to be diagnosed. In addition, as discussed in Chapter 4, many individuals with chronic infectious diseases would have died of some other cause before there was any skeletal response. According to Santos and Roberts (2001), in populations which pre-date antibiotics, between 1–9% of individuals with syphilis are estimated to show skeletal involvement. Thus, the crude prevalence for Park Street (0.6%) is not far off this, considering the issues associated with diagnosis. In addition, this prevalence is in keeping with other contemporary assemblages (eg St Pancras and Cross Bones, see Chapter 4). The cases identified at Park Street probably reflect individuals who lived with the disease for several years into its advanced stages. In this sense, a low prevalence may be taken to indicate a population with a low threshold for withstanding disease because few survived into the later stages.

Another infectious disease, leprosy, was not observed in the Park Street skeletons, but this finding is not surprising. Leprosy had declined in England by the post-medieval period, either because of climate change and/or because of the emergence of tuberculosis, which may have created an immunity to the disease (Roberts and Cox 2003). A case of leprosy from St Marylebone is a rare example of the presence of the disease in post-medieval London (Miles *et al.* 2008, 128).

Other aspects of the living conditions detrimental to health may also be reflected in the skeletal record. As mentioned above, rickets was observed in the assemblage, the cause of which is inconclusive, but infant feeding practices and a lack of exposure to sunlight are among the possibilities. A good proportion of the population engaged in occupations which predominantly involved indoor work (such as work in the soap factory, brewing, etc.), and housing occupied narrow, dimly lit alleyways (see Fig 6.6a). Most houses lacked basic social amenities such as a kitchen, but varied in size and quality (Boulton 1999, 194). For example, the alleys and yards which the Park Street individuals most likely occupied included some dwellings which were relatively spacious (see Fig 6.6b), while others were one room tenements, sometimes in cellars (Boulton 2005, 193). A similar picture is described by Brickley *et al.* (1999, 20–24) in respect of the Cross Bones individuals. It is easy, therefore, to understand how conditions such as rickets would have been prevalent in the population at the time.

Scurvy, caused by inadequate vitamin C in the diet, was also observed among the burial ground population (see Chapter 4). Scurvy resulting from a shortage of potatoes during the 'blight' has previously been cited in other post-medieval assemblages. The potato, introduced into the country in the 17th century, became a key component of the staple diet of the poor, and a key source of vitamin C. This may be reflected in a decrease in deaths attributed to scurvy recorded in the London Bills of Mortality at this time (Roberts and Cox 2003, 306). However, when potato crops were blighted during the middle of the 19th century, alternative sources of vitamin C, for example citrus fruits and marine fish, were beyond the means of the poor, predisposing them to the disease. The potato famine had a particularly devastating impact in Ireland, and recent analysis of 970 human skeletons from mass burials dating to the height of the famine in Kilkenny city (1847–1851) identified a number of individuals with scorbutic lesions (Geber and Murphy 2012). In addition, Brickley and Ives (2006) identified scurvy in infants from St Martin's-in-the-Bull Ring churchyard, Birmingham, and proposed that the condition may have related to potato famine during the 1840s, although in the absence of a secure date for the burials a direct link could not be made.

Fig. 6.6 a) The Ship Inn, Borough High Street (1827) by John Chessel Buckler (© London Metropolitan Archives); b) view of Pepper Alley, Southwark (1827) by John Chessel Buckler (© London Metropolitan Archives)

The excavated assemblage from Park Street is thought not to date beyond 1831, so could pre-date the potato famine of 1846–51, although this does not preclude earlier episodes of potato famine, or more generally, food shortage and subsequent malnourishment. For example, Boulton (2005, 47) identified an increase in mortality among St Saviour's parishioners in 1597, suggesting that this 'crisis peak' may have been a result of exceptionally high bread prices. Indeed, several famines resulting from climatic deterioration are known from the time of the Cure's burials, in particular during the 1550s, 1560s, 1594–7, 1692–8, 1709, 1740 and 1756 (Lamb 1981). One of the worst climatic events, which appears to have had a direct impact on mortality in Europe, was the 'Great Frost' of 1739–1741, when extremely cold conditions caused crops to fail and drove up food prices. According to Engler et al. (2013) an increase in grain prices caused a direct increase in child mortality, disease, and famine in Europe. Grain prices in England went up by 32.9% between 1737–1741, which appears to correlate with a 23.4% increase in mortality between 1735–42 (Engler et al. 2013).

Mass fatality

Roberts and Cox (2003, 295) state that, at this time 'famine ensued and epidemic disease such as smallpox hit a malnourished population'. Large numbers of individuals dying over a short space of time presented considerable problems in urban contexts where the need to prevent the spread of disease was keenly felt and mass graves were dug for this purpose. For example, plague epidemics in 1625 and 1665 resulted in a reported 35,000 and 69,000 deaths and, interestingly, extramural and suburban areas, such as Southwark, were more severely affected by plague mortality by the 17th century than the inner city, which had, on average, smaller parishes, wealthier inhabitants, and more resources to prevent deaths (Harding 1993).

One grave from Park Street is very interesting in this context because it contained a group of 36 individuals, believed to have been buried over a relatively short space of time, possibly as a result of an epidemic (see Chapter 3, grave [969]). This mass grave cannot be more securely dated than to the period which has been assigned to the entire burial assemblage (1587–1831), but was possibly early in the sequence, having been cut by subsequent burials.

This context is similar to several mass graves which have been identified in London's archaeological record. Within the borough, mass graves of paupers or victims of an epidemic have been found on the site of New London Bridge House, Southwark (Bekvalac 2007; Dawson 2002; Jones 1990; see Chapter 4). The graves were within a post-medieval cemetery north of St Thomas' Street, believed to be associated with St Thomas' hospital (ibid.). The individuals had been buried in rows and, in some cases, up to three layers deep (Dawson 2002). There was soil in between some layers but not all, suggesting at least some of the burials had been contemporary (Jones 1990, 31). St Thomas' was a secondary cemetery, created in the 16th century in the parish of St Olave because of a lack of space in the parish churchyard (ibid.). This was the same as its neighbouring parish, St Margaret's, which also created the secondary burial ground, St Margaret's New Churchyard, part of which became Cure's College burial ground, from which the Park Street skeletons derive (see Chapter 2). It has been suggested that the creation of the secondary burial grounds at St Thomas' and St Margaret's in Southwark was slightly earlier than elsewhere in London and reflects the pressure on burial space in this borough (Dawson 2002, 6). Given this context, the presence of a mass grave at Park Street is perhaps unsurprising.

Beyond Southwark, mass graves have been found at Bedlam, East Smithfield and St Mary's Christ Church, Spitalfields, as discussed in Chapter 4. East Smithfield is the only excavated and fully analysed burial ground specifically for victims of the mid 14th-century Black Death. Assemblages here and at Bedlam have been sampled and aDNA analysis performed, which identified the bacterium *Yersinia pestis*, claimed by some historians to have caused the Black Death (Bos *et al.* 2011; Crossrail 2016). At St Mary's Christ Church, Spitalfields, almost 4000 individuals had been buried in mass graves, the majority of which pre-date the 1348–9 Black Death, and are believed to relate to a series of epidemics and accompanying recurrent famines known from historical sources (Connell *et al.* 2012, 230–1). This was evidenced by the mortality patterns, such as high deaths among sub-adults, increased mortality with age, and equal numbers of males and females, coupled with a high prevalence of pathology reflective of health stress (ibid. and see Chapter 4).

A number of interpretations were considered in Chapters 3 and 4 that might explain the Park Street mass grave. The absence of any skeletal trauma, sustained around the time of death, rules out violence, as has been observed in some mass graves of different periods attributed to conflict or massacre (eg see Fiorato *et al.* 2000). Another possible explanation is the clearance of graves, perhaps when the burial ground and almshouses were reordered (see Chapter 2), but this is unlikely considering the lack of disarticulation of the skeletons and the fact that later graves cut into the feature (see Chapter 3).

Brown (1911, 25-6) observes that pits, equivalent to three of four ordinary plots, were a common way of burying the poor, and there are indications that they were kept open for up to a week and could contain up to about forty bodies. It is therefore conceivable that Park Street mass grave [969] is one such example, perhaps an extreme of other graves found at the site which contained several individuals (eg [2414] and [2426]; see Chapter 3). However, according to Harding (1993) mass graves were probably never dug in London outside epidemics, individual burial or stacked burial (unlike the Park Street grave [969]) being the norm at a time when funerary traditions were focussed on individual funeral, interment, and commemoration.

The Park Street mass grave dates to a period when there were several epidemics and concurrent endemics described as 'plague'. In addition to the 1625 and 1665 outbreaks mentioned above, there were also outbreaks recorded in the borough in 1543, 1563, 1593, 1603, 1636 and 1637 (Boulton 2005). Attributed to the bubonic plague ('the Black Death'), a tropical disease, some of these outbreaks are likely to have involved other infectious diseases as well (Roberts and Cox 2003, 332). The 1665 outbreak was the most devastating, with 3000 deaths in Southwark, one of the worst affected boroughs, the inhabitants being too poor to escape to the countryside (Boulton 2005).

The mass grave may date to the earlier part of burial activity at Cure's, as it did not truncate earlier burials. Therefore, a 16th- or 17th-century epidemic is a possible explanation for this burial event. Should the grave not be that early, it may also fall just within the timeframe of the main cholera epidemics which broke out during the 19th century, the first occurring between 1831–32 (Wohl 1983). Smallpox, which had a serious impact on mortality during the 17th and 18th centuries, is another possible contender. Other possibilities are influenza and dysentery, and are considered by Boulton (2005, 31, 50, 53) in relation to mortality peaks in the St Saviour's parish in 1578, 1581–2, 1597, 1609 and 1641. Typhus and ague are other contenders (see Roberts and Cox 2003, 330).

Confirming that the mass grave was the result of an epidemic is difficult based on the archaeology and osteology evidence alone. The depth of the grave may be considered in relation to regulations imposed on burial as a health measure to prevent the spread of plague. However, it has been widely observed that this and similar regulations which prevented the observation of traditional funerary rites (eg viewing the dead), were unpopular, and there was marked variation in the enforcement of such measures (Cherryson et al. 2012, 112). Thus, despite the stipulated six feet below ground level, victims of the 1665 plague have been found just half a metre below ground surface during recent excavations of the Bedlam burial ground (M Henderson pers. comm.).

Similarly, plague burials need not necessarily be careless, haphazard interments as the oft cited 'they died in heaps, and were buried in heaps' (Defoe 1772, 337) description of the 1665 plague epidemic may imply. For example, the Bedlam plague victims had been buried in coffins in orderly rows in a mass grave, and similar arrangements were observed at East Smithfield Black Death cemetery (1348/49), which included single interments as well as mass graves (Cowal et al. 2008). This latter example is a reminder that victims of plague or other epidemics were not necessarily buried in mass burial rites, but were also buried in single graves, and so cannot be certainly attributed to plague/epidemics. When the plague of the 16th and 17th centuries and the 19th-century cholera epidemics initially broke out, attempts were made to adhere to funerary traditions as long as possible, but as health concerns rose and capacity was overstretched, these were abandoned (Cherryson et al. 2012, 111–12). Most of the larger London suburban parishes probably ended up burying their dead in mass graves within existing churchyards to save space, but also to save money at a time when high mortality resulted in the parish carrying the costs of many burials, among other factors (Harding 1993). Of course, during epidemics, people continued to die of non-epidemic related conditions.

Plague and other such epidemic diseases leave no visible trace on human bone. Although mortality profiles can provide some clues, these are hampered by methods employed to estimate age at death in human skeletal remains (see Chapter 4). Further analysis, employing Bayesian statistics, may help to address this, but this is beyond the scope of the present analysis. That said, mortality patterns did seem to be most consistent with those of individuals with weakened immunity as a result of famine, struck down by an epidemic. Without direct identification of bacteria through aDNA analysis – the only way to positively identify plague or other epidemic in the archaeological record – interpretation remains unresolved.

Comparison of mortality and morbidity at Cure's College with Cross Bones and St Saviour's burial grounds

Park Street is the third burial assemblage to have been excavated from St Saviour's parish, the other two being the lower status Cross Bones (to *c* 1853) burial ground and higher status St Saviour's churchyard (*c* 1832–1853), both excavated in the 1990s. These assemblages cover different but overlapping periods of time beginning in the 16th century and ending in the mid-19th century (see above). Together, they provide a rare opportunity to consider the morbidity and mortality experience of three socially stratified groups, spanning three centuries, and from the same local parish. The sample sizes and level of reported information for these assemblages are variable, and therefore not all data are comparable. In particular, the limited scope of works undertaken at St Saviour's meant that only limited osteological data was obtained, specifically information on demography, and some pathology. However, some general observations are worth mentioning and are taken from Brickley *et al.* (1999) for Cross Bones, and Dodwell (2001) for St Saviour's (see Chapter 4 for detailed discussion).

Demographically, Park Street and Cross Bones were different, most notably because the latter had a much higher number of juveniles, virtually the same number of males (21) and females (20), and proportionally more individuals in the oldest age category. Conversely, Cure's lacked juveniles, in particular those less than five years of age, and individuals in the oldest age category, and had a greater number of males (104) than females (73). In particular, there were more individuals aged 18–35 in the Park Street assemblage (93/331; 28%) than the Cross Bones assemblage (11/148; 7%).

Like Park Street, very young individuals were uncommon in the St Saviour's assemblage, which comprised 21 adults and three juveniles, of which two were infants (Divers 2009 *et al.*, 91). Unlike Park Street, but similar to Cross Bones, most of the adults were over the age of 45 years, and the ratio of males to females was almost the same (ibid.).

Numbers from St Saviour's are too low for any meaningful discussion of demographic trends. The high number of juveniles at Cross Bones compared with Park Street most likely reflects the fact that more infant burials were truncated at Park Street, although cultural explanations cannot be entirely ruled out, for example extreme poverty resulting in higher infant deaths among Cross Bones individuals (Brickley *et al.* 1999, 31). The bias in favour of younger adults at Cure's compared with Cross Bones is perhaps surprising, considering that more deaths among the

Table 6.2: Summary comparison of pathology, Park Street and Cross Bones

	Relative prevalence	Park Street	Cross Bones
Schmorl's nodes	Higher		Y
	Lower	Y	
Periostitis (Adults)	Higher	Y	
	Lower		Y
Periostitis (Juveniles)	Higher		Y
	Lower	Y	
Enamel hypoplasia	Higher		Y
	Lower	Y	

young would be expected among the poorer individuals interred at Cross Bones. This may be the result of excavation bias, although it is worth noting also that Park Street attracted individuals who were established tradespeople, most likely within that age group, and more likely to have had the means to pay the burial fees (see Chapter 2).

Calculated statures present a mixed picture: mean statures for males (Cross Bones: 1.69m; Park Street: 1.67m) and females (Cross Bones: 1.58m; Park Street: 1.57m) from Cross Bones and Park Street were similar, although slightly higher for Cross Bones than Park Street. The shortest males (Cross Bones: 1.53m; Park Street: 1.60m) and shortest females (Cross Bones: 1.42m; Park Street: 1.44m) were from Cross Bones; the tallest female was from Cross Bones (Cross Bones: 1.72m; Park Street: 1.65) and the tallest males were at both sites (both 1.80 m). However, numbers of males and females for which stature could be calculated from each site were very low: 16 males and 19 females from Cross Bones and 24 males and 15 females from Park Street.

In terms of pathology (see Table 6.2), Schmorl's nodes, or herniation of the intervertebral discs, was observed at Park Street and Cross Bones, calculation of the crude prevalence suggesting that it was more common among Cross Bones males (67%; 14/21) and females (55%; 11/20) than Park Street (males: 48%, 50/104; females: 36%, 26/73). Schmorl's nodes can be caused by several factors, including heavy manual activity (see Chapter 4).

Both assemblages included examples of button osteomas. These benign neoplasms are the most common type of tumour observed in skeletal assemblages. In addition, one male skeleton, aged over 45 years, from Cross Bones had probable prostate cancer, identified from multiple metastatic lesions. Malignant cancer such as this is rarely diagnosed in skeletal assemblages of any date, and no such examples were observed at Park Street.

Interestingly, as at Park Street, few examples of specific infection were identified at Cross Bones. There was one case of venereal syphilis in an adult female and one example of bone infection (osteomyelitis). No confirmed cases of tuberculosis were observed in either assemblage. The lack of specific infection may reflect the fact that, as discussed above, individuals were not surviving long enough for infectious diseases to manifest on their bones.

Non-specific bone inflammation (periostitis) affected 13% (6/45) of adult skeletons from Cross Bones, compared with 16% (40/245) of adults from Park Street. In one or two cases from Park Street, it possibly referred to systemic disease, because it was observed on multiple bones from the upper and lower skeleton. No such patterns were observed at Cross Bones where cases involved lower leg bones, which are commonly affected as a result of minor trauma (Roberts and Manchester 1995), and in one case was associated with fused bones from trauma.

However, periostitis observed among the juveniles from both sites presents a different picture. This was observed on 38% (39/103) of juveniles (primarily aged from 0–5 years) from Cross Bones compared with just 7% (6/86) from Park Street. In the Cross Bones cases, the lesions may refer to rickets, but this is not suggested for the Park Street cases. Deformities, possibly caused by rickets, were observed in eight juveniles and three adults, or 7% of skeletons (11/148) from Cross Bones and six juveniles and seven adults, or 4% of skeletons (13/331) from Park Street. There was also evidence of scurvy in one adult and one juvenile from the Park Street assemblage, but this was not diagnosed in the Cross Bones' material. Cribra orbitalia, another form of deficiency, was identified in 6% juveniles (6/103) from Cross Bones compared with 15% juveniles (13/85) from Park Street. However, the rate estimated for Cross Bones is probably biased by poor preservation (Brickley *et al.* 1999, 47). Overall, both assemblages appeared to show evidence of nutritional deficiency, but this was perhaps more prevalent in the Cross Bones assemblage, especially among the juveniles, considering the high prevalence of periostitis.

Enamel hypoplasia, defects in the tooth enamel referring to episodes of growth arrest during childhood, was observed in individuals from both the Park Street and Cross Bones burial grounds. The crude prevalence was much higher at Cross Bones (males: 24%, 5/21; females: 38%, 8/21) than Park Street (males: 8%, 6/104; females: 15%, 11/73). It was more prevalent among females at both sites. Taken alone, this evidence points to greater childhood health stress among the Cross Bones individuals, especially females.

Healed fractures were identified at Park Street and Cross Bones, but commonly affected bones were different, these being ribs and femurs at Cross Bones and the cranial vault, foot and spine at Park Street. At both sites, the number of cases is too low to draw any conclusions. No peri-mortem trauma was observed in either assemblage, although evidence of autopsy was observed in two adults from Cross Bones. They included sectioning of the skull in the horizontal plane in order access the brain and related structures (craniotomy), and cuts down either side of the spinous process of the vertebrae, to access the structures of the spine (possibly a laminectomy). In neither case was there a skeletal pathology to suggest why these procedures had been performed. No such examples of autopsy/dissection were found at Park Street, but a skull from St Saviour's had cut marks associated with a craniotomy, thought to be reflective of a blade catching the skull while the scalp was being retracted before the skull cap was removed (Cherryson *et al.* 2012, 141; Dodwell 2001, 144). Unlike anatomisation, autopsy (post-mortem examination) was usually focussed on establishing the cause of death and was considered to be more respectable, less invasive and less destructive. The practice was performed on the poor and destitute from the voluntary hospitals and, at the other end of the social spectrum, the educated middle classes, in particular those with medical backgrounds, who had private physicians and supported scientific enquiry (Cherryson *et al.* 2012, 137). Although the evidence is somewhat anecdotal, it is interesting to note that the two examples of autopsy from St Saviour's parish come from the poorest and the wealthiest of the three burial grounds.

This brief consideration of the osteology data associated with Cross Bones, Park Street and St Saviour's is limited in scope by the size of the assemblages, the different levels of data presentation, and the date ranges of the assemblages. However, at a general level, it seems to suggest that the morbidity and mortality experience of the individuals was different, and this corresponds with the different sectors of society that were served by the burial grounds. This is most evident in the juvenile pathology (non-specific inflammation and enamel hypoplasia) and the mortality profiles of Cross Bones and Park Street.

Conclusions: Living and dying in Southwark, the perspective from Cure's College

In some respects, the burial assemblage excavated at Park Street could be considered to be relatively unremarkable. Although a sizeable assemblage of 331 individuals, the burials actually represent a very small proportion of the buried population, considering that they span some 300 years of activity and were excavated from an area representing only approximately 34% of the original burial ground, or a fraction of the estimated total number of inhumations (16,000–56,000). In addition, the burial assemblage represents a rather piecemeal sample due to the nature of the excavations, which was focussed within pile caps. Furthermore, there had been extensive earlier disturbances to the burial ground, especially during the 1860s, when a significant number of burials were exhumed prior to construction of the railway. In contrast with some other sites which have produced rich assemblages of grave goods and other associated funerary remains such as coffins and coffin fittings (eg New Bunhill Fields), very few artefacts were recovered from Park Street, and this hampered attempts at phasing.

However, when considered alongside historical records and other similar assemblages from the borough and elsewhere, this assemblage still contributes some important new evidence. Some of the Park Street graves contained multiple interments and one multiple grave in particular may be result of a catastrophic event, possibly famine and/or an epidemic. Combined with the heavy intercutting of burials and estimated density of burials (between 12 and 43 bodies every square metre, see above), this would seem to reflect a parish which was under pressure to provide burial space. This is consistent with historical sources, which also suggest that multiple, high density burial activity in large London suburban parishes, such as St Saviour's, was prompted by the parish's need to save on the cost of burial during epidemics (Harding 1993, and see above). It also supports archaeological evidence from elsewhere in the borough (St Thomas') which, it has been argued, was the earliest in London, dating from the 16th century, to create secondary burial grounds to manage the pressure on space (Dawson 2002, see above).

Park Street is the first sizeable collection of burials to be archaeologically recorded from an almshouse context in Britain. Cure's College was an almshouse established in the 16th century to serve the poor, and which operated for almost 300 years, but the overall impression gained from analysing the Park Street assemblage is of people who were predominantly not inmates but, rather, working class individuals engaged in local trades and of sufficient means to afford a burial and a funeral. This is reflected in the mortality profile, the coffin remains and decorative fittings, lower levels of disease compared with Cross Bones, but suggested higher levels of disease compared with assemblages of wealthier/higher status individuals, including St Saviour's. Thus, the Park Street skeletons are generally midway between low status and high status assemblages from Southwark and elsewhere in London. The burial assemblage therefore provides an invaluable new perspective on the individuals who used Cure's College burial ground between the 16th and 19th centuries, their lives and their deaths.

It is only relatively recently that the significance of post-medieval burial assemblages like the one from Park Street have begun to be appreciated and realised. This has been demonstrated through a number of publications which have explored numerous research questions relating to disease, the living environment, cultural practices, commemoration, grave goods, society, belief and religion (eg see Powers 2015 and Tarlow 2015). This work has added considerably to knowledge of the period, and in particular has demonstrated the value of the resource when considered alongside historical evidence. Perhaps most important is that it has helped to change attitudes towards post-medieval burial archaeology, once regarded as a subject that had little to offer because it is all documented (Powers *et al.* 2013,126), to one which is now considered to be interesting, rich in evidence and is a 'valuable part of our disciplinary endeavours' (Tarlow 2015, 1).

Bibliography

Anderson, J E, Becker, S, Guinena, A H, and McCarthy, B J, 1986 Breastfeeding effects on birth interval components: A prospective child health study in Gaza, *Studies in Family Planning* 17, 153–160

Aufderheide, A C, and Rodríguez-Martín, C, 1998 *The Cambridge Encyclopedia of Human Paleopathology*, Cambridge University Press, Cambridge

BABAO, 2010a *British Association of Biological Anthropology and Osteoarchaeology Code of Ethics*, BABAO Working group for ethics and practice

BABAO, 2010b *British Association of Biological Anthropology and Osteoarchaeology Code of Practice*, BABAO Working group for ethics and practice

Barker, C, Cox, M, Flavel, A, and Loe, L, 2008 Mortuary procedures II. Skeletal analysis I: basic procedures and demographic assessment, in M Cox, A Flavel, I Hanson, J Laver and R Wessling (eds) *The Scientific Investigation of Mass Graves: Towards Protocols and Standard Operating Procedures*, Cambridge University Press, Cambridge, 295–382

Barnes, E, 1994 *Developmental Defects of the Axial Skeleton in Palaeopathology*, University Press of Colorado, Colorado

Barnes, E, 2008 Congenital abnormalities, in R Pinhasi and S Mays (eds) *Advances in Human Palaeopathology*, John Wiley and Sons, Chichester, 329–362

Bashford, L, and Pollard, T, 1998 In the burying place – the excavation of a Quaker burial ground, in M Cox (ed), *Grave Concerns: Death and Burial in Post-Medieval England, 1700-1850,* CBA Research Report 113, York, 154–66

Bashford, L, and Sibun, L, 2007 Excavations at the Quaker Burial Ground, Kingston-upon-Thames, London, *Post-Medieval Archaeology,* 41, 100–154

Beaumont, J, Gledhill, A, Lee-Thorp, J, and Montgomery, J, 2012 Childhood diet: A closer examination of the evidence from dental tissues using stable isotope analysis of incremental human dentine, *Archaeometry* 55 (2), 1–19

Beaumont, J, Montgomery, J, and Wilson, A, 2013 Using stable isotope analysis to identify Irish immigrants, in M Henderson, A Miles, D Walker, B Connell and R Wroe-Brown, '*He being dead yet speaketh'. Excavations at three Post-medieval Burial Grounds in Tower Hamlets, East London, 2004–10*, MOLA Monogr 64, Museum of London Archaeology, 301–304

Bekvalac 2007 St. Thomas' Hospital Cemetery Summary, Museum of London Archaeological Archive Centre for Human Bioarchaeology Online at: https://www.museumoflondon.org.uk/collections/other-collection-databases-and-libraries/centre-human-bioarchaeology/osteological-database/post-medieval-cemeteries/st-thomas-hospital-post-medieval [Accessed February 2017]

Bekvalac, J, and Kausmally, T, 2008 Life and death in Chelsea, in R Cowie, J Bekvalac and T Kausmally, *Late 17th to 19th Century Burial and Earlier Occupation at All Saints, Chelsea Old Church, Royal Borough of Kensington and Chelsea*, MoLAS Archaeology Study Series 18, Museum of London Archaeology Service, London, 40–59

Berry, A C, and Berry, A J, 1967 Epigenetic variation in the human cranium, *Journal of Anatomy* 101, 361–379

Binder, M, and Roberts, C A, 2014 Calcified structures associated with human skeletal remains: possible atherosclerosis affecting the population buried at Amara West, Sudan (1300–800 BC), *International Journal of Palaeopathology* 6, 20–29

Bocquet-Appel, J, and Masset, C, 1982 Farewell to paleodemography, *Journal of Human Evolution* 11, 321–333

Bogaard, A, Heaton, T H E, Poulton, P, and Merbach, I, 2007 The impact of manuring on nitrogen isotope ratios in cereals: Archaeological implications for reconstruction of diet and crop management practices, *Journal of Archaeological Science* 34, 335–343

Bos K I, Schuenemann V J, Golding G B, Burbano H A, Waglechner N, Coombes B K, McPhee J B, DeWitte S N, Meyer M, Schmedes S, Wood J, Earn D J, Herring D A, Bauer P, Poinar H N, Krause J, 2011 A draft genome of Yersinia pestis from victims of the Black Death, *Nature* Oct 12; 478 (7370): 506–10. doi: 10.1038/nature10549

Boston, C, 2009 Burial practice and material culture, in C Boston, A Boyle, J Gill and A Witkin *'In the Vaults Beneath' Archaeological Recording at St George's Church, Bloomsbury*, Oxford Archaeology Monogr No. 8, Oxford Archaeology, Oxford, 147–172

Boston, C, 2010 Coffin furniture, in H Webb and A Norton, The medieval and post-medieval graveyard of St Peter-le-Bailey at Bonn Square, Oxford, 158–159, *Oxoniensia* 74, 137–179

Boston, C, Boyle, A and Witkin, A, 2009 *In the Vaults Beneath – An Archaeological Recording Action at St George's Church, Bloomsbury Way, London*, Oxford Archaeology Monogr 8, Oxford Archaeology, Oxford

Boston, C, Witkin, A, Boyle, A and Wilkinson, D R P, 2008 *Safe Moor'd in Greenwich Tier. A Study of the Skeletons of Royal Naval Sailors and Marines Excavated at the Royal Hospital, Greenwich*, Oxford Archaeology Monogr 5, Oxford Archaeology, Oxford

Boulle E L 2001 Evolution of Two Human Skeletal Markers of the Squatting Position: A Diachronic Study from Antiquity to the Modern Age, *American Journal of Physical Anthropology* 115, 50–56

Boulter, S. Robertson, D J, and Start, H 1998 *The Newcastle Infirmary at the Forth, Newcastle Upon Tyne. Volume II. The Osteology: People, Disease and Surgery*, Archaeological Research and Consultancy at the University of Sheffield, unpubl report

Boulton, J, 2005 *Neighbourhood and Society: A London Suburb in the Seventeenth Century*, Cambridge Studies in Population, Economy and Society in Past Time, Cambridge University Press, Cambridge

Boyle, A, 2015 Approaches to post-medieval burial in England: Past and present, in S Tarlow (ed.) *The Archaeology of Death and Burial in Post-medieval Europe*, De Gruyter Open, 39–60

Boyle, A, Boston, C and Witkin, A, *2005 The Archaeological Experience at St Luke's Church, Old Street, Islington*, Oxford Archaeology, unpubl report

Boylston, A, Wiggins, R, and Roberts, C, 1998 Material evidence. Human skeletal remains, in G Drinkall and M Foreman (eds), *The Anglo Saxon Cemetery at Castledyke South, Barton-On-Humber*, Sheffield Academic Reports 6, Sheffield Academic Press, Sheffield, 221–236

Brady, K, and Taylor, J, 2013 *Thameslink Archaeological Assessment 3: Archaeological Excavations at Green Dragon Court, London Borough of Southwark*, Oxford Archaeology – Pre-Construct Archaeology, unpubl report

Brickley, M, Barry, H, and Western, G, 2006 The People: Physical Anthropology, in J Adams, M Brickley, S Buteux, T Adams and R Cherrington, *St Martin's Uncovered: Investigations in the Churchyard of St. Martin's-in-the-Bull-Ring, Birmingham, 2001*, Oxbow, Oxford, 90–151

Brickley, M, and Ives, R, 2006 Skeletal manifestations of infantile scurvy, *American Journal of Physical Anthropology* 129 (2), 163–172

Brickley, M, and Ives, R, 2008 *The Bioarchaeology of Metabolic Bone Diseases*, Academic Press, Elsevier, Oxford and London

Brickley, M, Mays, S, and Ives, R, 2010 Evaluation and interpretation of residual rickets deformities in adults, *International Journal of Osteoarchaeology* 20, 54–66

Brickley, M, and McKinley, J, 2004 *Guidelines to the Standards for Recording Human Remains*, IFA Paper 7, BABAO, Southampton and IFA, Reading

Brickley, M, Miles, A, and Stainer, H, 1999 *The Cross Bones Burial Ground, Redcross Way, Southwark, London: Archaeological Excavations (1991–1998) for the London Underground Limited Jubilee Line Extension Project*, MoLAS Monogr 3, Museum of London Archaeology

Brickley, M, and Smith, M, 2006 Culturally determined patterns of violence: biological anthropological investigations at a historic urban cemetery, *American Anthropologist* 108, 163–177

Brooks, S T, and Suchey, J M, 1990 Skeletal age determination based on the os pubis: A comparison of the Acsádi-Nemeskéri and Suchey-Brooks Methods, *Human Evolution* 5, 227–238

Brothwell, D R, 1981 *Digging Up Bones*, Oxford University Press, Oxford

Buckberry, J, and Chamberlain, A, 2002 Age estimation from the auricular surface of the ilium: A revised method, *American Journal of Physical Anthropology* 119, 231–239

Brown, W E, 1911 *St Pancras Open Spaces and Disused Burial Grounds*, London, Metropolitan Borough of St Pancras

Buikstra, J E, and Ubelaker, D H (eds), 1994 *Standards for Data Collection from Human Skeletal Remains*, Arkansas Archaeological Survey Research Series 44, Arkansas

Caffell, A, and Holst, M, 2007 *Osteological Analysis: Whitefriars, Norwich*, York Osteoarchaeology Report No. 0806, York

Carbonell, V M, 1963 Variations in the frequency of shovel-shaped incisors in different populations, in D R Brothwell (ed.) *Dental Anthropology*, Pergamon Press, London, 211–234

Carlin, M, 1983 *The Urban Development of Southwark 1200–1500*, unpublished PhD thesis, University of Toronto

Carlin, M, 1996 *Medieval Southwark*, The Hambledon Press, London

Campanacho, V, and Santos, A L, 2013 Comparison of the entheseal changes of the os coxae of Portuguese males (19th–20th centuries) with known occupation, *International Journal of Osteoarchaeology* 23 (2), 229–236

Chamberlain, A, 2000 Problems and prospects in palaeodemography, in M Cox and S Mays, Human Osteology in Archaeology and Forensic Science, *Greenwich Medical Media*, London, 101–115

Champion, J A I, 1993 Epidemics and the built environment in 1665, in J A I Champion (ed.) *Epidemic Disease in London*, London, University of London, Institute of Historical Research, Working Paper Series 1, 35–54.

Cherryson, A, Crossland, Z, and Tarlow, S, 2012 *A Fine and Private Place. The Archaeology of Death and Burial in Post-medieval Britain and Ireland*, Leicester Archaeology Monogr No. 22, University of Leicester

Chisholm, B S, Nelson, D E, and Schwarcz, H P, 1982 Stable carbon isotope ratios as a measure of marine versus terrestrial protein in ancient diets, *Science* 216, 1131–1132

Church of England and English Heritage, 2005 *Guidance for Best Practice for Treatment of Human Remains Excavated from Christian Burial Grounds in England*, London

Concanen, M, and Morgan, A, 1795 *The History and the Antiquities of the Parish of St Saviour's Southwark*, London

Cole, S, 2010 *The Story of Mens Underwear*, Parkstone International, New York

Condon, K W, 1981 The correspondence of developmental enamel defects between the mandibular canine and the first premolar, *American Journal of Physical Anthropology* 54, 211

Connell, B, Gray Jones, A, Redfern, R, and Walker, D, 2012, *A bioarchaeological study of medieval burials on the site of St Mary Spital: excavations at Spitalfields Market, London E1, 1991–2007*, MOLA Monogr 60, London

Cowal, L, Mikulski, R and White, W, 2008 The human bone, in I Grainger, D Hawkins, L Cowal, and R Mikulski, *The Black Death Cemetery, East Smithfield, London*, MoLAS Monogr 43, London 42–55

Cowie, R, Bekvalac, J, and Kausmally, T, 2007 *Late 17th to 19th-Century Burial and Earlier Occupation at All Saints, Chelsea Old Church, Royal Borough of Kensington and Chelsea*, MoLAS Archaeological Study Series 18, Museum of London, London

Cox, M, 1996 *Life and Death in Spitalfields 1700-1850*, CBA Occasional Papers 21, Council for British Archaeology, York

Cox, M, 2000 Ageing adults from the skeleton, in M Cox and S Mays, *Human Osteology in Archaeology and Forensic Science*, Greenwich Medical Media, London, 61–81

Crossrail, 2016 http://www.crossrail.co.uk/news/articles/dna-of-bacteria-responsible-for-london-great-plague-of-1665-identified-for-first-time

Cushnaghan, J, and Dieppe, P A, 1991 Study of 500 patients with limb joint osteoarthritis, I: Analysis by age, sex and distribution of symptomatic joint sites, *Annals of the Rheumatic Diseases* 50, 8–13

Dawson, G, 2002 A plague pit in Southwark?, *Southwark and Lambeth Archaeological Society Newsletter* 89, 4–6

Defoe, D A, 1772 *Journal of the Plague Year*, online at http://www.gutenberg.org/ebooks/376 [accessed February 2017], Project Gutenberg

Deniro, M J, 1985 Postmortem preservation and alteration of *in vivo* bone collagen isotope ratios in relation to palaeodietary reconstruction, *Nature* 317, 806–809

Deniro, M J, and Epstein, S, 1978 Influence of diet on the distribution of carbon isotopes in animals, *Geochimica et Cosmochimica Acta* 42, 495–506

Deniro, M J, and Epstein, S, 1981 Influence of diet on the distribution of nitrogen isotopes in animals, *Geochimica et Cosmochimica Acta* 45, 341–351

DeWitte, S N, and Stojanowski, C M, 2015 The osteological paradox 20 years later: Past perspectives, future directions, *Journal of Archaeological Research* 23, 397–450

DeWitte, S N, 2016 Archaeological evidence of epidemics can inform future epidemics, *Annual Review of Anthropology* (DOI: 10.1146/annurev-anthro-102215-095929), online at https://www.academia.edu/28377944/Archaeological evidence of epidemics can inform future epidemics [Accessed February 2017]

Dias, G, and Tayles, N, 1997 'Abscess cavity' – a misnomer, *International Journal of Osteoarchaeology* 7, 548–554

Dieppe, P A, 1994 Osteoarthritis. Clinical features and diagnostic problems, in J H Klippel and P A Dieppe (eds), *Rheumatology*, Mosby, London, 74.1–74.16

Divers, D, Mayo, C, Cohen, N, and Jarrett, C, 2009 *A New Millennium at Southwark Cathedral. Investigations into the first two thousand years*, PCA Monogr 8, Pre-Construct Archaeology

Djuric, M, Milovanovic, P, Janovic, A, Draskovic, M, Djukic, K, Milenkovic, P, 2008 Porotic lesions in immature skeletons from Stara Torina, late medieval Serbia, *International Journal of Osteoarchaeology* 18, 458–475

Dodwell, N, 2001 The human remains, in D Divers, *Assessment of an Archaeological Excavation at Southwark Cathedral, London Borough of Southwark, SE1: Phases 1 and 2*, Pre-Construct Archaeology, unpubl report, 141–145

Duray, S M, 1996 Dental indicators of stress and reduced age at death in prehistoric Native Americans, *American Journal of Physical Anthropology* 99, 275–286

Dyson, T, and Ó Grada, C (eds), 2002 *Famine Demography: Perspectives from the Past and Present*, Oxford University Press, Oxford

Eggers, G W N, Burke Evans, E, Blumel, J, Nowlin, D H, and Butler, J K, 1963 Cystic Change in the Iliac Acetabulum, *Journal of Bone and Joint Surgery*, 45 (4), 669–722

Emery, P A, and Wooldridge, K, 2011, *St Pancras Burial Ground: Excavations for St Pancras International, the London terminus of High Speed 1, 2002–3*, Gifford Monogr

Emsley, C, Hitchcock, T, and Shoemaker, R, 2017 London history - A population history of London, *Old Bailey Proceedings Online* (www.oldbaileyonline.org, version 7.0 [accessed 27 January 2017]

Engler, S, Mauelshagen, F, Werner, J, and Luterbacher, J, 2013 The Irish famine of 1740–1741: famine vulnerability and "climate migration", *Climate of the Past* 9, 1161–79

English Heritage (EH) and The Church of England, 2005 *Guidance for best practice for treatment of human remains excavated from Christian burial grounds in England*, London

English Heritage (EH), 2004 *Human Bones from Archaeological Sites. Guidelines for producing assessment documents and analytical reports*, London

Eubanks, J D and Cheruvu, V K, 2009 Prevalence of Sacral Spina Bifida Occulta and Its Relationship to Age, Sex, Race, and the Sacral Table Angle: An Anatomic, Osteologic Study of Three Thousand One Hundred Specimens, *Spine* 34, 1539–1543

Fairman, A, Champness, C, and Taylor, J, 2013 *Thameslink Archaeological Assessment 10: Archaeological Excavations at London Bridge Station Improvement Works, London Borough of Southwark, vols 1 and 2*, Oxford Archaeology–Pre-Construct Archaeology, unpubl report

Fairman, A, and Taylor, J, 2013 *Thameslink Archaeological Assessment 2: Archaeological Excavations at 11–15 Borough High Street, London Borough of Southwark*, Oxford Archaeology–Pre-Construct Archaeology, unpubl report

Federico, D J, Lynch, J K, and Jokl, P, 1990 Osteochondritis dissecans of the knee: a historical review of etiology and treatment, *Arthroscopy* 6 (3), 190–7

Fernandes, R, Nadeau, M J, and Grootes, P M, 2012 Macronutrient-based model for dietary carbon routing in bone collagen and bioapatite, *Archaeological and Anthropological Sciences* 4, 291–301

Fidas, A, MacDonald, H L, Elton, R A, Wild, S R, Chrisholm, G D, and Scott, R, 1987 Prevalence and patterns of spina bifida occulta in 2707 normal adults, *Clinical Radiology* 38, 537–542

Fildes, V, 1986 *Breasts, Bottles and Babies. A History of Infant Feeding*, Edinburgh University Press, Edinburgh

Finnegan, M, 1978 Non-metric variation of the infracranial skeleton, *Journal of Anatomy* 125, 23–37

Fioarto, V, Boylston, A, and Knüsel, C (eds), 2000 *Blood Red Roses. The Archaeology of a Mass Grave from the Battle of Towton AD 1461*, Oxbow Books, Oxford

Flatt, A E, 2001 The Vikings and Baron Dupuytren's disease, *Proceedings Baylor University Medical Centre* 14, 378–384

Fogel, M L, Tuross, N, and Owsley, D W, 1989 Nitrogen isotope tracers of human lactation in modern and archaeological populations, *Annual Report to the Director, Geophysical Laboratory, Carnegie Institution, Washington DC*, 111–117

Friar, S, 2003 *The Sutton Companion to Churches*, Sutton Publishing, Stroud

Galloway, A, 1999 *Broken Bones: Anthropological Analysis of Blunt Force Trauma*, Charles C Thomas, Springfield

Geber, J, and Murphy, E, 2012 Scurvy in the Great Irish Famine: Evidence of vitamin C deficiency from a mid-19th century skeletal population, *American Journal of Physical Anthropology* 148 (4), 512–524

Glencross, B, and Stuart-Macadam, P, 2000 Childhood trauma in the archaeological record, *International Journal of Osteoarchaeology* 10 (3), 198–209

Gilchrist, R, and Sloane, B, 2005 *Requiem – The*

Medieval Monastic Cemetery in Britain, Museum of London Archaeology Service, London

Gill, G W, 1986 Craniofacial criteria in forensic race identification, in K J Reichs (ed.), *Forensic Osteology: Advances in the Identification of Human Remains,* Springfield, Charles C Thomas, 293–318.

Gill, G W and Rhine, J S, 1990 Skeletal Attribution of Race: Methods of Forensic Anthropology, *Anthropological Papers* 4, Maxwell Museum of Natural History, Albuquerque

Gittings, C, 1999 Sacred and secular: 1558–1660, in P C Jupp and C Gittings (eds), *Death in England, an Illustrated History*, Manchester University Press, Manchester, 147–173

Goodman, A H, and Armelagos, G J, 1985 Factors affecting the distribution of enamel hypoplasias within the human permanent dentition, *American Journal of Physical Anthropology* 68, 479–493

Goodman, A H and Rose, J C, 1991 Dental enamel hypoplasias as indicators of nutritional stress, in M A Kelley and C S Larsen (eds), *Advances in Dental Anthropology*, 279–293

Gowland, R L, 2015 Entangled lives: Implications of the developmental origins of health and disease hypothesis for bioarchaeology and the life course, *American Journal of Physical Anthropology* 158 (4), 530–540

Gowland, R L, and Chamberlain, A T, 2005 Detecting plague: palaeodemographic characterisation of a catastrophic death assemblage, *Antiquity* 79 (303), 146–157

Grainger, I, Hawkins, D, Cowal, L, and Mikulski, R, 2008 *The Black Death Cemetery, East Smithfield, London*, MoLAS Monogr 43, London

Gravlee C C, Bernard H R and Leonard, W R, 2003 New answers to old questions: Did Boas Get it Right? Heredity, environment and cranial form: A reanalysis of Boas's immigrant data, *American Anthropologist* 105 (1), 125–138

Groves, S, Roberts, C, Johnstone, C, Hall, R, and Dobney, K, 2003 A high status burial from Ripon Cathedral, North Yorkshire, England: Differential diagnosis of a chest deformity, *International Journal of Osteoarchaeology* 13 (6), 358–368

Hancox, E, 2006 Coffins and coffin furniture, in Brickley et al. 2006, 152–60

Hannan, A, Li, R, Benton-Davis, S, and Grummer-Strawn, G, 2005 Regional variation of public opinion about breastfeeding in the United States, *Journal of Human Lactation* 21, 284–288

Harding, V, 1993 Burial of the plague dead in early modern London, in J A I Champion (ed.), *Epidemic Disease in London*, Centre for Metropolitan History, Institute of Historical Research, University of London, 53–64

Haslam, A, 2014 *An Archaeological Excavation on Land at the Elephant and Castle Leisure Centre, London Borough of Southwark, SE11 4TW*, Pre-Construct Archaeology, report no. R11773, unpubl report

Hasler, P W (ed), 1981 *The History of Parliament: The House of Commons 1558–1603*, Boydell and Brewer

Henderson, C, and Cardoso, F A, 2013 Special issue on enthesial changes and occupation: Technical and theoretical advances and their applications, *International Journal of Osteoarchaeology* 23 (2), 127–134

Henderson, C Y, Mariotti, V, Pany-Kucera, S, Villotte, S, and Wilczak, C, 2013 Recording specific enthesial changes of fibrocartilaginous enthuses: Initial tests using the Coimbra method, *International Journal Osteoarchaeology* 23 (2), 147–151

Henderson, M, Miles, A, Walker, D, Connell B and Wroe-Brown R, 2013, *'He being dead yet speaketh' Excavations at three post-medieval burial grounds in Tower Hamlets, East London, 2004–10*, MOLA Monogr 64, Museum of London Archaeology, London

Henderson, R C, Lee-Thorp, J, and Loe, L, 2014 Early life histories of the London Poor using Using $\delta^{13}C$ and $\delta^{15}N$ Stable Isotope Incremental Dentine Sampling, *American Journal of Physical Anthropology* 154, 585–593

Hillson, S, 1986 *Teeth*, Cambridge University Press, Cambridge

Hillson, S, 1996 *Dental Anthropology* (3rd edn), Cambridge University Press, Cambridge

Holmes, I, 1896 *The London Burial Grounds*, London

Houlbrooke, R, 1999 The age of decency: 1660–1760, in P C Jupp and C Gittings (eds), *Death in England, an Illustrated History*, Manchester University Press, Manchester, 174–201

Howie, P W, Forsyth, J S, Ogston, S A, Clark, A, and Florey C D, 1990 Protective effect of breast feeding against infection, *British Medical Journal* 300, 11–16

Hughs, V, and Taylor, J, 2013 *Thameslink Archaeological Assessment 1: Archaeological Excavations at Vaults 2, 5 and 9, Railway Approach, London Borough of Southwark*, Oxford Archaeology-Pre-Construct Archaeology, unpubl report

Humphrey, L, 2000 Growth studies of past populations: an overview and an example, in M Cox and S Mays (eds) *Human Osteology in Archaeology and Forensic Science*, Greenwich Medical Media, London, 23–38

IFA, 1993 *Excavation and Post-excavation Treatment of Cremated and Inhumed Human Remains*, Technical Paper No. 13

Ineichen, B, Pierce, M, and Lawrenson, R, 1997 Jewish and Celtic attitudes to breast feeding compared, *Midwifery* 13, 40–43

Ives, R, 2015 Insights into health, life and death in Victorian London's East end, *London Archaeologist*, 14 (6), 150–154

Ives, R, MacQuarrie, H, Hogg, I, forthcoming *An East End Opportunity. Insights into Post-medieval Life, Death and Burial from Excavations at Kilday's Ground, Bethnal Green*, AOC Archaeology Monogr

İşcan, M Y, and Loth, S R, 1998 Estimation of age and determination of sex from the sternal rib ends, in K Reichs (ed.), *Forensic osteology: Advances in the Identification of Human Remains* (2nd edn), Charles C Thomas, Springfield, 68–89

Janaway, R C, 1993 The textiles, in J Reeves and M Adams, *The Spitalfields Project Vol. 1, The Archaeology, Across the Styx*, CBA Res Rep 85, York, 93–119

Jim, S, Jones, V, Ambrose, S H, and Evershed, R P, 2006 Quantifying dietary macronutrient sources of carbon for bone collagen biosynthesis using natural abundance stable carbon isotope analysis, *British Journal of Nutrition* 95, 1055–1062

Jones, H, 1990 *Archaeological Excavations on New London Bridge House, London Bridge Street, SE1*, Museum of London Department of Greater London Archaeology, unpubl report

Judd, M A, 2002a Ancient injury recidivism: an example from Kerma period of ancient Nubia, *International Journal of Osteoarchaeology* 12, 89–106

Judd, M A, 2002b One accident too many? *British Museum Studies in Ancient Egypt and Sudan* 3, 42–54

Jurmain, R D, 1999 *Stories from the Skeleton – Behavioural Reconstruction in Human Osteology*, Gordon and Breach, Netherlands

Jurmain, R, Alves Cardoso, F, Henderson, C, and Villotte, S, 2012 Bioarchaeology's Holy Grail: The reconstruction of activity, in A L Grauer (ed.), *A Companion to Paleopathology*, Blackwell Publishing, Oxford

Katzenberg, M A, Saunders, S R, and Fitzgerald, W R, 1993 Age differences in stable carbon and nitrogen isotope ratios in a population of prehistoric maize horticulturalists, *American Journal of Physical Anthropology* 90, 267–281

Keene, D, 2000 Changes in London's economic hinterland as indicated by debt cases in the Court of Common pleas, in J Galloway (ed.), *Trade, urban hinterlands and market integration c. 1300–1600*, Centre for Metropolitan History Working Papers Series No. 3, London, 59–81

Kendall, E J, Montgomery, J, Evans, J A, Stantis, C, and Mueller, V, 2013 Mobility, mortality, and the middle ages: Identification of migrant individuals in a 14th century Black Death cemetery population, *American Journal of Physical Anthropology* 150, 210–222

Knight, H, 2002 *Aspects of Medieval and Later Southwark: Archaeological Excavations (1991–8) for the London Underground Limited Jubilee Line Extension Project*, MoLAS Monogr 13, Museum of London Archaeology, London

Knüsel, C J, 2000a Activity-related skeletal change, in V Fiorato, A Boylston and C Knüsel, *Blood Red Roses. The Archaeology of a Mass Grave from the Battle of Towton AD 1461*, Oxford, 103–118

Knüsel, C J, 2000b Bone adaptation and its relationship to physical activity in the past, in M Cox and S Mays, *Human Osteology in Archaeology and Forensic Science*, London, 381–40

Kumar, A, and Tubbs, S R, 2011 Spina bifida: A diagnostic dilemma in palaeopathology, *Clinical Anatomy* 24, 19–33

Lamb, H H, 1981 Climate from 1000 BC to 1000 AD, in M Jones and D Dimbleby (eds), *The Environment of Man: The Iron Age to the Anglo-Saxon Period*, BAR Brit Ser 87, Archaeopress, Oxford, 53–65

Langthorne, J, 2014 Assessment of the human remains in A Haslam, *An Archaeological Excavation on Land at the Elephant and Castle Leisure centre, London Borough of Southwark, SE11 4TW*, Pre-Construct Archaeology Report No. R11773, 107–121

Langthorne, J, and Taylor, J, 2013 *Thameslink Archaeological Assessment 4: Archaeological Excavations at 2–4 Bedale Street, London Borough of Southwark*, Oxford Archaeology–Pre-Construct Archaeology, unpubl report

Larsen, C S, 1997 *Bioarchaeology. Interpreting behaviour from the human skeleton*, Cambridge University Press, Cambridge

Lewis, M, 2002 *Urbanisation and Child Health in Medieval and Post-Medieval England*, BAR Brit Ser 339, Archaeopress, Oxford

Lewis, M E, 2004 Endocranial lesions in non-adult skeletons: Understanding their aetiology, *International Journal of Osteoarchaeology* 14, 82–97

Lewis, M, 2007 *The Bioarchaeology of Children*, Cambridge University Press, Cambridge

Lewis, M, and Roberts, C, 1997 Growing pains: the interpretation of stress indicators, *International Journal of Osteoarchaeology* 7, 581–586

Lewis, M E, Roberts, C A, and Manchester, K, 1995 Comparative study of the prevalence of maxillary sinusitis in later medieval urban and rural populations in northern England, *American Journal of Physical Anthropology* 98, 497–506

Litten, J, 1991 *The English Way of Death - The Common Funeral Since 1450*, Robert Hale, London

Longin, R, 1971 New method of collagen extraction for radiocarbon dating, *Nature* 230, 241–242

Lönnerdal, B, 2000 Breast milk: A truly functional food, *Nutrition* 16, 509–511

Lovejoy, C O, Meindl, R S, Pryzbeck, T R, and Mensforth, R P, 1985 Chronological metamorphosis of the auricular surface of the ilium: A new method for the determination of adult skeletal age at death, *American Journal of Physical Anthropology* 68, 15–28

Lovell, N C, 1994 Spinal arthritis and physical stress at Bronze Age Harappa, *American Journal of Physical Anthropology* 93, 149–164

Lovell, N, 1997 Trauma analysis in palaeopathology, *Yearbook Physical Anthropology* 40, 139–70

Macintyre, K, 2002 Famine and the female mortality advantage, in T Dyson and C O'Grada, (eds) *Famine Demography. Perspectives from the Past and Present*, International Studies in Demography Series, Oxford University Press, Oxford, 240–260

Malden, H E (ed.), 1912 *The Victoria History of the Counties of England. A History of the County of Surrey: Volume 4*, London

Maresh, M M, 1970 Measurements from roentgenograms, in R W McCammon (ed.), *Human Growth and Development*, 157–200

Margerison, B J, and Knüsel, C J, 2002 Palaeodemographic comparison of a catastrophic and an attritional death assemblage, *American Journal of Physical Anthropology* 119, 134–143

Massler, M, Schour, I and Poncher, H G, 1941 Developmental pattern of the child as reflected in the calcification pattern of the teeth, *American Journal of Diseases of Children* 62, 33–67

May, H, Peled, N, Dar, G, Abbas, J and Hershkovitz, I, 2011 Hyperstosis Frontalis Interna: What Does It Tell Us About our Health?, *American Journal of Human Biology* 23, 392–397

May, T, 2003 *The Victorian Undertaker*, Shire Publications, London

Mays, S A, 2003 The rise and fall of rickets in England, in R Murphy and P E J Wiltshire, *The Environmental Archaeology of Industry*, Symposia of the Association for Environmental Archaeology 20, Oxford, 144–53

Mays, S A, 2005 Palaeopathological study of hallux valgus, *American Journal of Physical Anthropology* 126 (2), 139–149

Mays, S A, 2006 Spondylolysis, spondylolisthesis, and lumbo-sacral morphology in a medieval English skeletal population, *American Journal of Physical Anthropology* 131, 352–62

Mays, S, 2007 Spondylolysis in the lower thoracic–upper lumbar spine in a British medieval population, *International Journal of Osteoarchaeology* 17, 608–618

Mays, S, 2013 A discussion of some recent methodological developments in the Osteoarchaeology of childhood, *Childhood in the Past: An International Journal* 6 (1), 4–21

Mays, S, Brickley, M and Dodwell, N, 2002, *Human Bones from Archaeological Sites: Guidelines for Producing Assessment Documents and Analytical Reports*, English Heritage, Swindon

Mays, S A, Brickley, M, and Ives, R, 2008 Growth in an English population from the Industrial Revolution, *American Journal of Physical Anthropology* 136 (1), 85–92

Mays, S A, Brickley, M, and Ives, R, 2009 Growth and vitamin D deficiency in a population from 19th century Birmingham, England, *International Journal Osteoarchaeology* 19 (3), 406–415

Mays, S A and Dungworth, D, 2009 Intervertebral Chondrocalcinosis: An Exercise in Differential Diagnosis in Palaeopathology. *International Journal of Osteoarchaeology* 19, 36–49

Mays, S, Taylor, G M, Legge, A J, Young, D B and Turner-Walker, G, 2001 Palaeopathological and Biomolecular Study of Tuberculosis in a Medieval Skeletal Collection from England, *American Journal of Physical Anthropology* 114, 298–311.

McCarthy, R, Clough, S and Norton, A, 2010 *Excavations at the Baptist Chapel Burial Ground, Littlemore, Oxford,* Oxford Archaeology, unpubl report

McCarthy, R, and Clough, S, 2010 Osteological analysis, in C Raynor, R McCarthy and S Clough, *Coronation Street, South Shields, Tyne and Wear. Archaeological Excavation and Osteological Analysis Report*, Oxford Archaeology North, unpubl report, 43–81

McKinley, J I, 2004 Compiling a skeletal inventory: Disarticulated and co-mingled human remains, in M Brickley and J I McKinley (eds), *Guidelines to the Standards for Recording Human Remains*, IFA Technical Paper 7, Reading, 14–17

McKinley, J I, 2008, *The 18th Century Baptist Chapel*

and *Burial Ground at West Butts Street, Poole*, Wessex Archaeology, Salisbury

Medline Plus, 2015 *Dwarfism*. Online at: https://www.nlm.nih.gov/medlineplus/dwarfism.html Maryland, Usa, Medline Plus, service of the National Library of Medicine, National Institute of Health [accessed: 16.11.15]

Meindl, R S, and Lovejoy, C O, 1985 Ectocranial suture closure: A revised method for the determination of skeletal age at death based on the lateral-anterior sutures, *American Journal of Physical Anthropology* 68, 29–45

Merbs, C F, 1996 Spondylolysis and spondylolisthesis: A cost of being an erect biped or a clever adaptation?, *American Journal of Physical Anthropology* 101, 201–228

Merbs C F, 1989 Trauma, in M Y Iscan and K A R Kennedy (eds), *Reconstruction of Life from the Skeleton*, New York, Liss, 161–189

Michopoulou, E, Nikita, E, and Valakos, E, 2015 Evaluating the efficiency of different recording protocols for entheseal changes in regards to expressing activity patterns using archival data and cross-sectional geometric properties, *American Journal of Physical Anthropology* 158 (4), 557–568

Miles, A, 1962 Assessment of the ages of a population of Anglo-Saxons from their dentitions, *Proceedings of the Royal Society of Medicine* 55, 881–886

Miles, A, 2002 *The Davenant Centre, 179–181 Whitechapel Road* Archaeological Assessment Report, November 2002, unpubl client report

Miles, A, 2011 Coffins and coffin fittings, in P Emery and K Wooldridge, *St Pancras Burial Ground Excavations for St Pancras International, the London Terminus of High Speed 1, 2002–3* Gifford Monogr, 166–179

Miles A, with Connell, B, 2012 *New Bunhill Fields Burial Ground, Southwark: Excavations at Globe Academy, 2008*, MOLA Archaeology Studies Series 21, London

Miles, A, and Powers, N, 2010, *The Bow Baptist Burial Ground*, MoLAS unpubl report

Miles, A, Powers, N, Wroe-Brown, R and Walker, D, 2008 *St Marylebone Church and Burial Ground in the 18th to 19th Centuries. Excavations at St Marylebone School, 1992 and 2004–6*, MoLAS Monogr 46, MoLAS, London

Miles, A, and White, W, 2008 *Burial at the Site of the Parish Church of St Benet Sherehog Before and After the Great Fire: Excavations at 1 Poultry, City of London*, Museum of London Archaeology Service Monogr 39, London

Minagawa, M, and Wada, E, 1984 Stepwise enrichment of 15N along food chains: Further evidence and the relation between $\delta15N$ and animal age, *Geochimica et Cosmochimica Acta* 48, 1135–1140

Miquel-Feucht, M J, Polo-Cerdá, M and Villalaín-Blanco, J D, 1999 El síndrome criboso: cribra femoral vs cribra orbitaria, in J A Sánchez (ed), *Sistematización metodológica en Paleopatología, Actas V Congreso Nacional AEP,* Associatión Española de Paleopatología, Alcalá la Real, Jaén, Spain, 221–237

Mitchell, P D, Boston, C, Chamberlain, A T, Chaplin, S, Chauhan, V, Evans, J, Fowler, L, Powers, N, Webb, H and Witkin, A, 2011 The study of anatomy in England from 1700 to the early 20th century, *Journal of Anatomy* 219, 91–99

Mitchell, P D and Redfern, R G, 2011 Brief Communication: Developmental Dysplasia of the Hip in Medieval London. *American Journal of Physical Anthropology* 144, 479–484

MoL, 1994 (3rd edition), *Archaeological Site Manual: Museum of London Archaeology Service*, Museum of London

MoLAS, 2003 (Knight, H) *Thameslink 2000 Borough Viaduct London SE1, London Borough of Southwark, Detailed desk-based assessment*, MoLAS for Network Rail, unpubl report

Molleson, T and Cox, M, 1993 *The Spitalfields Project. Volume 2: The Anthropology. The Middling Sort*, CBA Res Rep 86, York

Moore, J, and Buckberry, J, 2016 The use of corsetry to treat Pott's disease of the spine from 19th century Wolverhampton, England, *International Journal of Paleopathology* 14, 74–80

Moorrees, C F A, Fanning, E A, and Hunt, E E, 1963a Formation and resorption of three deciduous teeth in children, *American Journal of Physical Anthropology* 21, 205–213

Moorrees, C F A, Fanning, E A, and Hunt, E E, 1963b Age variation of formation stages for ten permanent teeth, *Journal of Dental Research* 42, 1490–1502

Nitsch, E K, Humphrey, L T, and Hedges, R E M, 2011 Using stable isotope analysis to examine the effect of economic change on breastfeeding practices in Spitalfields, London, UK, *American Journal of Physical Anthropology* 146 (4), 619–628

NWR, 2009a *Thameslink Programme: Written Scheme of Investigation for Archaeological Works at: Park Street and Hop Exchange Viaduct; Borough Market Viaduct; Borough High Street Bridge; and Railway Approach Viaduct, London Borough of Southwark*, Network Rail, unpubl report

NWR, 2009b *Thameslink Programme. Written*

Scheme of Investigation for Archaeological Works at: Borough Viaduct and London Bridge Station, London Borough of Southwark, Network Rail, unpubl report

OA, forthcoming, *Excavations at St Paul's Church, Hammersmith, London,* Oxford Archaeology, Oxford

Ortner, D J, 2003 *Identification of Pathological Conditions in Human Skeletal Remains*, Academic Press, London and San Diego

Ortner, D J, and Erikson, M F, 1997 Bone changes in the human skull probably resulting from scurvy in infancy and childhood, *International Journal of Osteoarchaeology* 7, 212–220

Ortner, D J, Kimmerle, E, and Diez, M, 1999 Skeletal evidence of scurvy in archaeological skeletal samples from Peru, *American Journal of Physical Anthropology* 108, 321–331

Ortner, D J, Butler, W, Cafarella, J, and Milligan, L, 2001 Evidence of probable scurvy in subadult from archaeological sites in north America, *American Journal of Physical Anthropology* 114, 343–351

Paine, R R, 2000 If a population crashes in prehistory, and there is no palaeodemographer there to hear it, does it make a sound?, *American Journal of Physical Anthropology* 112, 181–90

Pearson, O M, and Buikstra, J E, 2006 Behavior and the Bones, in J E Buikstra and L A Beck (eds), *Bioarchaeology: The Contextual Study of Human Remains*, Academic Press, Burlington MA, 207–225

Pilloud, M A, and Canzonieri, C, 2014 The occurrence and possible aetiology of spondylolysis in a pre-contact California population, *International Journal of Osteoarchaeology* 24 (5), 602–613

Pindborg, J J, 1982 Aetiology of developmental defects not related to fluorosis, *International Dental Journal* 32, 123–134

Pinhasi, R, Shaw, P, White B, Ogden, A R, 2006 Morbidity, rickets and long-bone growth in post-medieval Britain, a cross-population analysis, *Annals of Human Biology* 33 (3), 372–89

Porter, R, 1994 *London, a social history*, London

Powers, N, 2005 *Evaluation of disarticulated remains recovered from the Royal London Hospital, Whitechapel*, MoLAS upubl report

Powers, N, 2006 *Assessment of human remains excavated from the Church of St George the Martyr, Borough High Street, Southwark SE1*, MoLAS upubl report

Powers, N, 2009 *St Marylebone (Post-medieval) Cemetery Summary*, Museum of London Archaeological Archive Centre for Human Bioarchaeology Online at https://www.museum oflondon.org.uk/collections/other-collection-databases-and-libraries/centre-human-bio archaeology/osteological-database/post-medieval-cemeteries/st-marylebone [Accessed July 2016]

Powers, N, 2011, Osteological evidence, in P Emery and K Wooldridge, *St Pancras Burial Ground Excavations for St Pancras International, the London Terminus of High Speed 1, 2002–3*, Gifford Monogr, 127–153

Powers, N, 2015 *A Draft Agenda for the Archaeological Study of Historic Burials in Greater London*, Allen Archaeology Report No. 2015083 prepared for Historic England, Allen Archaeology

Powers, N, Wilson, A S, Montgomery, J, Bowsher, D, Brown, T, Beaumont, J, and Janaway, R C, 2013 No Certain Roof but the Coffin Lid. Exploring the commercial and academic need for a high level research framework to safeguard the future of the post-medieval burial resource, in C Dalglish (ed.), *Archaeology, the Public and the Recent Past*, The Boydell Press, Woodbridge, 125–144

Pre-Construct Archaeology (PCA), 2005a *St Paul's Church, Hammersmith, London Borough of Hammersmith and Fulham, Archaeological desk top assessment*, Pre-Construct Archaeology unpubl report, 2005

Pre-Construct Archaeology (PCA), 2005b *St Paul's Church, Hammersmith, London Borough of Hammersmith and Fulham, Archaeological watching brief*, Pre-Construct Archaeology unpubl report, 2005

Pre-Construct Archaeology (PCA), 2007 *Written Scheme of Investigation for archaeological excavation and watching brief at St Paul's Churchyard, Hammersmith, London Borough of Hammersmith and Fulham*, Pre-Construct Archaeology unpubl report, 2007

Prowse, T L, Saunders, S R, Schwarcz, H P, Garnsey, P, Macchiarelli, R, and Bondioli, L, 2008 Isotopic and dental evidence for infant and young child feeding practices in an Imperial Roman skeletal sample, *American Journal of Physical Anthropology* 137, 294–308

Raynor, C, McCarthy, M and Clough, S, 2011 *Coronation Street, South Shields, Tyne and Wear: Archaeological Excavation and Osteological Analysis Report*, Oxford Archaeology, unpubl report

Reeve, J and Adams, M, 1993 *The Spitalfields Project-The Archaeology, Across the Styx*; Vol. 1, CBA Research Report 85

Rendle, W, 1878 *Old Southwark and its People*, Southwark

Resnick, D, and Niwayama, G (eds), 1995 *Diagnosis of Bone and Joint Disorders*, W B Saunders Company, Philadelphia, London, Toronto, Montreal, Sydney and Tokyo

Ribot, I, and Roberts, C, 1996 A study of non-specific stress indicators and skeletal growth in two medieval sub-adult populations, *Journal of Archaeological Science* 23, 67–79

Richmond, M, 1999 Archaeologia Victoriana: The archaeology of the Victorian funeral, in J Downes and T Pollard (eds), *The Loved Body's Corruption – Archaeological Contributions to the Study of Human Mortality*, Cruithne Press, Glasgow, 145–58

Robb, J, 1998 The interpretation of skeletal muscle sites, *International Journal of Osteoarchaeology* 8, 363–377

Roberts, C A, 1991 Trauma and treatment in the British Isles in the historic period: A design for multidisciplinary research, in D J Ortner and A C Aufderheide (eds), *Human Palaeopathology: Current Synthesis and Future Options*, Smithsonian Inst. Press, Washington DC, 225–240

Roberts, C A, 1988 *Trauma and Treatment in British Antiquity*, PhD Thesis, University of Bradford

Roberts, C A, 1999 Rib lesions and tuberculosis: The current state of play, in G Pálfi, O Dutour, J Deák and I Hutás (eds), *Tuberculosis Past and Present*, Golden Book Publishers and Tuberculosis Foundation, Budapest/Szeged, 311–316

Roberts, C, and Cox, M, 2003 *Health and Disease in Britain from Prehistory to the Present Day*, Sutton Publishing, Stroud, Gloucestershire

Roberts, C, and Manchester, K, 1995 *The Archaeology of Disease*, Sutton Publishing, Stroud, Gloucestershire

Roberts, H, and Godfrey W H, 1950 *Survey of London: Volume 22, Bankside (The Parishes of St. Saviour and Christchurch Southwark)*, London

Roberts, H, and Godfrey, W H (eds), 1950 Park Street, in H Roberts and W H Godfrey (eds), *Survey of London: Vol 22, Bankside (The Parishes of St. Saviour and Christchurch Southwark)*, London, British History Online http://www.british-history.ac.uk/survey-london/vol22/pp82-83, [accessed 14 October 2016]

Rogers, J, Shepstone, L and Dieppe, P, 1997 Bone former: osteophyte and enthesophyte formation are positively associated, *Annals of Rheumatic Diseases* 56, 85–90

Rogers, J, and Waldron, T, 1995 *A Field Guide to Joint Disease in Archaeology*, John Wiley and Sons, Chichester

Rogers, J, and Waldron, T, 2001 DISH and the monastic way of life. *International Journal of Osteoarchaeology* 11, 357–365.

Ross, C, and Clark, J, (eds) 2008 *London, the Illustrated History*, Museum of London

Rugg, J, 1999 From reason to regulation: 1760–1850, in P C Jupp and C Gittings (eds), *Death in England, an Illustrated History*, Manchester University Press, Manchester, 202–229

Santos, A L and Roberts, C A, 2001 A picture of tuberculosis in young Portuguese people in the early 20th century: A multidisciplinary study of the skeletal and historical evidence, *American Journal of Physical Anthropology* 115 (1), 38–49

Sarnat, B G, and Schour, I, 1941 Enamel hypoplasias (chronologic enamel aplasia) in relation to systemic disease: A chronologic, morphologic and etiologic classification, *Journal of the American Dental Association* 28, 1989–2000

Scheuer, L, and Black, S, 2000 *Developmental Juvenile Osteology*, Elsevier Academic Press, Oxford

Schoeninger, M J, Deniro, M J, and Tauber, H, 1983 Stable nitrogen isotope ratios of bone collagen reflect marine and terrestrial components of prehistoric human diet, *Science* 220, 1381–1383

Schurr, M R, 1997 Stable nitrogen isotopes as evidence for the age of weaning at the Angel Site: A comparison of isotopic and demographic measures of weaning age, *Journal of Archaeological Science* 24, 919–927

Schwartz, J H, 1995 *Skeleton Keys: An Introduction to Human Skeletal Morphology, Development and Analysis*, Oxford University Press, Oxford

Start, H, and Kirk, L, 1998 The bodies of friends – the osteological analysis of a Quaker burial ground, in M Cox (ed.) *Grave Concerns. Death and Burial in England 1700–1850*, CBA Research Report 113, Council for British Archaeology, York

Steckel, R H, 1995 Stature and the standard of living, *Journal of Economic Literature* 33, 1903–1940

Steele, V, 2001 *The Corset: A Cultural History*, Yale University Press, London

Stirland, A, 1987 A possible correlation between os acromiale and occupation in the burials from the Mary Rose, *Proceedings of the Vth European Meeting of the Paleopathology Association*, Siena, 327–333

Stirland, A, 1998 Musculoskeletal evidence for activity: Problems of evaluation, *International Journal of Osteoarchaeology* 8, 354–362

Stock J T, 2006 Hunter-gatherer postcranial robusticity relative to patterns of mobility, climatic adaptation, and selection for tissue economy, *American Journal of Physical*

Anthropology, 131(2), DOI: 10.1002/ajpa.20398, 194–204

Stone, P K, 2012 Binding women: ethnology, skeletal deformations and violence against women, *International Journal of Paleopathology* 2, 53–60

Stuart-Macadam 1989, Nutritional deficiency diseases: a survey of scurvy, rickets, and iron deficiency anaemia, in M Y Iscan and K A R Kennedy (eds), *Reconstruction of Life from the Skeleton*, New York, 201–222

Stuart-Macadam, P, 1991 Anaemia in Roman Britain: Poundbury Camp, in H Bush and M Zvelebil, *Health in Past Societies, Biocultural Interpretations of Human Skeletal Remains in Archaeological Contexts*, BAR Int Ser 567, Tempus Reparatum, 101–113

Tarlow, S, 2015 Introduction: death and burial in post-medieval Europe, in S Tarlow (ed.) *The Archaeology of Death and Burial in Post-medieval Europe*, De Gruyter Open, 1–18

Taylor, J, 1999 Nails and Wood Screws, reproduced from *The Building Conservation Directory* http://www.buildingconservation.com/articles/nails/nails.htm [Accessed July 2012]

Taylor, J, 2013 *Thameslink Archaeological Assessment 6: Archaeological Excavations at 6-7 Stoney Street, London Borough of Southwark*, Oxford Archaeology–Pre-Construct Archaeology, unpubl report

Taylor, J, and Brown, G, 2009 *Operations Manual I*, Pre-Construct Archaeology

Taylor, J, and Champness, C, 2013 *Thameslink Archaeological Assessment 9: Archaeological Excavations at Western Approach Viaduct, London Borough of Southwark*, Oxford Archaeology–Pre-Construct Archaeology, unpubl report

Taylor, W, 1833 *Annals of St Mary Overy, a historical and descriptive account of St Saviour's Church and parish with numerous illustrations*, London

Teague, S, 2013 *Thameslink Archaeological Assessment 8: Archaeological Investigations at Blackfriars Station, City of London and London Borough of Southwark*, Oxford Archaeology–Pre-Construct Archaeology, unpubl report

Teague, S, Loe, L, and Taylor, J, 2013 *Thameslink Archaeological Assessment 7: Archaeological Investigations on land to the rear of the Hop Exchange and Park Street, London Borough of Southwark*, Oxford Archaeology–Pre-Construct Archaeology, unpubl report

Teague, S and Taylor, J, 2013 *Thameslink Archaeological Assessment 5: Archaeological Excavations at Borough Market, London Borough of Southwark Site*, Oxford Archaeology–Pre-Construct Archaeology, unpubl report

Trotter, M, 1970, Estimation of stature from intact long bones, in T.D. Stewart (ed.) *Personal Identification in Mass Disasters*. Washington DC: Smithsonian Institution Press, 71–83

Trotter, M and Gleser, G C, 1952 Estimation of stature from long bones of American Whites and Negroes, *American Journal of Physical Anthropology* 9, 427–440.

Trotter, M and Gleser, G C, 1958 A re-evaluation of estimation of stature based on measurements of stature taken during life and on long bones after death, *American Journal of Physical Anthropology* 16, 79–123

Tucker, F, 2007 Kill or cure? The osteological evidence of the mercury treatment of syphilis in 17th- to 19th-century London, *London Archaeologist*, 11 (8), 220–224

Turner, J, 1838 *Burial Fees of the Principal Churches, Chapels and New Burial-grounds, in London and Its Environs ...: And All ... Information for Undertakers*, London

Tyrell, A, 2000 Skeletal Non-Metric Traits and The Assessment of Inter and Intra Population Diversity: Past Problems and Future Potential, in M Cox and S Mays (eds*)*, *Human Osteology In Archaeology and Forensic Science,* Greenwich Medical Media Ltd, London, 289–306

Van der Merwe, N J, and Vogel, J C, 1978 13C content of human collagen as a measure of prehistoric diet in woodland North America, *Nature* 276, 815–816

Waldron, H A, 1991 Prevalence and distribution of osteoarthritis in a population from Georgian and Early Victorian London, *Annals of the Rheumatic Diseases* 50, 301–307

Waldron, I, 1998 Sex differences in infant and early childhood mortality: Major causes of death and possible biological causes, in United Nations (ed.), *Too young to die: Genes or gender*, New York, 64–83

Waldron, T, 1994 *Counting the Dead. The Epidemiology of Skeletal Populations*, John Wiley and Sons, Chichester

Waldron, T, 2007 *St Peter's, Barton-upon-Humber, Lincolnshire. A Parish Church and its Community. Volume 2: The Human Remains*, Oxbow Books, Oxford

Waldron, T, 2009 *Palaeopathology,* Cambridge University Press, Cambridge

Waldron, T, and Cox, M, 1989 Occupational arthropathy: evidence from the past, *British Journal of Industrial Medicine* 46, 420–422

Walford, E, 1878 Southwark: Old St Thomas's and Guy's Hospitals, in *Old and New London: Volume 6*, 89-100, *British History Online* http://www.british-history.ac.uk/old-new-london/vol6/pp89-100 [accessed 27 February 2017]

Walker, D, and Henderson, M, 2010 Smoking and health in London's East End in the first half of the 19th century, *Post-Medieval Archaeology* 44 (1), 209–22

Walker, D, 2012 *Disease in London, 1st–19th Centuries. An Illustrated Guide to Diagnosis*, MOLA Monogr 56, Museum of London Archaeology, London

Walker, G A, 1839 *Gatherings from graveyards, particularly those from London and a detail of dangerous and fatal results produced by the unwise and revolting custom of inhumating the dead in the midst of the living*, London

Walker, K, 1990 *Guidelines for the preparation of excavation archives for long term storage*, London

Walker, P L, 1997 Wife beating, boxing and broken noses: skeletal evidence for the cultural patterning of violence, in D W Frayer and D C Martin (eds), *Troubled Times: Osteological and Archaeological Evidence of Violence*, Gordon and Breach, Amsterdam, 145–179

Walker, P L, Bathurst, R R, Richman, R, Gjerdum, T, Andrushko, V A, 2009 The Causes of Porotic Hyperostosis and Cribra orbitalia: a Reappraisal of the Iron-Deficiency-Anaemia Hypothesis. *American Journal of Physical Anthropology* 139, 109–125

Wapler, U, Crubézy, E, Schultz, M, 2003 Is cribra orbitalia synonymous with anaemia? Analysis and interpretation of cranial pathology in Sudan, *American Journal of Physical Anthropology* 123, 333–339

Watts, R, 2015 The long-term impact of developmental stress. Evidence from later medieval and post-medieval London (AD1117–1853), *American Journal of Physical Anthropology* 158, 569–580

Weinreb, B, Hibbert, C, Keay, J, and Keay, J, 2008 *The London Encyclopaedia* (3rd edn), Macmillan, Essex

Wells, C, 1964 *Bones, Bodies and Disease: Evidence of Disease and Abnormality in Early Man*, Frederick A Praeger, New York

Werner, A, 2005 Trade and industry, in C Ross and J Clark (eds), *London, the Illustrated History*, London, 170–1

Weston, D A, 2008 Investigating the Specificity of Periosteal Reactions in Pathology Museum Specimens, *American Journal of Physical Anthropology* 127, 48–59

White, W, 2011, Osteological evidence, in P Emery and K Wooldridge, *St Pancras Burial Ground Excavations for St Pancras International, the London Terminus of High Speed 1, 2002–3*, Gifford Monogr, 112–117

Wohl, A S, 1983 *Endangered Lives: Public Health in Victorian Britain*, Methuen, London

Wolff, J, 1892 *The Law of Bone Remodelling*, Springer-Verlag, Berlin

Wood, J W, Milner, G R, Harpending, H C and Weiss, K M, 1992 The osteological paradox: problems of inferring prehistoric health from skeletal samples, *Current Anthropology* 33, 343–370

Wright, R, 2008 Detection of Likely Ancestry using CRANID, in M F Oxenham (ed.), *Forensic Approaches to Death, Disaster and Abuse*, Australian Academic Press, Queensland, 111–122

Wright, R, 2012 *Guide to Using the CRANID programs Cr6blnd: for linear and nearest neighbours discriminant analysis*

Yammine, K, 2014 The prevalence of os acromiale: A systematic review and meta-analysis, *Clinical Anatomy* 27, 610–621

Yeomans, L, 2006 *A zooarchaeological and historical study of the animal product based industries operating in London during the post-medieval period*, unpubl. PhD thesis, Institute of Archaeology, University College London

Zimmerman, M R, and Kelley, M A, 1982 *Atlas of Human Paleopathology*, Praeger Publishers, New York

Primary archives

BPP 1849 XXI (1087) 92, http://www.histpop.org

British Museum, College Almshouses and burial ground facing north west, 1851 (1880,1113.5300)

British Museum, College Almshouses and burial ground, probably facing north, 1851 (1880,1113.5299)

British Museum, College Almshouses and burial ground facing south east towards the chapel, 1852. (1880,1113.5298)

British Museum, Alleyne's Almshouses in Soap Yard, Southwark; a row of almshouses, with washing hanging across the street outside. 1839 (1874,0314.22)

British Museum, View of the old almshouses founded by Edward Alleyn, in Soap Yard, Deadman Place, Southwark; laundry hanging on line across yard, a few figures outside almshouses. 1851 Watercolour (1880,1113.5302)

Census for England and Wales, 1841, 1851, 1861

Bibliography

Charles Booth's poverty maps online, 2015, (London School of Economics) http://booth.lse.ac.uk/cgi-bin/do.pl?sub=view_booth_only&args=532450,180154,2,large,1

Churchwardens of St Saviour, broadsheet 1613,

Daily News (London, England), Monday, September 26, 1853; Issue 2293

Locating London's Past, 2011, Estimating London's Population, Version 1.0, Population Statistics and Notes. URL: http://www.locatinglondon.org/static/Population.html#toc2 Date accessed: 08 May 2014

London Metropolitan Archives, Insured: Edward Miller Wheelers Yard Red Cross Street Borough wheelwright, Reference Code: CLC/B/192/F/001/MS11936/474/936943, Date 1817 Dec 24

London Metropolitan Archives: P92/SAV/449: Vestry Minutes for St Saviour's, 1557-1581

London Metropolitan Archives: P92/SAV/450: Vestry Minutes for St Saviour's, 1582-1628

London Metropolitan Archives P92/SAV/1263 (1821) Plan of College of Poor and burial ground by Geo. Gwilt

London Metropolitan Archives P92/SAV/1305 (1844) Printed ground plans of Cure's College and Soap Yard almshouses Showing disposition of houses maintained by various charities. Signed Jn. Howe

London Metropolitan Archives P92/SAV/3091 (1766-1774) Fee book of burials

London Metropolitan Archives, P92/SAV/3093 (1782-1791) Fee book of burials

London Metropolitan Archives, P92/SAV/3094 (1791-1797) Fee book of burials

London Metropolitan Archives, P92/SAV/3095 (1797-1802) Fee Book of Burials

London Metropolitan Archives: P92/SAV/0025: Records of the Parish of St Margaret, Southwark: Notes on purchase of the 'Lord Ferrers Place' for the new Churchyard, temp. Henry VIII 1485 *(an archivist has mis dated this, Julian Munby has dated this as 1534-1536 which it notes on the page, also the 27th year of Henry VIII's reign was 1534 not 1485)*

National Archives, RAIL 107/3, Reports from Surveyor and Architect concerning removal of 7950 bodies from burial ground of College Almshouses (photographic copies – originals with Curator of Relics), October 1862

National Archives, prob 11/1579

Copyright of maps referred to

Braun and Hogenberg's map of 1572 http://talus.artsci.wustl.edu/RenEpicClass/Books/Other/London%201572.jpg The Hebrew University of Jerusalem & The Jewish National & University Library (copyright available at several locations)

Tallis London Street Views 1838–1840, published by Nattali and Maurice, London, 1969. Original collection the Goss Collection – The Corporation of the City of London – The Guildhall Library

Gwilt's plan of the Alsmhouse estate in 1814. London Metropolitan Archives

Horwood's map of 1792–99 – Southwark Archives

Horwood's map of 1819 – Southwark Archives Map 546

Londinvm Feracissimi Angliae circa 1572 (line drawing, not coloured version) – Southwark Archives http://www.southwark.gov.uk/info/200212/egovernment/1776/old_maps_of_southwark

OS map 1873-75 1:1056, sheets VII.76/ V.II 86 (Godfrey edition) http://www.alangodfreymaps.com/

Rocque's map of 1746 – MOTCO http://www.motco.com/

Index

abscess 55
almshouse
    Cure's College 7, 10, 12–14, 16–18, 27, 29, 37–8, 100, 105, 112–13, 117, 120
    Lower Norwood 17
    Soap Yard 12, 16, 37, 100
ancestry 43–4, 84–5
ankylosis 41, 71, 79
ante-mortem tooth loss (AMTL) 53–4, 57, 90

beliefs 108–10, 121
Black Death 83, 117
body fluids 112
breast milk 80–1
breastfeeding 81
Buckler, John Chessel 115–16
burial fees 7, 10, 18–23, 108–9, 113, 119
burial ground
    Cross Bones 54
    Cure's College 1, 5, 7, 9–10, 13, 17–18, 20–3, 30, 35, 37–8, 103–4, 106, 108–9, 112, 117–18
    New Bunhill Fields 107
    Sheen's 84, 112
    St Bride's, City of London 46, 104
    St George the Martyr, Southwark 7, 104
    St George's, Bloomsbury 42, 48, 54, 58, 68, 77, 99, 104
    St Luke's, Islington 42, 46, 48, 53–4
    St Margaret's, Southwark 7–10, 14, 18, 117
    St Martin's-in-the-Bull-Ring, Birmingham 42, 46, 48, 54, 58, 60, 65–6, 69, 72, 86–7, 95, 115
    St Marylebone, London 42, 46, 48, 54, 58, 60–1, 64–6, 68, 72, 86–7, 90, 115
    St Pancras, London 42, 46, 48–9, 54, 61, 64–5, 72, 76, 84
    St Paul's, Hammersmith 95
    Union Workhouse 18, 20, 113
burial registers 7, 20–2, 100, 113
burials
    adolescent 31–4, 45–7, 50–1, 57, 60, 76–8, 83, 88–9, 99
    adult females 51, 57, 64, 67–8, 70, 74, 76, 78–9, 119
    adult males 64, 66–7, 75–6, 83
    child 31–3, 38, 45–7, 50–1, 57, 60–1, 64, 78, 89, 108
    crypt 42
    double 31, 35
    increasing costs of 19
    infant 21, 23, 32–3, 45–7, 64, 80–1, 87, 99–100, 106, 108–9, 113–15, 118
    juveniles 41–2, 44–7, 50, 53, 58–60, 64–6, 82–3, 86–7, 94, 118–19
    mature adult 31–4, 69, 75, 88
    neonates 45–7, 83, 99, 113
    pauper 83, 104
    prime adult 31–3, 47, 84, 88
    triple 31, 35
    young adult 31–3, 88

calculus 53–4, 57
catastrophic event 83–4, 120
cavities, periapical 55, 57
ceramic building material (CBM) 4, 28, 32
charnel pits 27, 31, 37, 98
child growth 48
childhood 76, 81, 88, 90–1, 103, 119
    diet 80–1, 83
children 10, 12, 22, 83, 86–7, 91, 100, 106, 108, 114
Church, St Margaret's 8
churchwardens 8, 10, 12–13, 16–18, 21
class 1, 8, 42, 81–2, 88–90, 108, 112
  middle 42
  upper 42, 104
  working 1, 8, 42, 90, 108, 112
coffin 5, 18, 28, 30–6, 38, 93–101, 103–5, 108–12, 118, 120
  construction 93, 109
  datum plate 97, 99–100
  decorations 93, 112
  fittings 29, 38, 93–4, 99, 120
  furnishings 93, 95, 97, 99, 101
  furniture 27, 38, 98, 104, 110–11
  grips 3, 30, 94–5, 98–100, 104, 112
  lid 95, 131
  nails 34, 104
  plates 6, 100, 106–7, 113

shape 3, 94
studs 33, 93, 98
wood 34, 38
coffined burials 28, 111
  stacked 104
coffins, wooden 93, 112
congenital condition 41
corsetry 80, 89–90
cranial non-metric traits 50–1
cribra orbitalia 64–6, 82, 88–90, 119
crude prevalence rate (CPR) 43, 54, 57–8, 60–1, 65–6, 68–70, 72, 76–7, 79, 83, 86
Cure, Thomas 10–11, 18

deformities 64, 72, 80, 89, 119
demography 118
dental anomalies 56–7
dental caries 53–5, 57, 90
dental enamel hypoplasia (DEH) 53, 55–7, 127
dentitions 53–7, 87
diet 54, 56, 64–5, 80–1, 83, 85, 91, 115
disease
  dental 53, 59–60, 64, 88, 90
  infectious 8, 60, 115, 117, 119
  metabolic 58, 74, 88–9
  neoplastic 41, 57–8, 61, 75, 77–8, 82
  periodontal 53–4
dislocations 72, 75–6, 86, 103
disorders, circulatory 76
Dupuytren's disease 80

enamel hypoplasia 56, 65, 82, 88–90, 119–20
enthesial changes 41, 49–50, 85
epidemics 32, 83–5, 91, 114, 116–18, 120

famine 83–5, 91, 115–16, 120
footstones 30, 38, 106–7
fractures 59, 64–6, 70, 72, 74–6, 86
funeral costs 7, 22–3
funerals 22–3, 93, 108–10, 113, 120

good death (ars moriendi) 108–9
granuloma 55
grave goods 108, 120–1
grave markers 10, 28, 30

hallux valgus 70
headstones 30, 105–7
human bone, disarticulated 30, 32–3, 98
hyperostosis frontalis interna (HFI) 79

infants, feeding practices 81–2, 87, 115
infection 57–8, 60, 64, 82, 90, 103, 114–15, 119
inflammation 55, 57–60, 88–90, 120
iron nails 33, 98

isotope analysis 80, 85, 87

leprosy 57, 60, 114–15
lesions 41, 50, 55, 59–61, 64–5, 71, 74–5, 77–8, 80, 86, 103, 114, 119
London Bills of Mortality 114–15
London Bridge Station 1, 3

mass graves 38, 45, 47, 82–4, 103, 116–18
maxillary sinusitis 60, 89–90
measles 21, 56, 114
migrants 83–5, 112, 114
mortality 8, 43, 46–7, 83–4, 90, 109, 113–18, 120

nutrition 87–8, 103

oral hygiene 54
os acromiale 76
ossified haematoma 75, 86
osteitis 57, 59, 72
osteoarthritis 59, 66–7, 70–1, 82, 85
osteochondritis dissecans 76–7
Osteoid osteomas 78
osteomyelitis 55, 57, 60, 119
osteoporosis 65, 86

Paris Garden 8
parishes 7
pensioners 21–3, 100, 109, 113
periostitis 57–61, 65, 70, 83, 89, 119
pipe smoking 56, 90–1
plague 8, 19, 83–5, 117–18
population of London 84
porosity 41, 61, 64–5, 70
porotic hyperostosis 65–6
post-cranial non-metric traits 50–2
potato famine 115–16
pottery 4, 28–30, 37
probate record 100

reburial 3, 5–6, 17, 83
rickets 41, 60–1, 64, 86–7, 89–91, 114–15, 119
robusticity 49

Schmorl's nodes 69, 119
scurvy 58–9, 64, 86–8, 90–1, 114–15, 119
sinusitis 58, 88
skull 41, 64, 74, 78, 95, 97–8, 100–1, 120
smallpox 21, 83–4, 91, 114, 116–17
Southwark, Foul Lane 21, 114–15
Southwark Cathedral 6, 11, 18, 104
spina bifida occulta (SBO) 78
spine 41, 68–9, 74, 76, 82, 90, 119–20
Spitalfields 42, 46–8, 60, 66, 76, 81, 84–5, 87, 93–4, 104, 117, 130

spondylolisis 51, 75–6, 86
spondylosis deformans 69
squatting 49–50
St Saviour's Parish, Southwark 1–2, 7, 10, 12, 16–23, 42, 100, 103–4, 108, 112–18, 120
stable isotope analysis 80–1
stature 43, 47–8, 85, 88, 91, 119
stress
   indicators 82, 88–9
   physiological 56, 83
symphalangism 41, 51, 78–9
syphilis 57, 59–60, 62, 64, 83, 90, 115

teeth 21, 41, 43, 53–7, 80–1, 90

Thames 1–2, 8, 66, 86, 103
Tower Hamlets
   Bow Baptist Church 90, 106
   Lukin Street cemetery 81, 85, 113
trauma 53, 56–9, 68–9, 72, 75–6, 78, 80, 83, 85–6, 90–1, 103, 114, 119
   soft tissue 75, 86
true prevalence rate (TPR) 43, 53–8, 60, 66–9, 74, 79
tuberculosis 57, 60–1, 64, 90, 114–15, 119

vaults 2, 18–20, 104, 109
vestry minutes 7, 10, 12–13, 16, 108, 115
violence 72, 74, 86, 91, 114, 117, 124
vitamin deficiency 41, 64–5, 86–7, 115